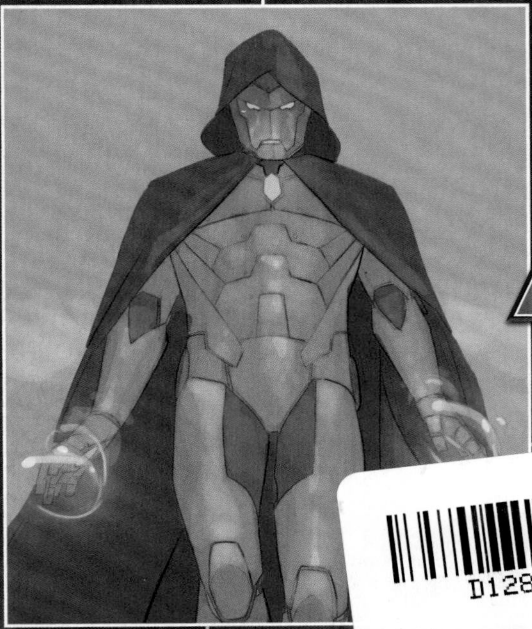

The Avengers

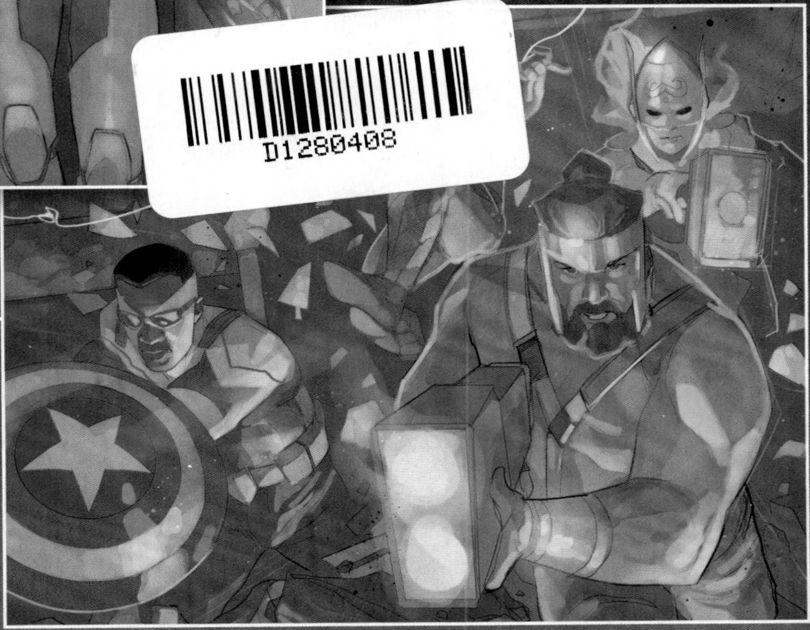

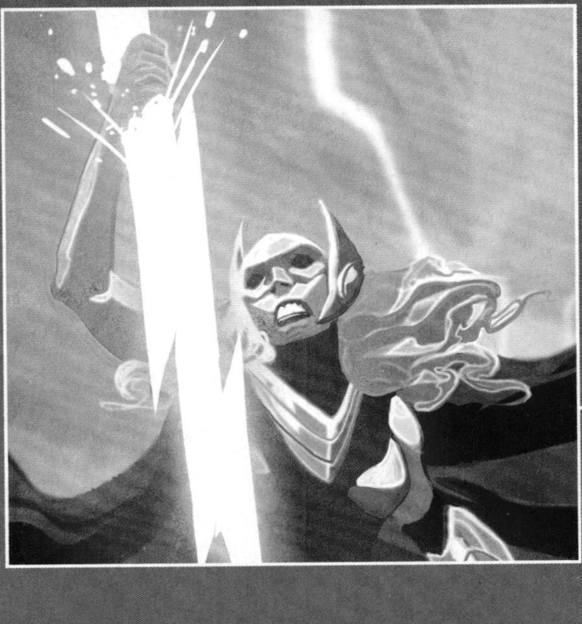

Secret Empire

After the near-fatal incapacitation
of Tony Stark during the second
super hero civil war, Victor Von Doom
abandoned his villainous ways and
took up the mantle of Iron Man.

But his past actions as Doctor Doom
have made it difficult for the
world to accept him as a hero.

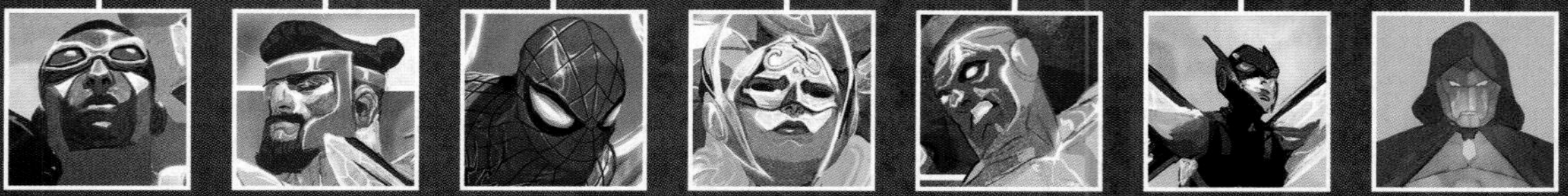
CAPTAIN AMERICA
Sam Wilson
HERCULES
SPIDER-MAN
Peter Parker
THOR
Jane Foster
VISION
WASP
Nadia Pym
IRON MAN
Victor Von Doom

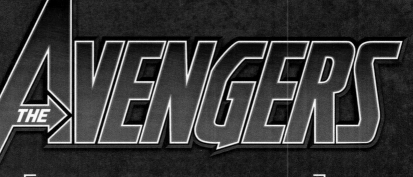

THE AVENGERS

[Secret Empire]

WRITERS Mark Waid with Jeremy Whitley (#7-8)

[#7-8]

ARTIST Phil Noto

[#9-11]

ARTIST Mike del Mundo

COLOR ARTISTS Mike del Mundo with Marco D'Alfonso

LETTERER VC's Cory Petit

COVER ART Alex Ross

ASSISTANT EDITOR Alanna Smith

EDITOR Tom Brevoort

[AVENGERS CREATED BY STAN LEE & JACK KIRBY]

COLLECTION EDITOR JENNIFER GRÜNWALD
ASSISTANT EDITOR CAITLIN O'CONNELL
ASSOCIATE MANAGING EDITOR KATERI WOODY
EDITOR, SPECIAL PROJECTS MARK D. BEAZLEY
VP PRODUCTION & SPECIAL PROJECTS JEFF YOUNGQUIST
SVP PRINT, SALES & MARKETING DAVID GABRIEL
BOOK DESIGNERS ADAM DEL RE WITH JAY BOWEN

EDITOR IN CHIEF AXEL ALONSO
CHIEF CREATIVE OFFICER JOE QUESADA
PRESIDENT DAN BUCKLEY
EXECUTIVE PRODUCER ALAN FINE

AVENGERS: UNLEASHED VOL. 2 — SECRET EMPIRE. Contains material originally published in magazine form as AVENGERS #7-11. First printing 2017. ISBN# 978-1-302-90612-2. Published by MARVEL WORLDWIDE, INC., a subsidiary of MARVEL ENTERTAINMENT, LLC. OFFICE OF PUBLICATION: 135 West 50th Street, New York, NY 10020. **Printed in Canada.** DAN BUCKLEY, President, Marvel Entertainment; JOE QUESADA, Chief Creative Officer; TOM BREVOORT, SVP of Publishing; DAVID BOGART, SVP of Business Affairs & Operations, Publishing & Partnership; C.B. CEBULSKI, VP of Brand Management & Development, Asia; DAVID GABRIEL, SVP of Sales & Marketing, Publishing; JEFF YOUNGQUIST, VP of Production & Special Projects; DAN CARR, Executive Director of Publishing Technology; ALEX MORALES, Director of Publishing Operations; SUSAN CRESPI, Production Manager; STAN LEE, Chairman Emeritus. For information regarding advertising in Marvel Comics or on Marvel.com, please contact Vit DeBellis, Integrated Sales Manager, at vdebellis@marvel.com. For Marvel subscription inquiries, please call 888-511-5480. **Manufactured between 9/22/2017 and 10/24/2017 by SOLISCO PRINTERS, SCOTT, QC, CANADA.**

10 9 8 7 6 5 4 3 2 1

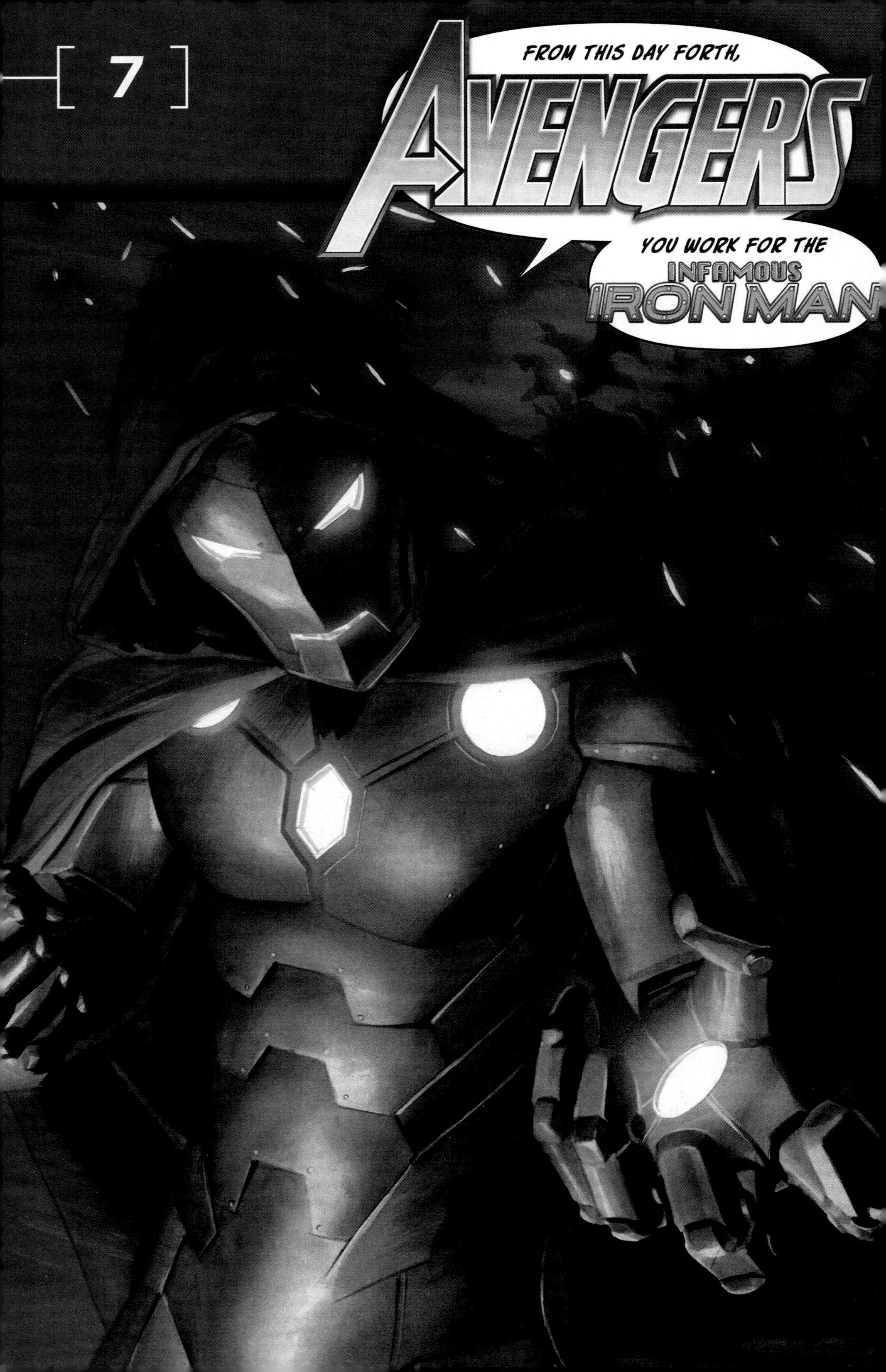
7
FROM THIS DAY FORTH,
AVENGERS
YOU WORK FOR THE
INFAMOUS
IRON MAN

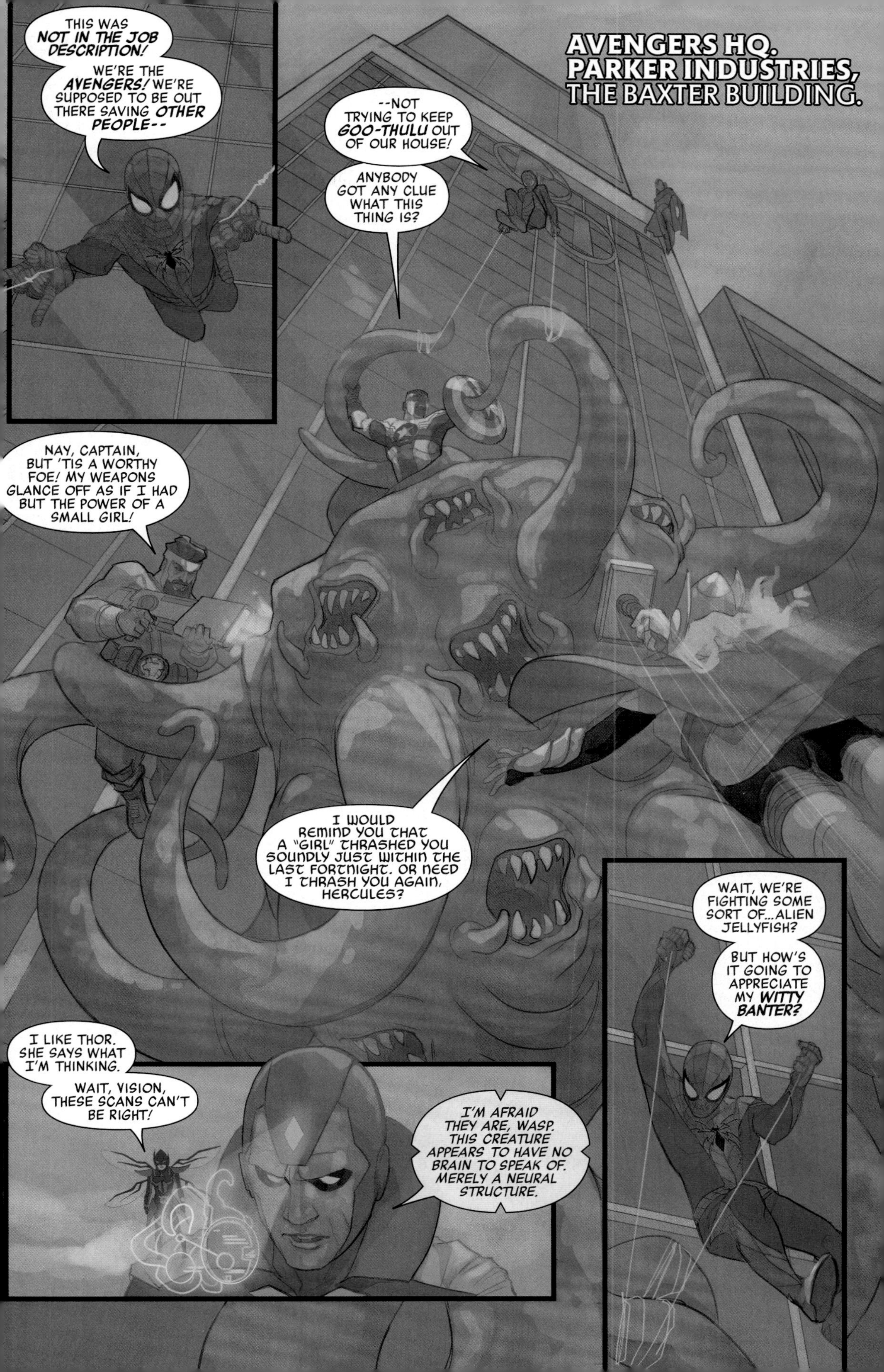
AVENGERS HQ. PARKER INDUSTRIES, THE BAXTER BUILDING.
THIS WAS NOT IN THE JOB DESCRIPTION!
WE'RE THE AVENGERS! WE'RE SUPPOSED TO BE OUT THERE SAVING OTHER PEOPLE--
--NOT TRYING TO KEEP GOO-THULU OUT OF OUR HOUSE!
ANYBODY GOT ANY CLUE WHAT THIS THING IS?
NAY, CAPTAIN, BUT 'TIS A WORTHY FOE! MY WEAPONS GLANCE OFF AS IF I HAD BUT THE POWER OF A SMALL GIRL!
I WOULD REMIND YOU THAT A "GIRL" THRASHED YOU SOUNDLY JUST WITHIN THE LAST FORTNIGHT. OR NEED I THRASH YOU AGAIN, HERCULES?
WAIT, WE'RE FIGHTING SOME SORT OF...ALIEN JELLYFISH?
BUT HOW'S IT GOING TO APPRECIATE MY WITTY BANTER?
I LIKE THOR. SHE SAYS WHAT I'M THINKING.
WAIT, VISION, THESE SCANS CAN'T BE RIGHT!
I'M AFRAID THEY ARE, WASP. THIS CREATURE APPEARS TO HAVE NO BRAIN TO SPEAK OF. MERELY A NEURAL STRUCTURE.

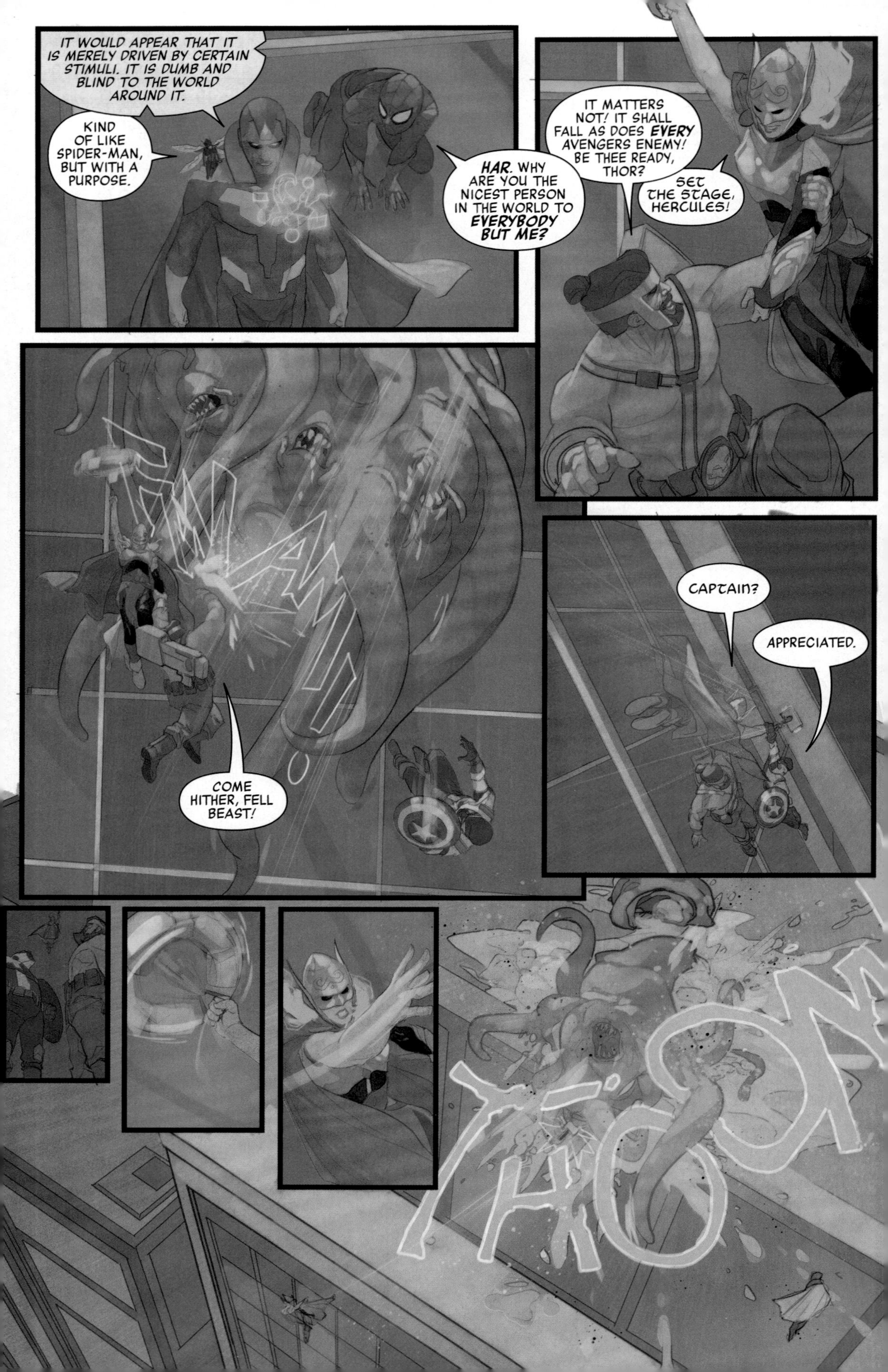
IT WOULD APPEAR THAT IT IS MERELY DRIVEN BY CERTAIN STIMULI. IT IS DUMB AND BLIND TO THE WORLD AROUND IT.
KIND OF LIKE SPIDER-MAN, BUT WITH A PURPOSE.
HAR. WHY ARE YOU THE NICEST PERSON IN THE WORLD TO EVERYBODY BUT ME?
IT MATTERS NOT! IT SHALL FALL AS DOES EVERY AVENGERS ENEMY! BE THEE READY, THOR?
SET THE STAGE, HERCULES!
COME HITHER, FELL BEAST!
CAPTAIN?
APPRECIATED.
THOOM

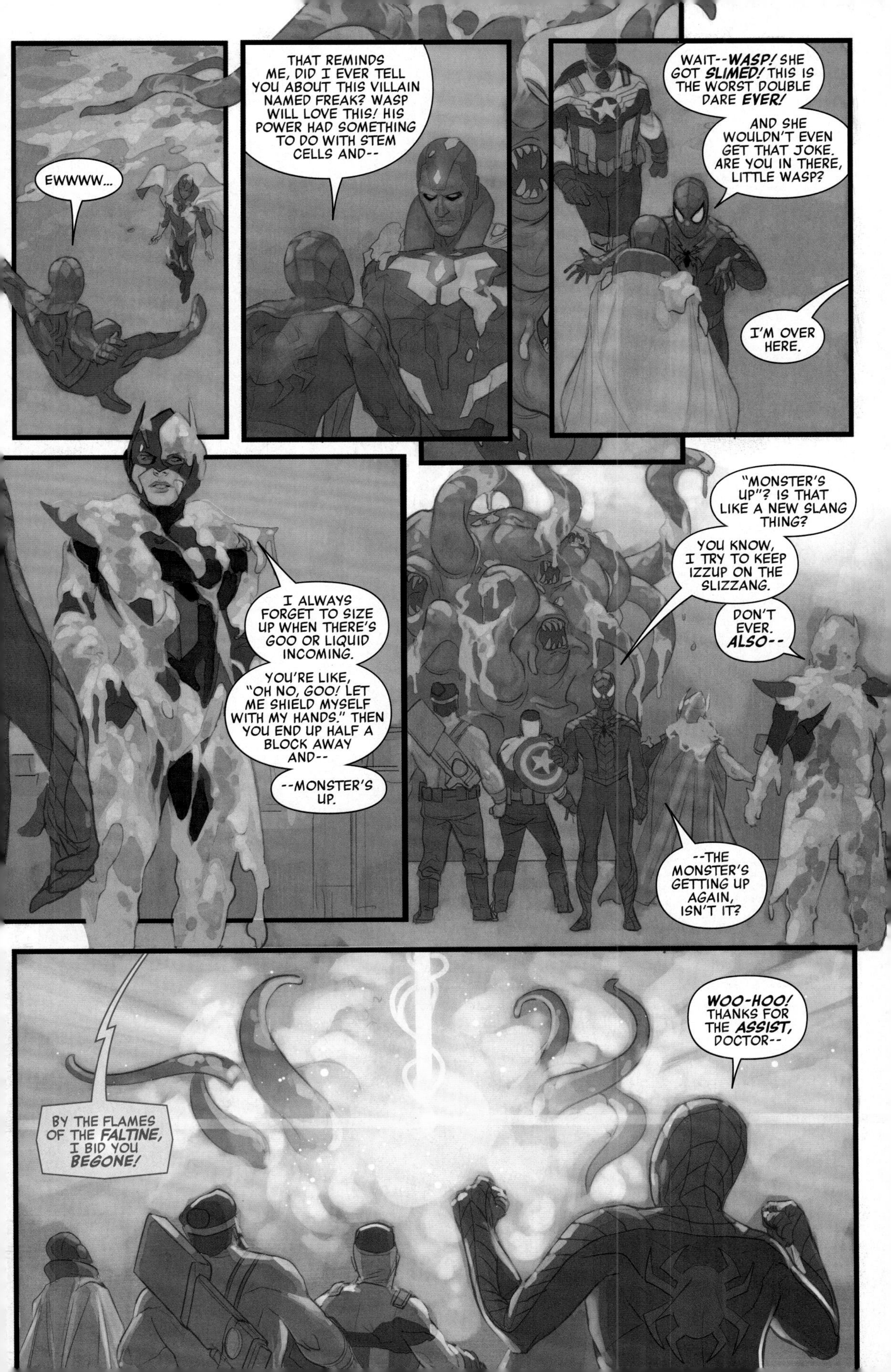
EWWWW...
THAT REMINDS ME, DID I EVER TELL YOU ABOUT THIS VILLAIN NAMED FREAK? WASP WILL LOVE THIS! HIS POWER HAD SOMETHING TO DO WITH STEM CELLS AND--
WAIT--WASP! SHE GOT SLIMED! THIS IS THE WORST DOUBLE DARE EVER!
AND SHE WOULDN'T EVEN GET THAT JOKE. ARE YOU IN THERE, LITTLE WASP?
I'M OVER HERE.
I ALWAYS FORGET TO SIZE UP WHEN THERE'S GOO OR LIQUID INCOMING.
YOU'RE LIKE, "OH NO, GOO! LET ME SHIELD MYSELF WITH MY HANDS." THEN YOU END UP HALF A BLOCK AWAY AND--
--MONSTER'S UP.
"MONSTER'S UP"? IS THAT LIKE A NEW SLANG THING?
YOU KNOW, I TRY TO KEEP IZZUP ON THE SLIZZANG.
DON'T EVER. ALSO--
--THE MONSTER'S GETTING UP AGAIN, ISN'T IT?
BY THE FLAMES OF THE FALTINE, I BID YOU BEGONE!
WOO-HOO! THANKS FOR THE ASSIST, DOCTOR--

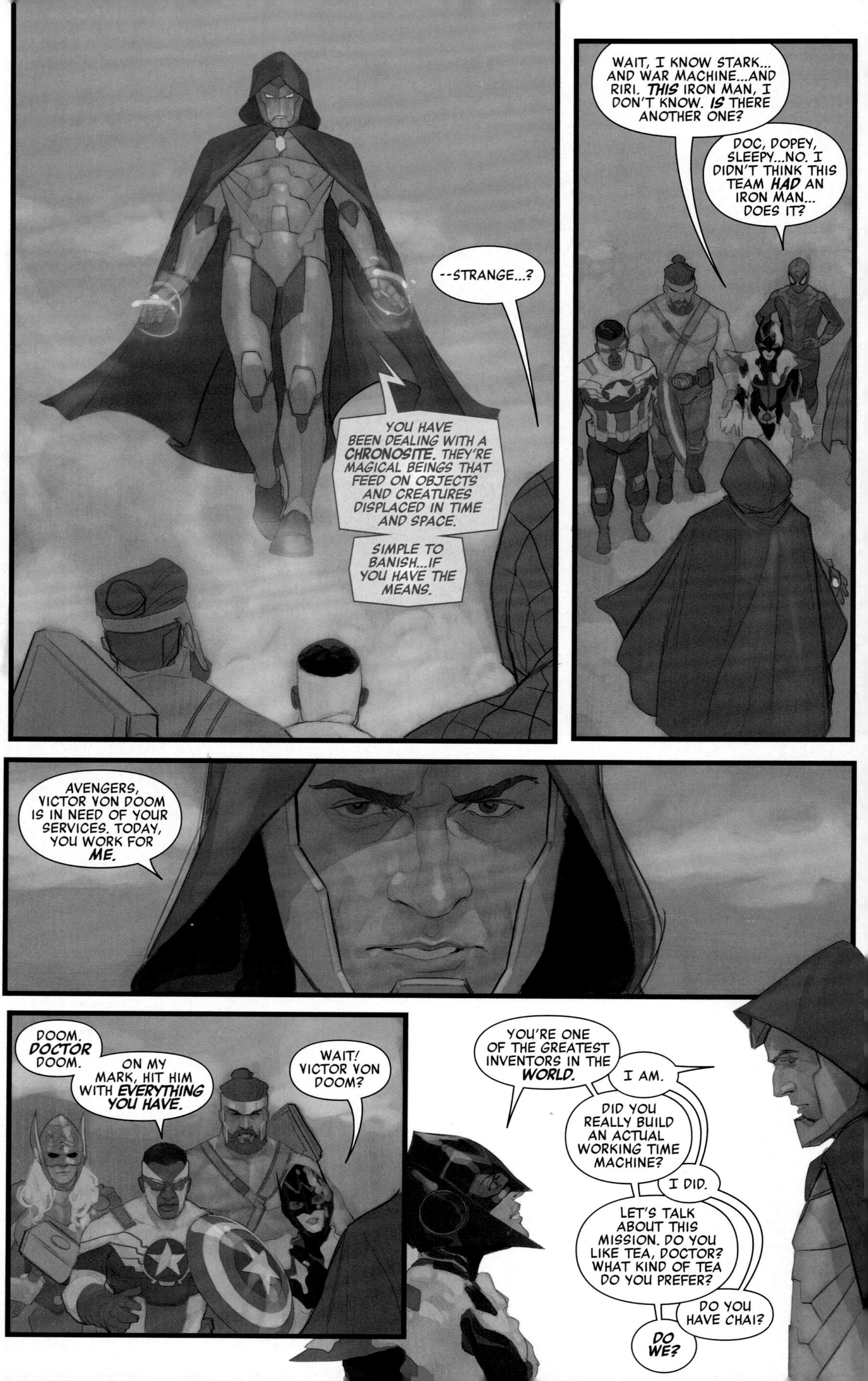
--STRANGE...?
YOU HAVE BEEN DEALING WITH A CHRONOSITE. THEY'RE MAGICAL BEINGS THAT FEED ON OBJECTS AND CREATURES DISPLACED IN TIME AND SPACE.
SIMPLE TO BANISH...IF YOU HAVE THE MEANS.
WAIT, I KNOW STARK... AND WAR MACHINE...AND RIRI. THIS IRON MAN, I DON'T KNOW. IS THERE ANOTHER ONE?
DOC, DOPEY, SLEEPY...NO. I DIDN'T THINK THIS TEAM HAD AN IRON MAN... DOES IT?
AVENGERS, VICTOR VON DOOM IS IN NEED OF YOUR SERVICES. TODAY, YOU WORK FOR ME.
DOOM. DOCTOR DOOM.
ON MY MARK, HIT HIM WITH EVERYTHING YOU HAVE.
WAIT! VICTOR VON DOOM?
YOU'RE ONE OF THE GREATEST INVENTORS IN THE WORLD.
I AM.
DID YOU REALLY BUILD AN ACTUAL WORKING TIME MACHINE?
I DID.
LET'S TALK ABOUT THIS MISSION. DO YOU LIKE TEA, DOCTOR? WHAT KIND OF TEA DO YOU PREFER?
DO YOU HAVE CHAI?
DO WE?

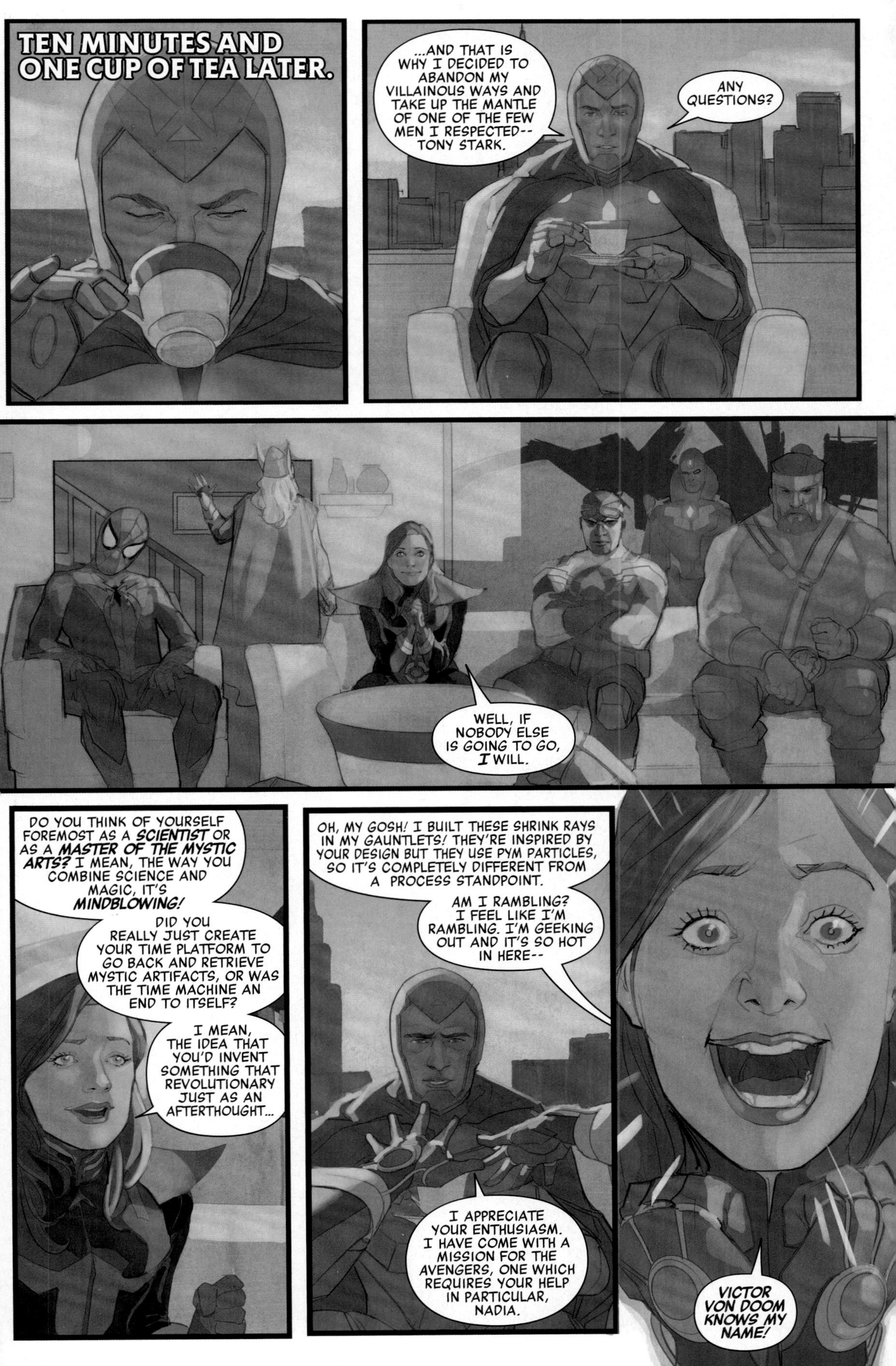
TEN MINUTES AND ONE CUP OF TEA LATER.
...AND THAT IS WHY I DECIDED TO ABANDON MY VILLAINOUS WAYS AND TAKE UP THE MANTLE OF ONE OF THE FEW MEN I RESPECTED-- TONY STARK.
ANY QUESTIONS?
WELL, IF NOBODY ELSE IS GOING TO GO, I WILL.
DO YOU THINK OF YOURSELF FOREMOST AS A SCIENTIST OR AS A MASTER OF THE MYSTIC ARTS? I MEAN, THE WAY YOU COMBINE SCIENCE AND MAGIC, IT'S MINDBLOWING!
DID YOU REALLY JUST CREATE YOUR TIME PLATFORM TO GO BACK AND RETRIEVE MYSTIC ARTIFACTS, OR WAS THE TIME MACHINE AN END TO ITSELF?
I MEAN, THE IDEA THAT YOU'D INVENT SOMETHING THAT REVOLUTIONARY JUST AS AN AFTERTHOUGHT...
OH, MY GOSH! I BUILT THESE SHRINK RAYS IN MY GAUNTLETS! THEY'RE INSPIRED BY YOUR DESIGN BUT THEY USE PYM PARTICLES, SO IT'S COMPLETELY DIFFERENT FROM A PROCESS STANDPOINT.
AM I RAMBLING? I FEEL LIKE I'M RAMBLING. I'M GEEKING OUT AND IT'S SO HOT IN HERE--
I APPRECIATE YOUR ENTHUSIASM. I HAVE COME WITH A MISSION FOR THE AVENGERS, ONE WHICH REQUIRES YOUR HELP IN PARTICULAR, NADIA.
VICTOR VON DOOM KNOWS MY NAME!

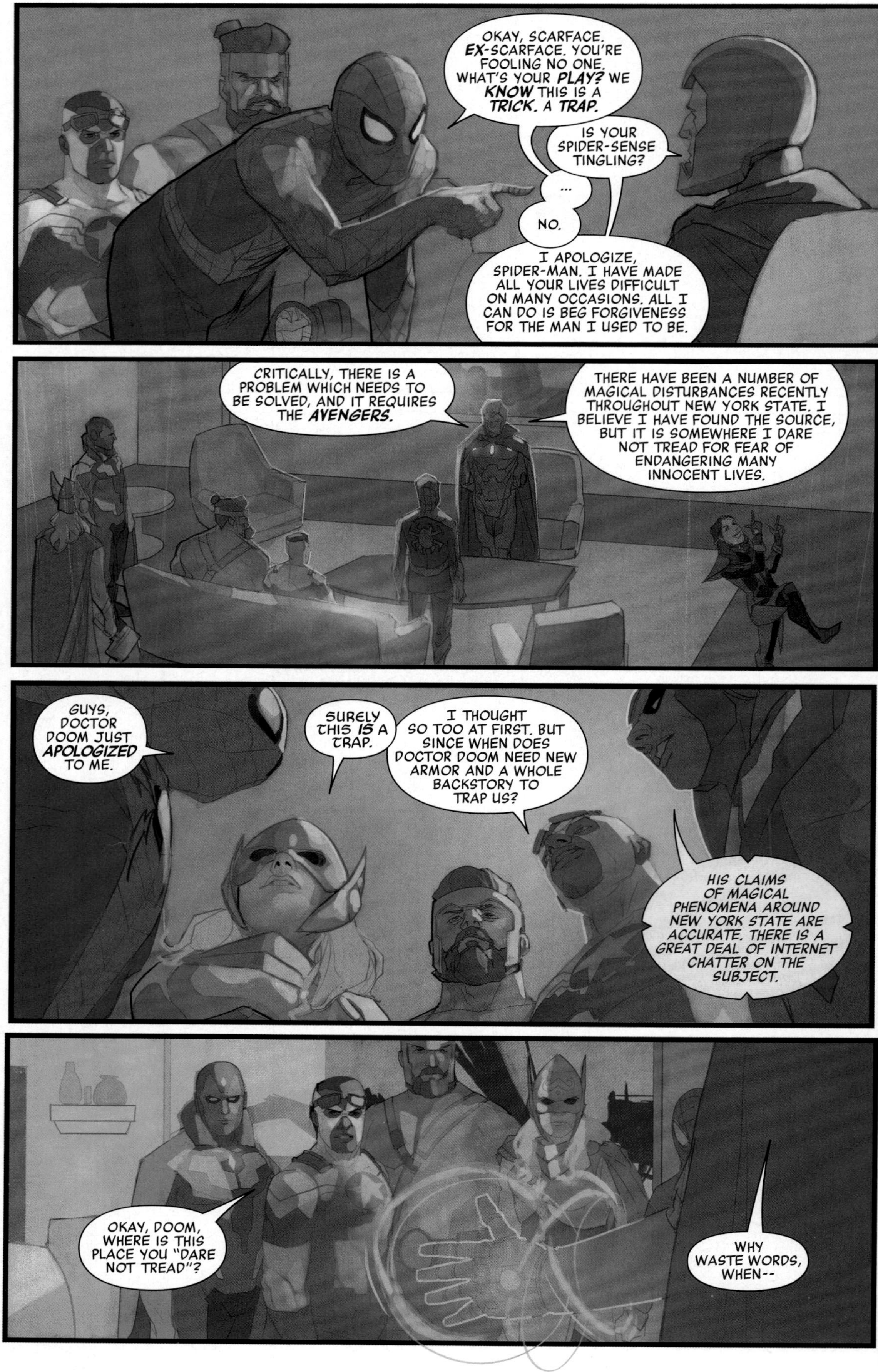
OKAY, SCARFACE. EX-SCARFACE. YOU'RE FOOLING NO ONE. WHAT'S YOUR PLAY? WE KNOW THIS IS A TRICK. A TRAP.
IS YOUR SPIDER-SENSE TINGLING?
...
NO.
I APOLOGIZE, SPIDER-MAN. I HAVE MADE ALL YOUR LIVES DIFFICULT ON MANY OCCASIONS. ALL I CAN DO IS BEG FORGIVENESS FOR THE MAN I USED TO BE.
CRITICALLY, THERE IS A PROBLEM WHICH NEEDS TO BE SOLVED, AND IT REQUIRES THE AVENGERS.
THERE HAVE BEEN A NUMBER OF MAGICAL DISTURBANCES RECENTLY THROUGHOUT NEW YORK STATE. I BELIEVE I HAVE FOUND THE SOURCE, BUT IT IS SOMEWHERE I DARE NOT TREAD FOR FEAR OF ENDANGERING MANY INNOCENT LIVES.
GUYS, DOCTOR DOOM JUST APOLOGIZED TO ME.
SURELY THIS IS A TRAP.
I THOUGHT SO TOO AT FIRST. BUT SINCE WHEN DOES DOCTOR DOOM NEED NEW ARMOR AND A WHOLE BACKSTORY TO TRAP US?
HIS CLAIMS OF MAGICAL PHENOMENA AROUND NEW YORK STATE ARE ACCURATE. THERE IS A GREAT DEAL OF INTERNET CHATTER ON THE SUBJECT.
OKAY, DOOM, WHERE IS THIS PLACE YOU "DARE NOT TREAD"?
WHY WASTE WORDS, WHEN--

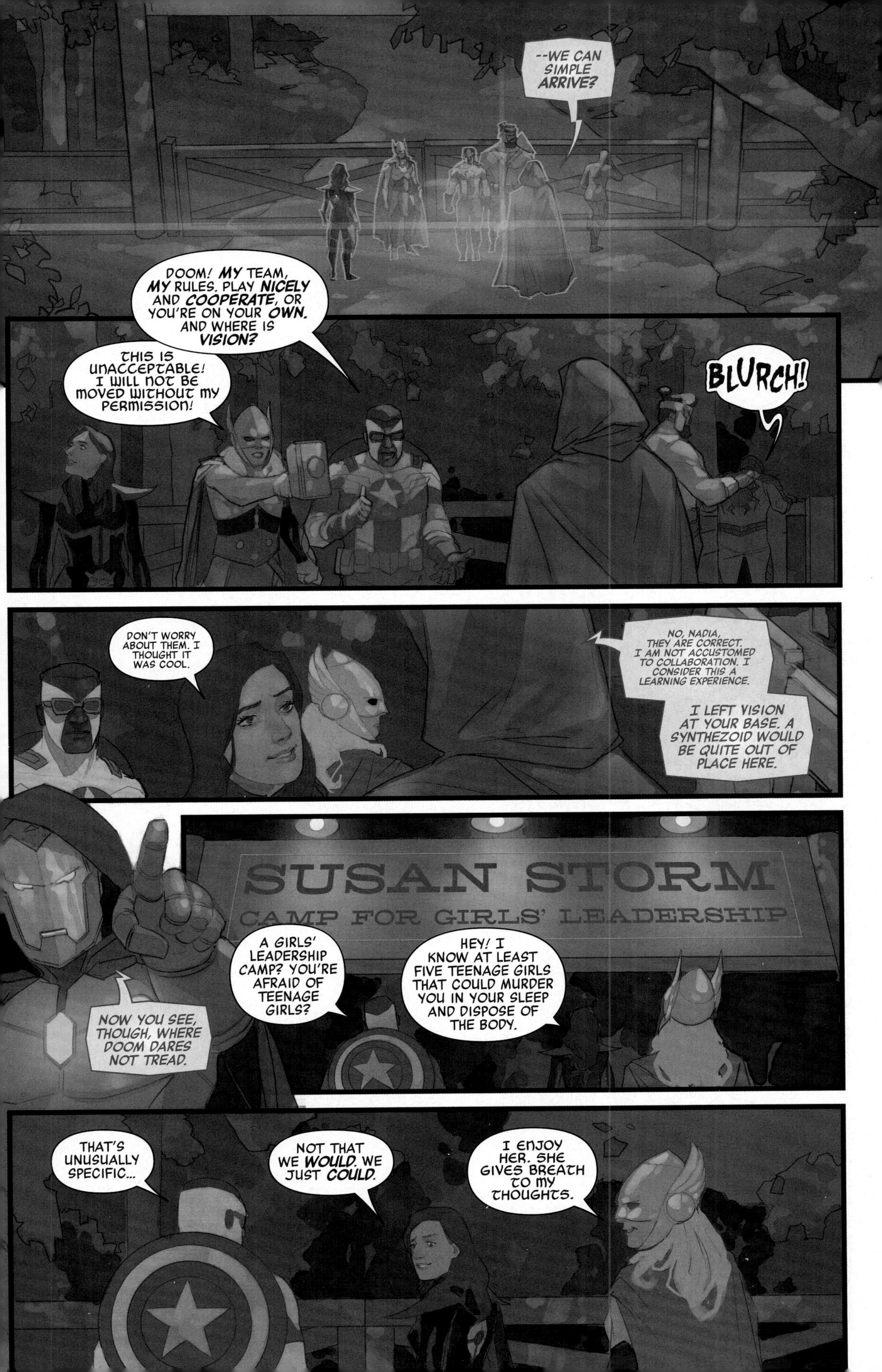
--WE CAN SIMPLE ARRIVE?
DOOM! MY TEAM, MY RULES. PLAY NICELY AND COOPERATE, OR YOU'RE ON YOUR OWN. AND WHERE IS VISION?
THIS IS UNACCEPTABLE! I WILL NOT BE MOVED WITHOUT MY PERMISSION!
BLURCH!
DON'T WORRY ABOUT THEM. I THOUGHT IT WAS COOL.
NO, NADIA, THEY ARE CORRECT. I AM NOT ACCUSTOMED TO COLLABORATION. I CONSIDER THIS A LEARNING EXPERIENCE.
I LEFT VISION AT YOUR BASE. A SYNTHEZOID WOULD BE QUITE OUT OF PLACE HERE.
SUSAN STORM
CAMP FOR GIRLS' LEADERSHIP
NOW YOU SEE, THOUGH, WHERE DOOM DARES NOT TREAD.
A GIRLS' LEADERSHIP CAMP? YOU'RE AFRAID OF TEENAGE GIRLS?
HEY! I KNOW AT LEAST FIVE TEENAGE GIRLS THAT COULD MURDER YOU IN YOUR SLEEP AND DISPOSE OF THE BODY.
THAT'S UNUSUALLY SPECIFIC...
NOT THAT WE WOULD. WE JUST COULD.
I ENJOY HER. SHE GIVES BREATH TO MY THOUGHTS.

I'M SORRY. PERHAPS I MISSED IT IN MY UNCONTROLLABLE VOMITING, BUT WHY ARE THE AVENGERS GOING TO HELP YOU RAID A GIRLS' LEADERSHIP CAMP?

THIS PLACE WAS CREATED BY SOMEONE DEAR TO ME. I WISH NOT TO SEE IT DESTROYED OR SHUT DOWN. BUT THERE IS SOMETHING ROTTEN LURKING UPON ITS GROUNDS.

WERE DOOM TO KNOCK ON THE COUNSELOR'S DOOR OR WALK AMONG THE CAMPERS, NOT ONLY WOULD IT CAUSE A PANIC, BUT THE PERPETRATORS WOULD LIKELY SLIP BETWEEN MY FINGERS.

HOWEVER, IF AN AGE-APPROPRIATE GIRL WERE ABLE TO HAVE A LOOK INSIDE--

I'M NOT BIG ON THE IDEA OF NADIA GOING ON A MISSION, FOR *YOU, ALONE.*

CAP, I ESCAPED A SECRET RUSSIAN GULAG ON MY OWN. I CAN HANDLE *SLEEPAWAY CAMP.*

THOUGH I AM SUDDENLY AWARE OF A WEAKNESS. MY HAIR BRAIDING SKILLS ARE MEDIOCRE AT BEST.

OH, AND I DON'T HAVE A CAMP UNIFORM.

FEAR NOT!

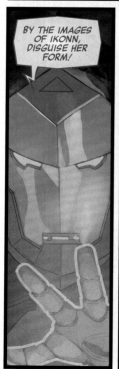

BY THE IMAGES OF IKONN, DISGUISE HER FORM!

SHOOM

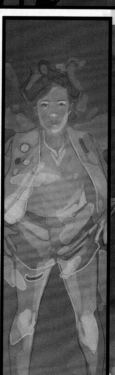

THE COMBAT BOOTS ARE A WEIRD TOUCH, DOOM. YOU NEED A TIM GUNN.

I *LOVE* THEM!

ALSO, YOU WILL FIND THAT YOU HEAR MY VOICE DIRECTLY IN YOUR EAR. AS AN EARPIECE WOULD BE A GIVEAWAY, I EMPLOYED A COMMUNICATION SPELL.

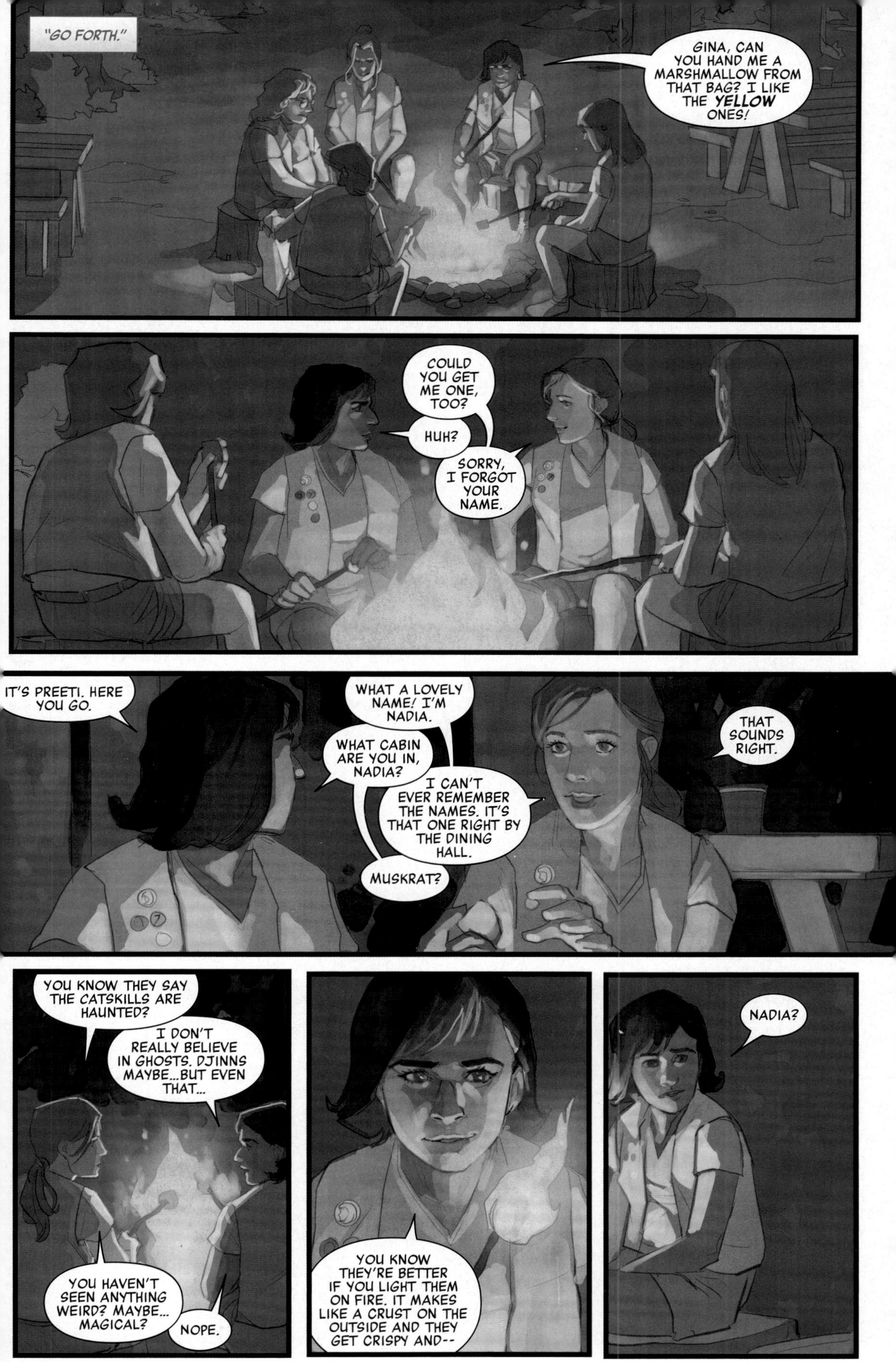
"GO FORTH."
GINA, CAN YOU HAND ME A MARSHMALLOW FROM THAT BAG? I LIKE THE YELLOW ONES!
COULD YOU GET ME ONE, TOO?
HUH?
SORRY, I FORGOT YOUR NAME.
IT'S PREETI. HERE YOU GO.
WHAT A LOVELY NAME! I'M NADIA.
WHAT CABIN ARE YOU IN, NADIA?
I CAN'T EVER REMEMBER THE NAMES. IT'S THAT ONE RIGHT BY THE DINING HALL.
MUSKRAT?
THAT SOUNDS RIGHT.
YOU KNOW THEY SAY THE CATSKILLS ARE HAUNTED?
I DON'T REALLY BELIEVE IN GHOSTS. DJINNS MAYBE...BUT EVEN THAT...
YOU HAVEN'T SEEN ANYTHING WEIRD? MAYBE... MAGICAL?
NOPE.
YOU KNOW THEY'RE BETTER IF YOU LIGHT THEM ON FIRE. IT MAKES LIKE A CRUST ON THE OUTSIDE AND THEY GET CRISPY AND--
NADIA?

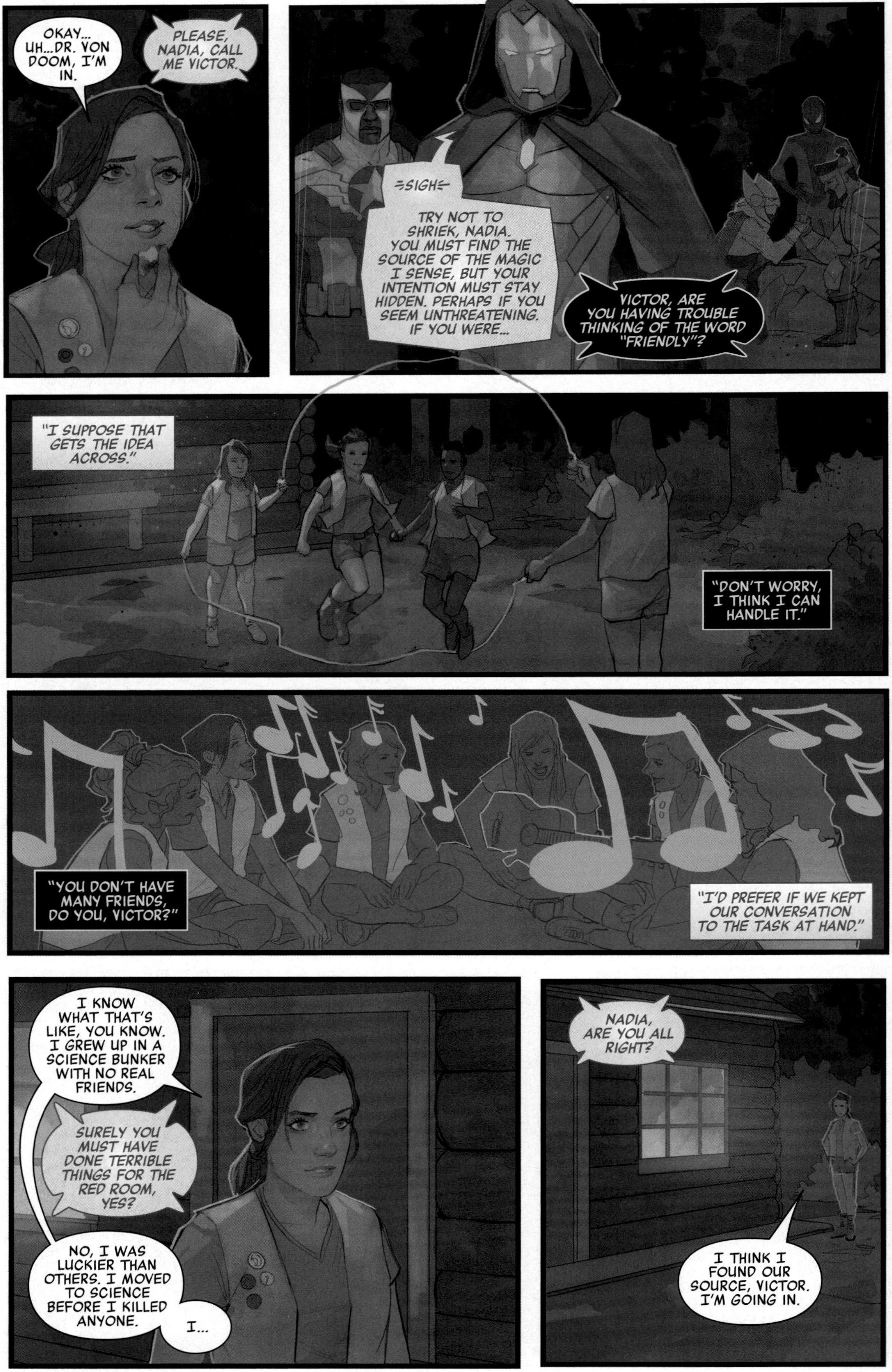

OKAY... UH...DR. VON DOOM, I'M IN.
PLEASE, NADIA, CALL ME VICTOR.
=SIGH=
TRY NOT TO SHRIEK, NADIA. YOU MUST FIND THE SOURCE OF THE MAGIC I SENSE, BUT YOUR INTENTION MUST STAY HIDDEN. PERHAPS IF YOU SEEM UNTHREATENING. IF YOU WERE...
VICTOR, ARE YOU HAVING TROUBLE THINKING OF THE WORD "FRIENDLY"?
"I SUPPOSE THAT GETS THE IDEA ACROSS."
"DON'T WORRY, I THINK I CAN HANDLE IT."
"YOU DON'T HAVE MANY FRIENDS, DO YOU, VICTOR?"
"I'D PREFER IF WE KEPT OUR CONVERSATION TO THE TASK AT HAND."
I KNOW WHAT THAT'S LIKE, YOU KNOW. I GREW UP IN A SCIENCE BUNKER WITH NO REAL FRIENDS.
SURELY YOU MUST HAVE DONE TERRIBLE THINGS FOR THE RED ROOM, YES?
NO, I WAS LUCKIER THAN OTHERS. I MOVED TO SCIENCE BEFORE I KILLED ANYONE.
I...
NADIA, ARE YOU ALL RIGHT?
I THINK I FOUND OUR SOURCE, VICTOR. I'M GOING IN.

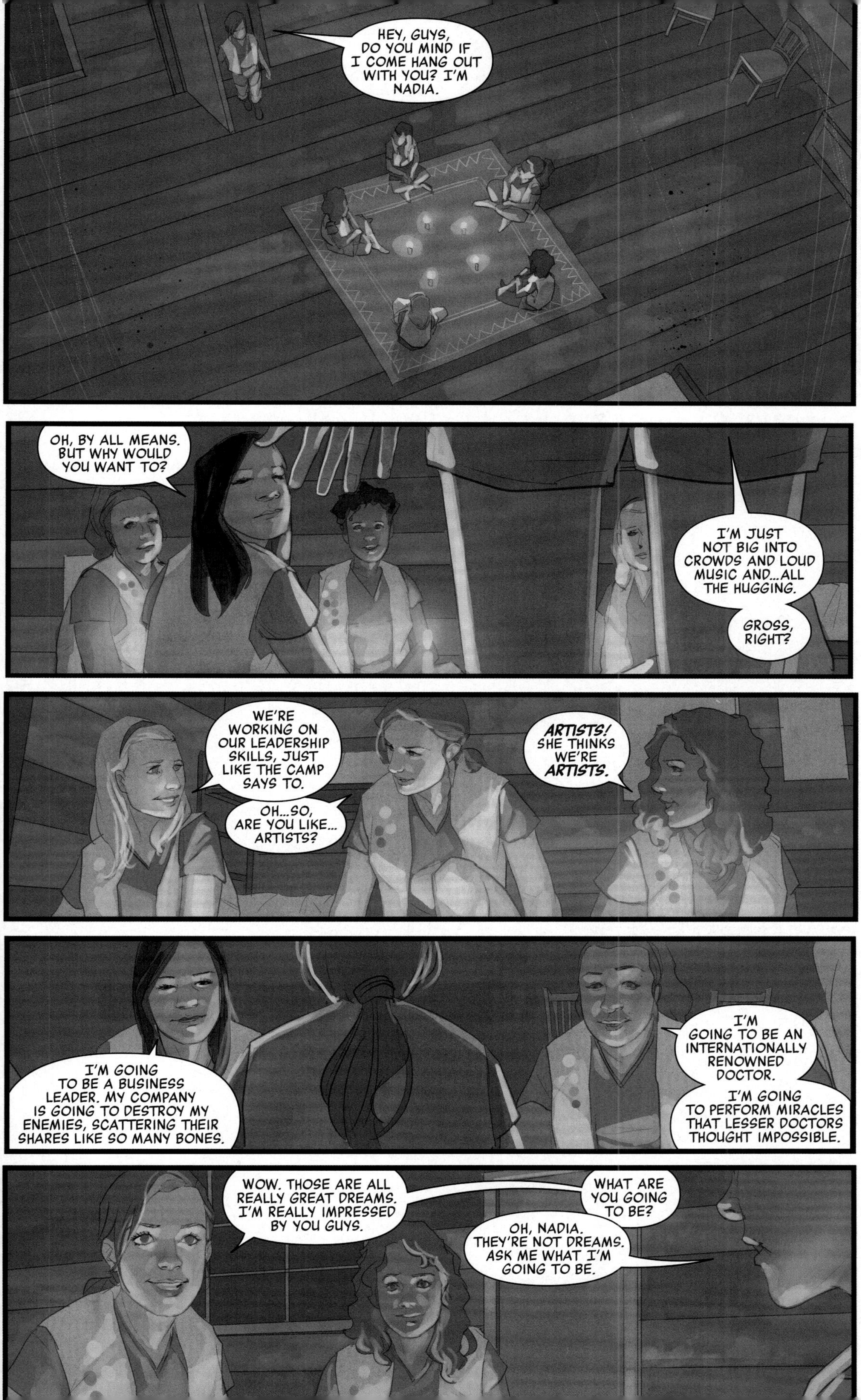
HEY, GUYS, DO YOU MIND IF I COME HANG OUT WITH YOU? I'M NADIA.
OH, BY ALL MEANS. BUT WHY WOULD YOU WANT TO?
I'M JUST NOT BIG INTO CROWDS AND LOUD MUSIC AND...ALL THE HUGGING.
GROSS, RIGHT?
WE'RE WORKING ON OUR LEADERSHIP SKILLS, JUST LIKE THE CAMP SAYS TO.
OH...SO, ARE YOU LIKE... ARTISTS?
ARTISTS! SHE THINKS WE'RE *ARTISTS.*
I'M GOING TO BE A BUSINESS LEADER. MY COMPANY IS GOING TO DESTROY MY ENEMIES, SCATTERING THEIR SHARES LIKE SO MANY BONES.
I'M GOING TO BE AN INTERNATIONALLY RENOWNED DOCTOR.
I'M GOING TO PERFORM MIRACLES THAT LESSER DOCTORS THOUGHT IMPOSSIBLE.
WOW. THOSE ARE ALL REALLY GREAT DREAMS. I'M REALLY IMPRESSED BY YOU GUYS.
WHAT ARE YOU GOING TO BE?
OH, NADIA. THEY'RE NOT DREAMS. ASK ME WHAT I'M GOING TO BE.

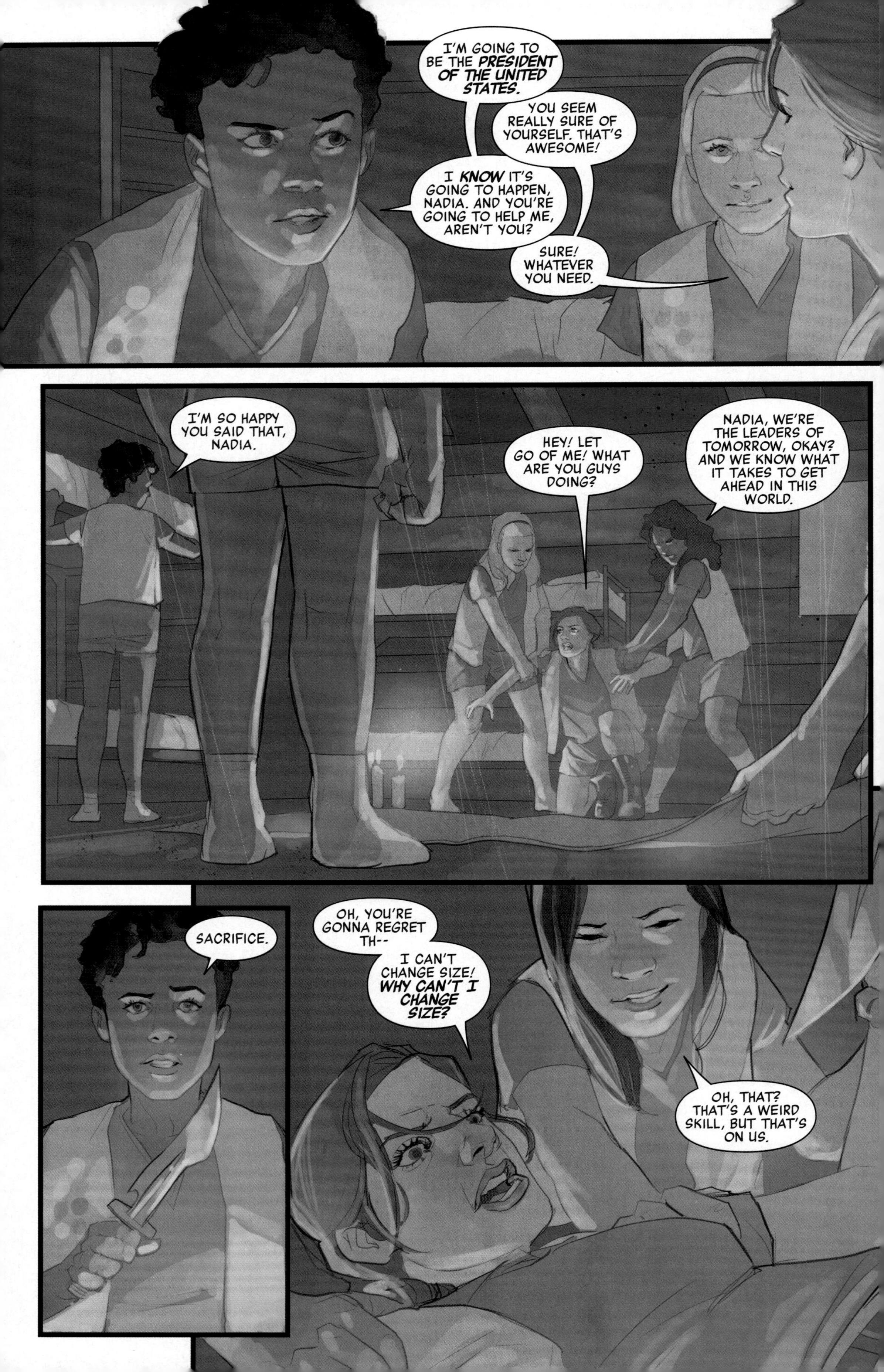
I'M GOING TO BE THE PRESIDENT OF THE UNITED STATES.
YOU SEEM REALLY SURE OF YOURSELF. THAT'S AWESOME!
I KNOW IT'S GOING TO HAPPEN, NADIA. AND YOU'RE GOING TO HELP ME, AREN'T YOU?
SURE! WHATEVER YOU NEED.
I'M SO HAPPY YOU SAID THAT, NADIA.
HEY! LET GO OF ME! WHAT ARE YOU GUYS DOING?
NADIA, WE'RE THE LEADERS OF TOMORROW, OKAY? AND WE KNOW WHAT IT TAKES TO GET AHEAD IN THIS WORLD.
SACRIFICE.
OH, YOU'RE GONNA REGRET TH--
I CAN'T CHANGE SIZE! WHY CAN'T I CHANGE SIZE?
OH, THAT? THAT'S A WEIRD SKILL, BUT THAT'S ON US.

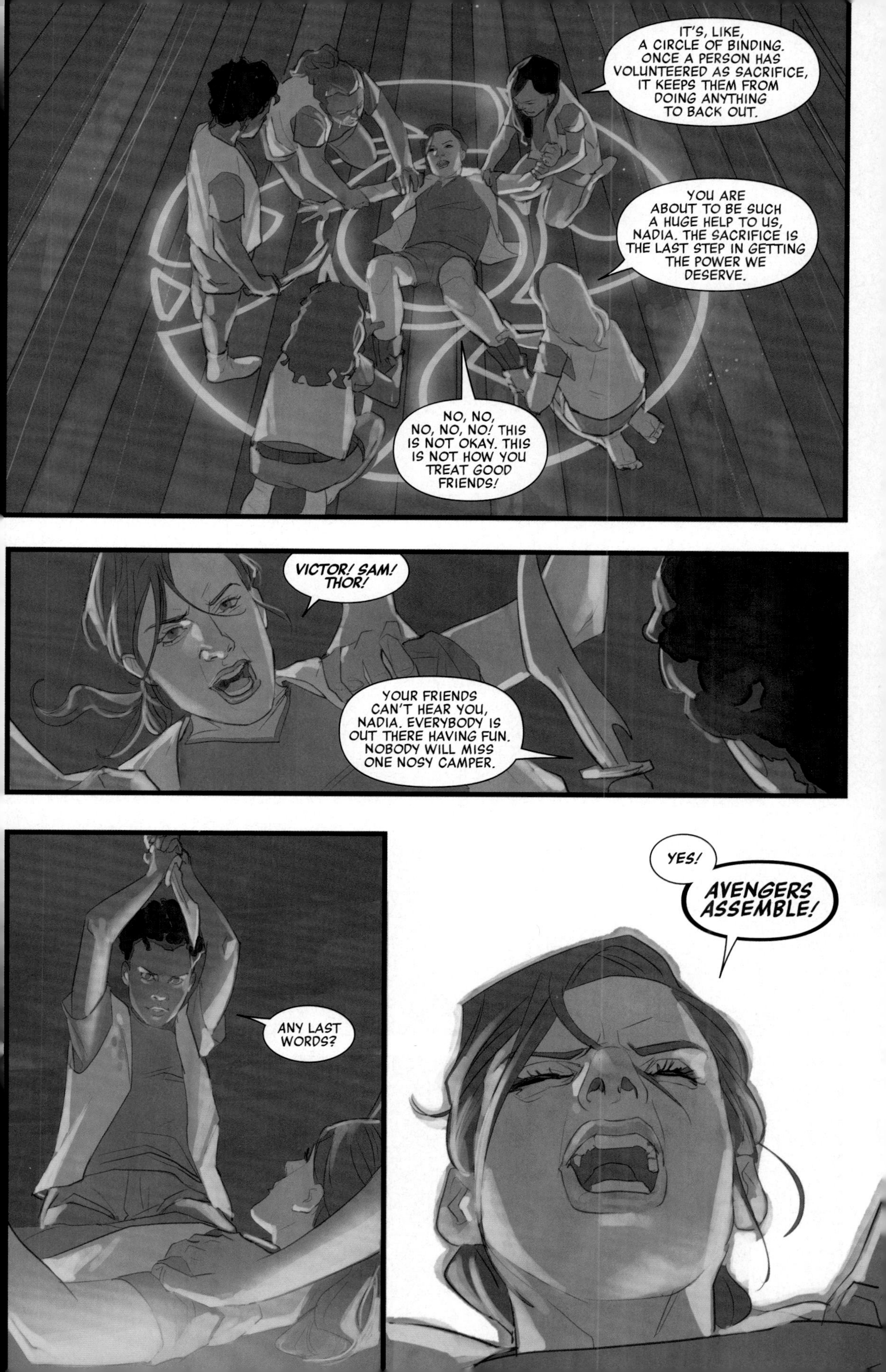
IT'S, LIKE, A CIRCLE OF BINDING. ONCE A PERSON HAS VOLUNTEERED AS SACRIFICE, IT KEEPS THEM FROM DOING ANYTHING TO BACK OUT.
YOU ARE ABOUT TO BE SUCH A HUGE HELP TO US, NADIA. THE SACRIFICE IS THE LAST STEP IN GETTING THE POWER WE DESERVE.
NO, NO, NO, NO, NO! THIS IS NOT OKAY. THIS IS NOT HOW YOU TREAT GOOD FRIENDS!
VICTOR! SAM! THOR!
YOUR FRIENDS CAN'T HEAR YOU, NADIA. EVERYBODY IS OUT THERE HAVING FUN. NOBODY WILL MISS ONE NOSY CAMPER.
ANY LAST WORDS?
YES!
AVENGERS ASSEMBLE!

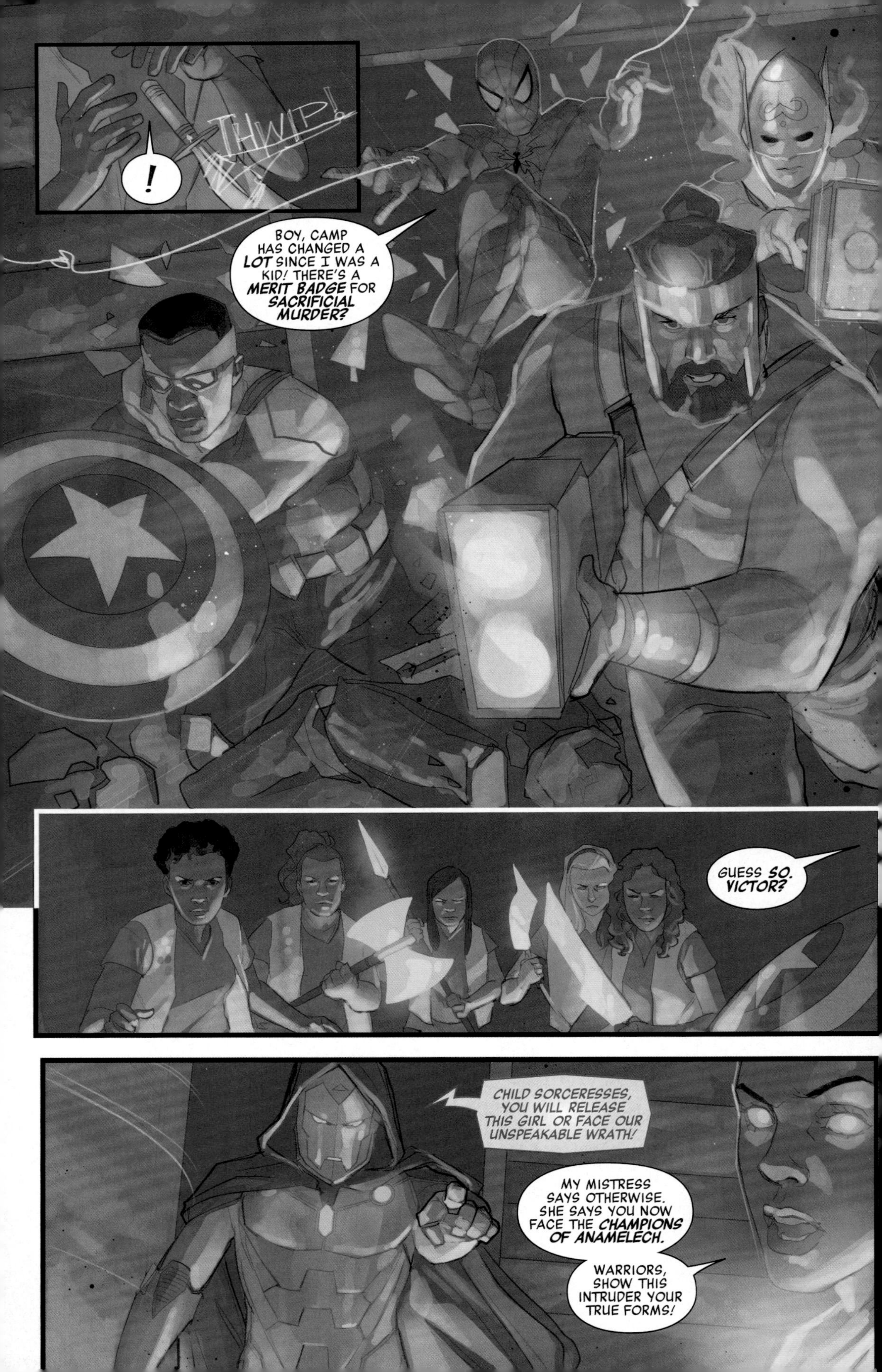
!
THWIP!
BOY, CAMP HAS CHANGED A LOT SINCE I WAS A KID! THERE'S A MERIT BADGE FOR SACRIFICIAL MURDER?
GUESS SO. VICTOR?
CHILD SORCERESSES, YOU WILL RELEASE THIS GIRL OR FACE OUR UNSPEAKABLE WRATH!
MY MISTRESS SAYS OTHERWISE. SHE SAYS YOU NOW FACE THE CHAMPIONS OF ANAMELECH.
WARRIORS, SHOW THIS INTRUDER YOUR TRUE FORMS!

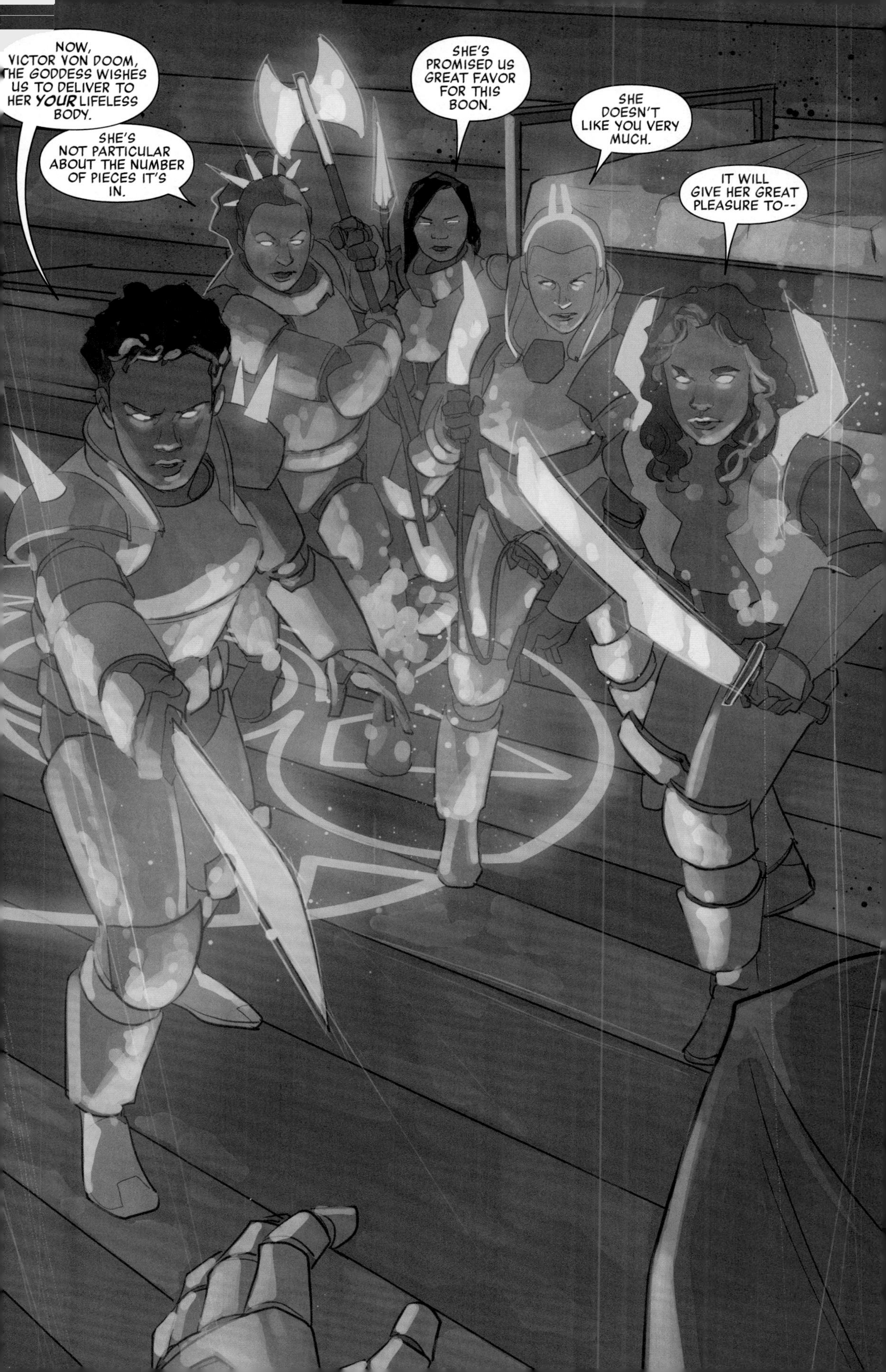
NOW, VICTOR VON DOOM, THE GODDESS WISHES US TO DELIVER TO HER *YOUR* LIFELESS BODY.
SHE'S NOT PARTICULAR ABOUT THE NUMBER OF PIECES IT'S IN.
SHE'S PROMISED US GREAT FAVOR FOR THIS BOON.
SHE DOESN'T LIKE YOU VERY MUCH.
IT WILL GIVE HER GREAT PLEASURE TO--

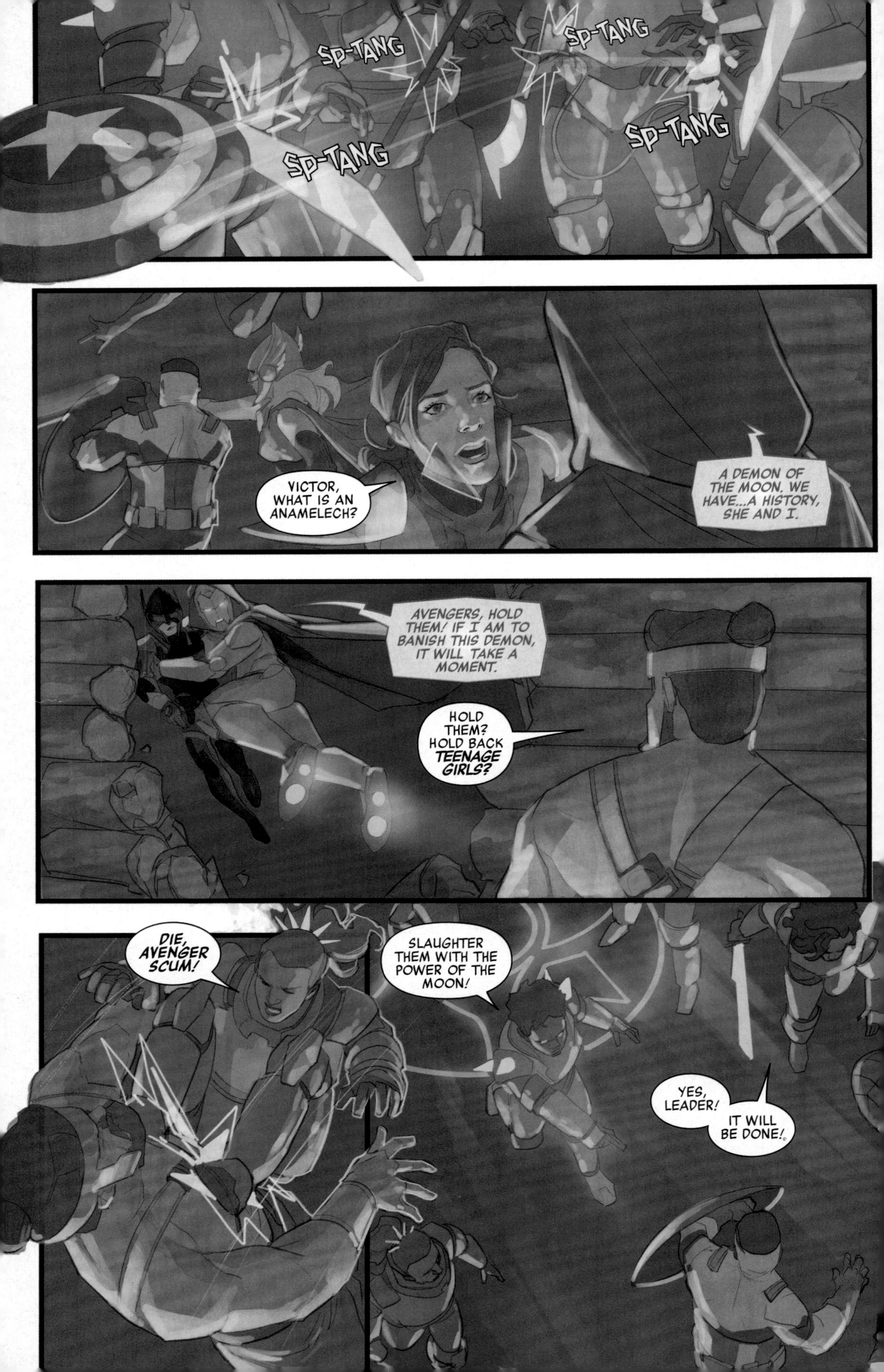
SP-TANG
SP-TANG
SP-TANG
SP-TANG
VICTOR, WHAT IS AN ANAMELECH?
A DEMON OF THE MOON. WE HAVE...A HISTORY, SHE AND I.
AVENGERS, HOLD THEM! IF I AM TO BANISH THIS DEMON, IT WILL TAKE A MOMENT.
HOLD THEM? HOLD BACK *TEENAGE GIRLS?*
DIE, AVENGER SCUM!
SLAUGHTER THEM WITH THE POWER OF THE MOON!
YES, LEADER!
IT WILL BE DONE!

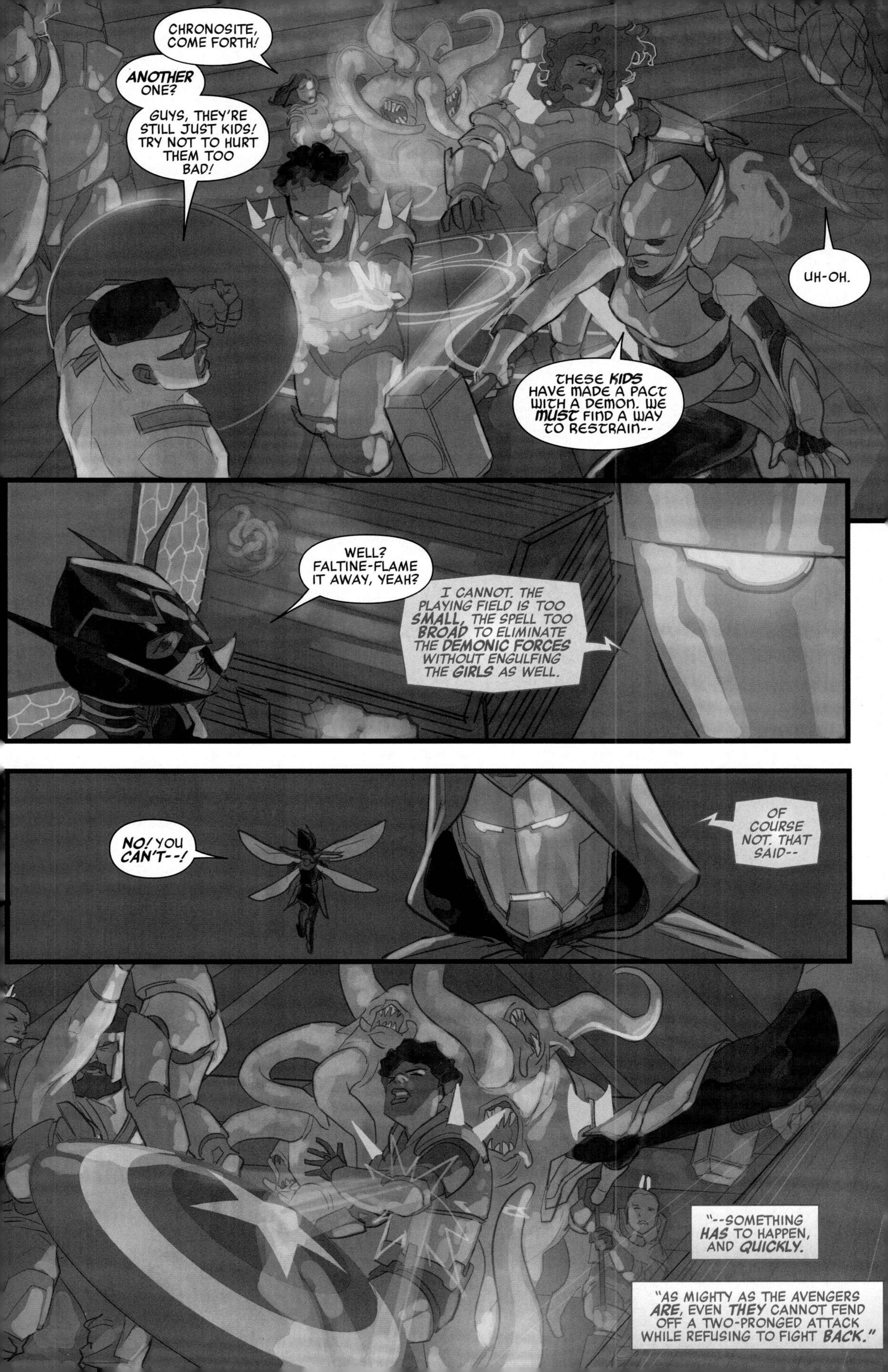

CHRONOSITE, COME FORTH!
ANOTHER ONE?
GUYS, THEY'RE STILL JUST KIDS! TRY NOT TO HURT THEM TOO BAD!
UH-OH.
THESE KIDS HAVE MADE A PACT WITH A DEMON. WE MUST FIND A WAY TO RESTRAIN--
WELL? FALTINE-FLAME IT AWAY, YEAH?
I CANNOT. THE PLAYING FIELD IS TOO SMALL, THE SPELL TOO BROAD TO ELIMINATE THE DEMONIC FORCES WITHOUT ENGULFING THE GIRLS AS WELL.
NO! YOU CAN'T--!
OF COURSE NOT. THAT SAID--
"--SOMETHING HAS TO HAPPEN, AND QUICKLY.
"AS MIGHTY AS THE AVENGERS ARE, EVEN THEY CANNOT FEND OFF A TWO-PRONGED ATTACK WHILE REFUSING TO FIGHT BACK."

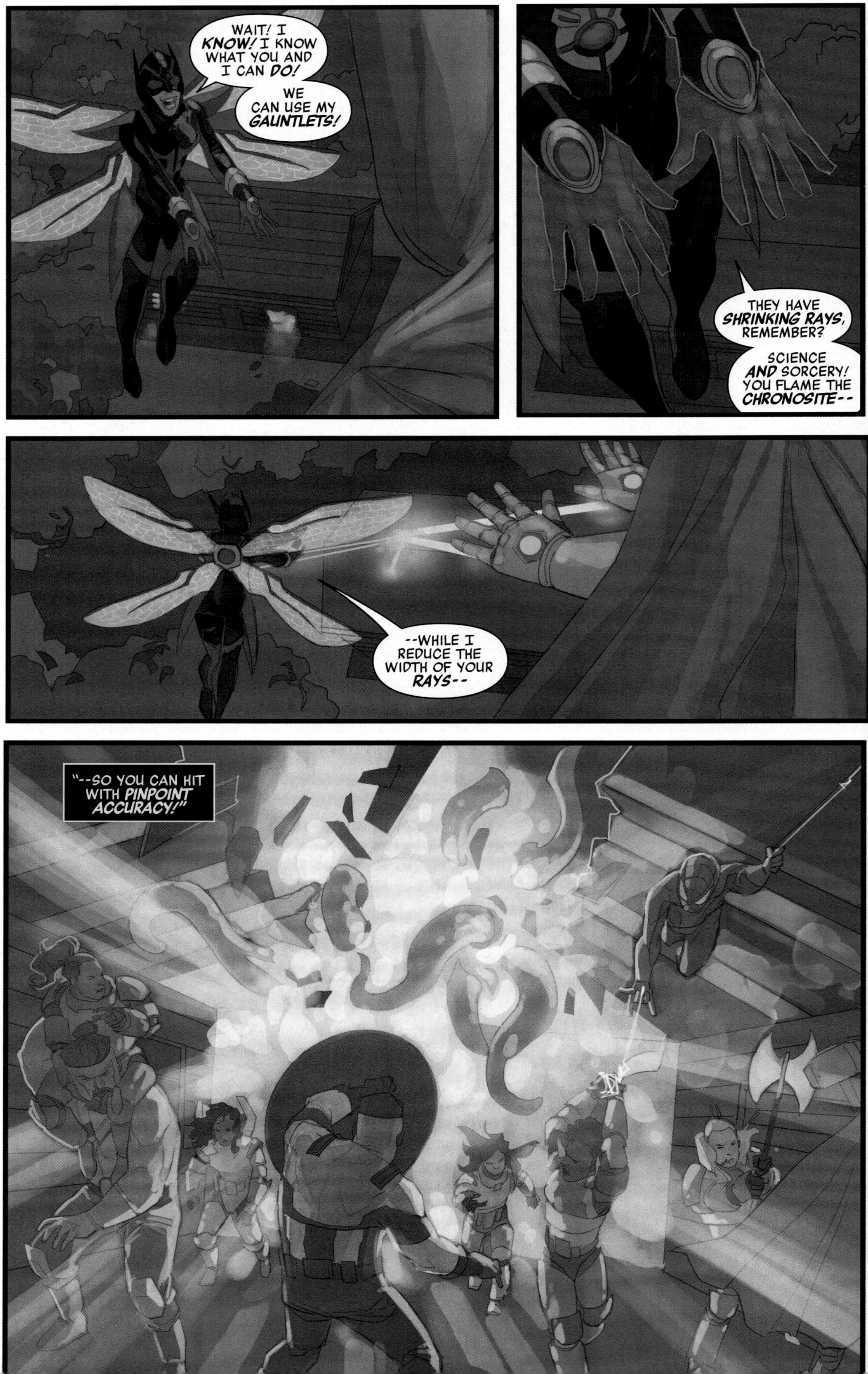
WAIT! I KNOW! I KNOW WHAT YOU AND I CAN DO!
WE CAN USE MY GAUNTLETS!
THEY HAVE SHRINKING RAYS, REMEMBER?
SCIENCE AND SORCERY! YOU FLAME THE CHRONOSITE--
--WHILE I REDUCE THE WIDTH OF YOUR RAYS--
"--SO YOU CAN HIT WITH PINPOINT ACCURACY!"

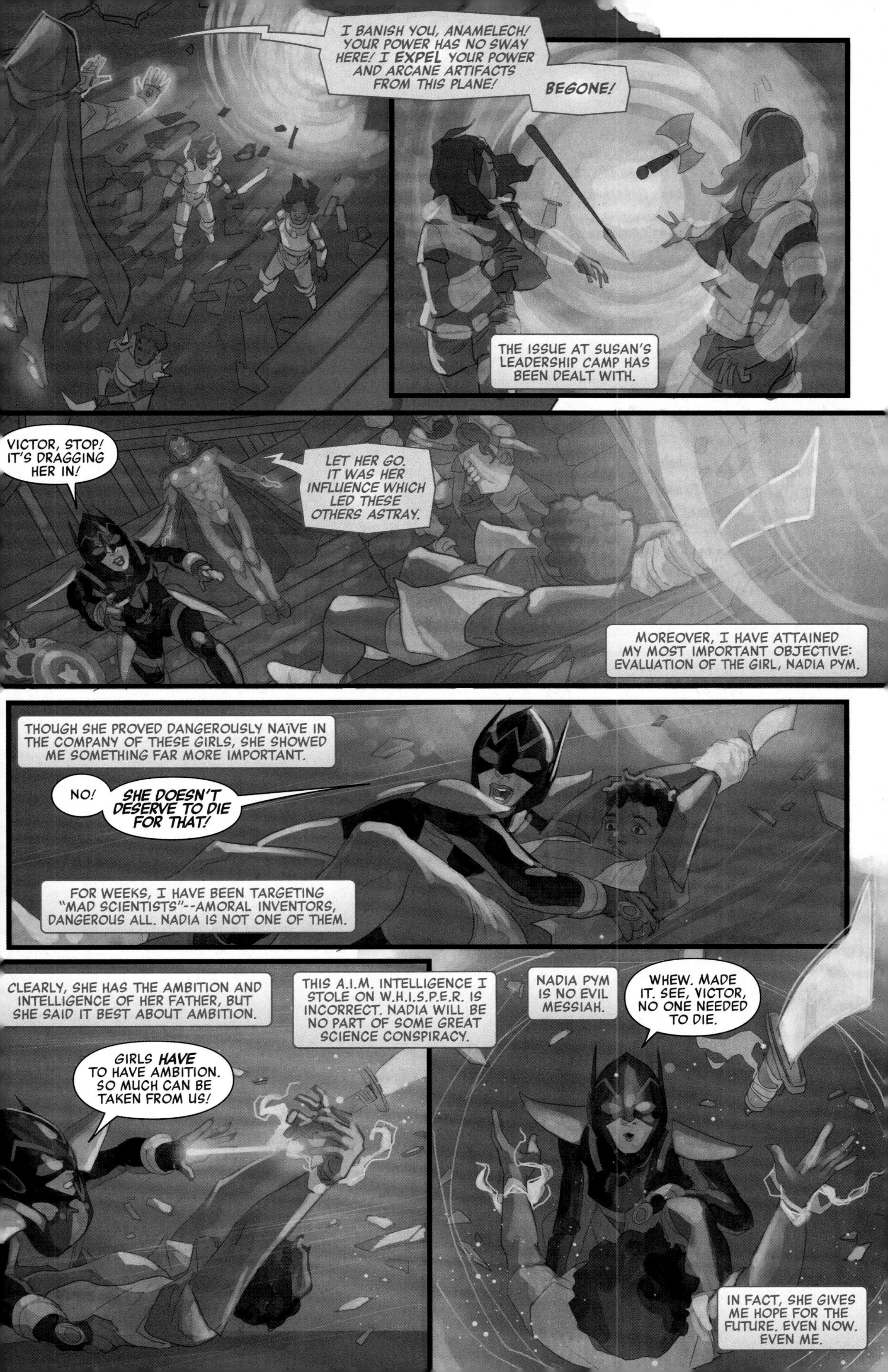

I BANISH YOU, ANAMELECH! YOUR POWER HAS NO SWAY HERE! I EXPEL YOUR POWER AND ARCANE ARTIFACTS FROM THIS PLANE!
BEGONE!
THE ISSUE AT SUSAN'S LEADERSHIP CAMP HAS BEEN DEALT WITH.
VICTOR, STOP! IT'S DRAGGING HER IN!
LET HER GO. IT WAS HER INFLUENCE WHICH LED THESE OTHERS ASTRAY.
MOREOVER, I HAVE ATTAINED MY MOST IMPORTANT OBJECTIVE: EVALUATION OF THE GIRL, NADIA PYM.
THOUGH SHE PROVED DANGEROUSLY NAÏVE IN THE COMPANY OF THESE GIRLS, SHE SHOWED ME SOMETHING FAR MORE IMPORTANT.
NO!
SHE DOESN'T DESERVE TO DIE FOR THAT!
FOR WEEKS, I HAVE BEEN TARGETING "MAD SCIENTISTS"--AMORAL INVENTORS, DANGEROUS ALL. NADIA IS NOT ONE OF THEM.
CLEARLY, SHE HAS THE AMBITION AND INTELLIGENCE OF HER FATHER, BUT SHE SAID IT BEST ABOUT AMBITION.
THIS A.I.M. INTELLIGENCE I STOLE ON W.H.I.S.P.E.R. IS INCORRECT. NADIA WILL BE NO PART OF SOME GREAT SCIENCE CONSPIRACY.
GIRLS HAVE TO HAVE AMBITION. SO MUCH CAN BE TAKEN FROM US!
NADIA PYM IS NO EVIL MESSIAH.
WHEW. MADE IT. SEE, VICTOR, NO ONE NEEDED TO DIE.
IN FACT, SHE GIVES ME HOPE FOR THE FUTURE. EVEN NOW. EVEN ME.

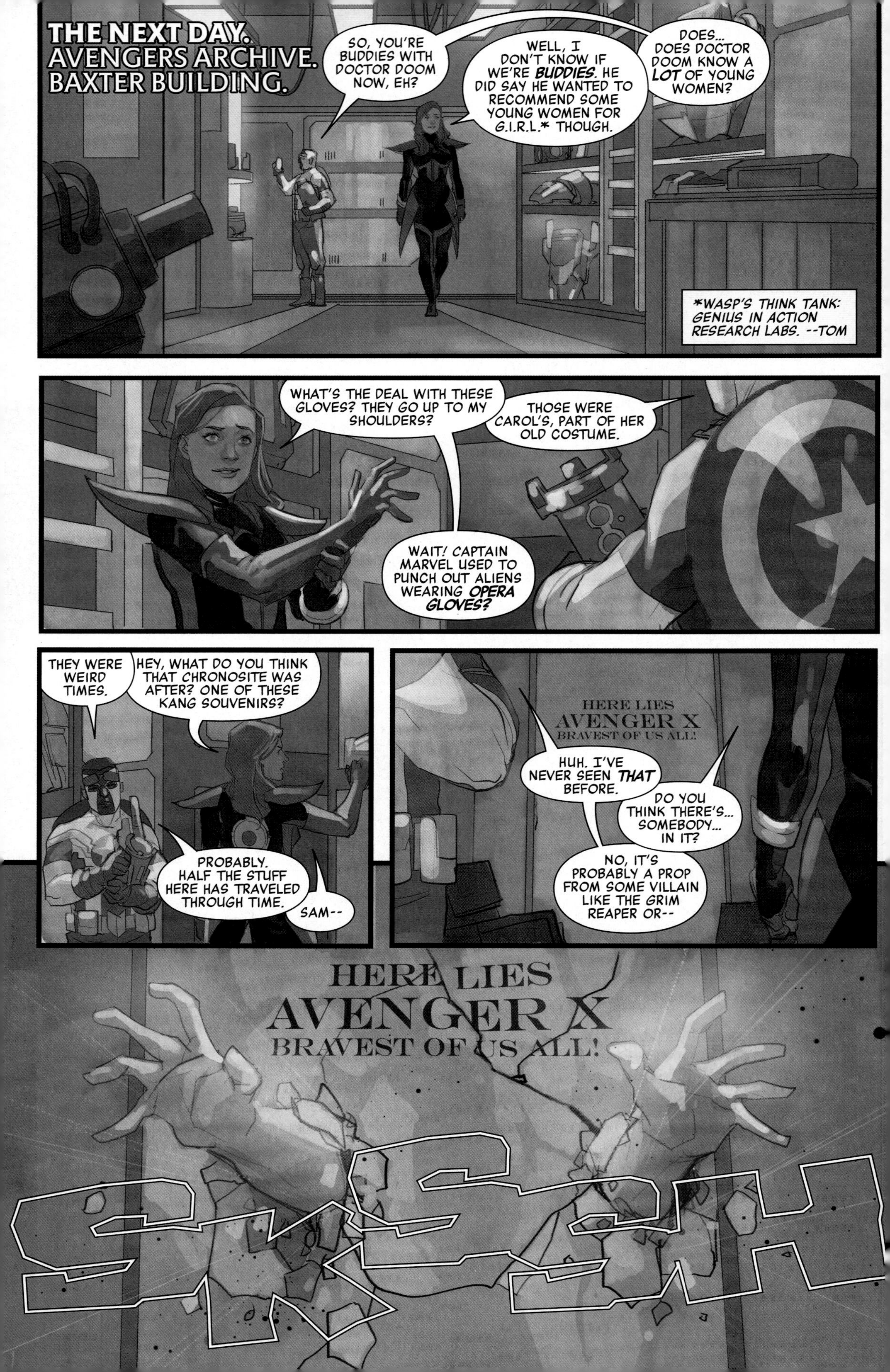
THE NEXT DAY. AVENGERS ARCHIVE. BAXTER BUILDING.
SO, YOU'RE BUDDIES WITH DOCTOR DOOM NOW, EH?
WELL, I DON'T KNOW IF WE'RE BUDDIES. HE DID SAY HE WANTED TO RECOMMEND SOME YOUNG WOMEN FOR G.I.R.L.* THOUGH.
DOES... DOES DOCTOR DOOM KNOW A LOT OF YOUNG WOMEN?
*WASP'S THINK TANK: GENIUS IN ACTION RESEARCH LABS. --TOM
WHAT'S THE DEAL WITH THESE GLOVES? THEY GO UP TO MY SHOULDERS?
THOSE WERE CAROL'S, PART OF HER OLD COSTUME.
WAIT! CAPTAIN MARVEL USED TO PUNCH OUT ALIENS WEARING OPERA GLOVES?
THEY WERE WEIRD TIMES.
HEY, WHAT DO YOU THINK THAT CHRONOSITE WAS AFTER? ONE OF THESE KANG SOUVENIRS?
PROBABLY. HALF THE STUFF HERE HAS TRAVELED THROUGH TIME.
SAM--
HERE LIES AVENGER X BRAVEST OF US ALL!
HUH. I'VE NEVER SEEN THAT BEFORE.
DO YOU THINK THERE'S... SOMEBODY... IN IT?
NO, IT'S PROBABLY A PROP FROM SOME VILLAIN LIKE THE GRIM REAPER OR--
HERE LIES AVENGER X BRAVEST OF US ALL!
SMASH

[8]

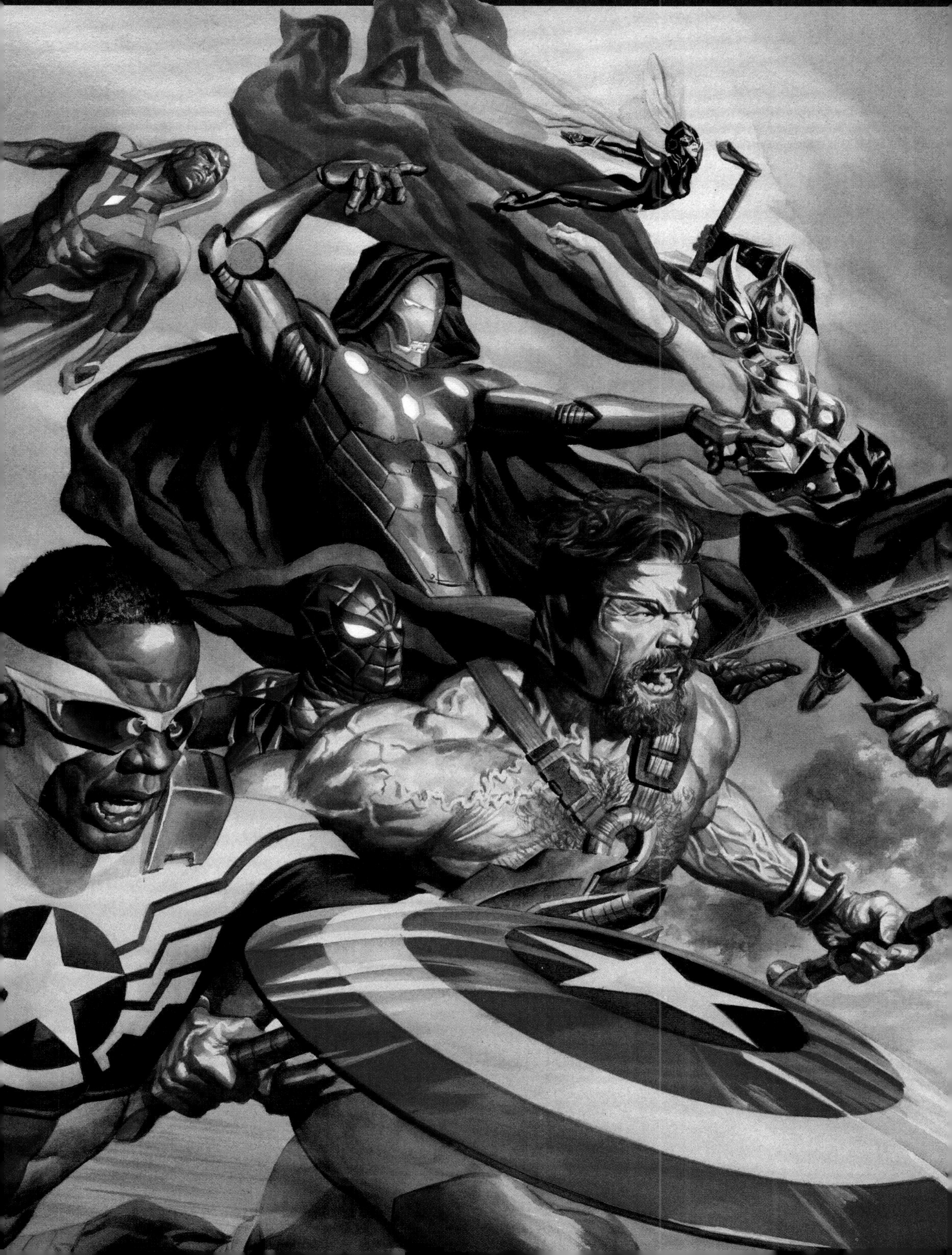

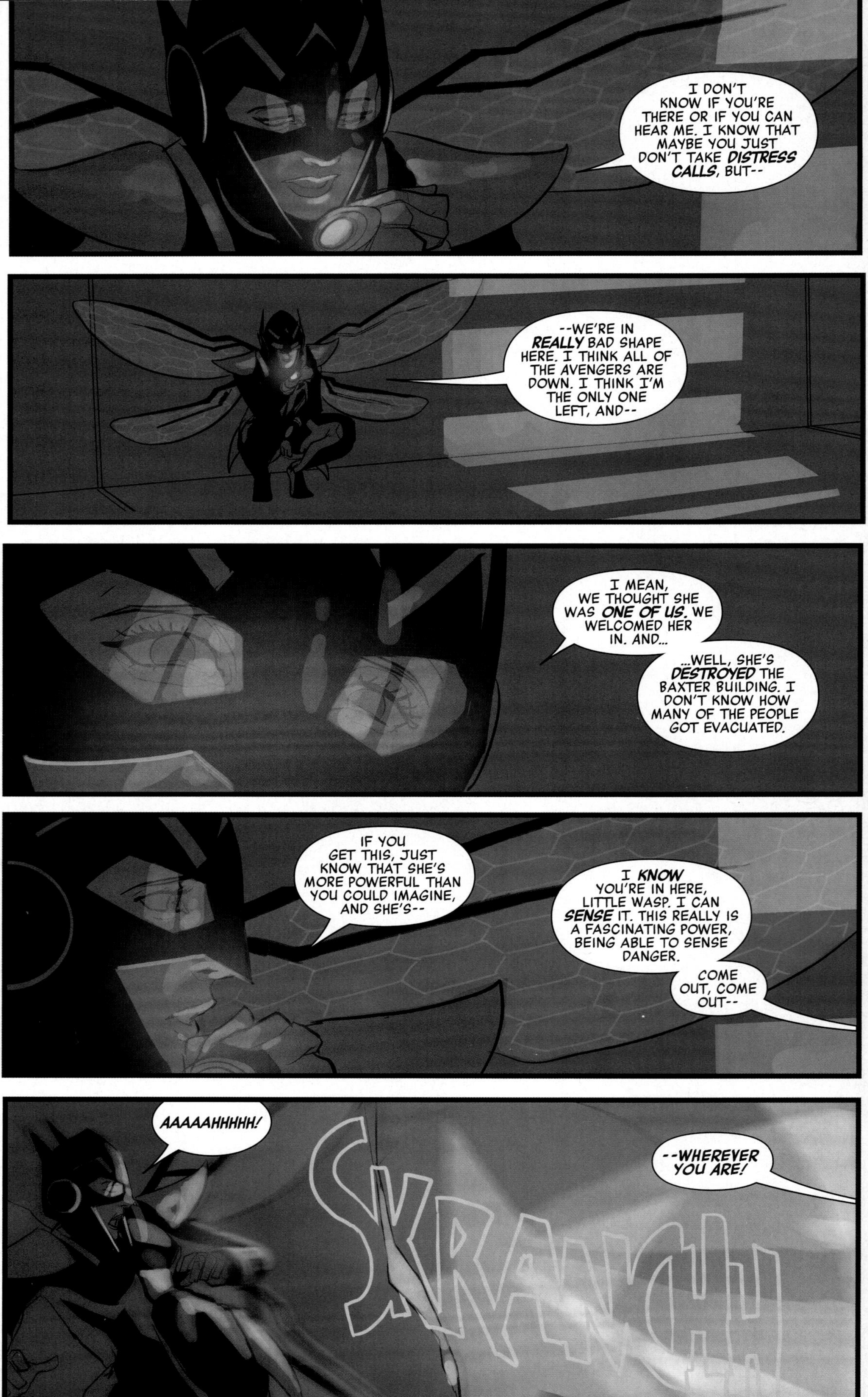

I DON'T KNOW IF YOU'RE THERE OR IF YOU CAN HEAR ME. I KNOW THAT MAYBE YOU JUST DON'T TAKE DISTRESS CALLS, BUT--
--WE'RE IN REALLY BAD SHAPE HERE. I THINK ALL OF THE AVENGERS ARE DOWN. I THINK I'M THE ONLY ONE LEFT, AND--
I MEAN, WE THOUGHT SHE WAS ONE OF US. WE WELCOMED HER IN. AND...
...WELL, SHE'S DESTROYED THE BAXTER BUILDING. I DON'T KNOW HOW MANY OF THE PEOPLE GOT EVACUATED.
IF YOU GET THIS, JUST KNOW THAT SHE'S MORE POWERFUL THAN YOU COULD IMAGINE, AND SHE'S--
I KNOW YOU'RE IN HERE, LITTLE WASP. I CAN SENSE IT. THIS REALLY IS A FASCINATING POWER, BEING ABLE TO SENSE DANGER.
COME OUT, COME OUT--
AAAAAHHHHH!
SKRANCH
--WHEREVER YOU ARE!

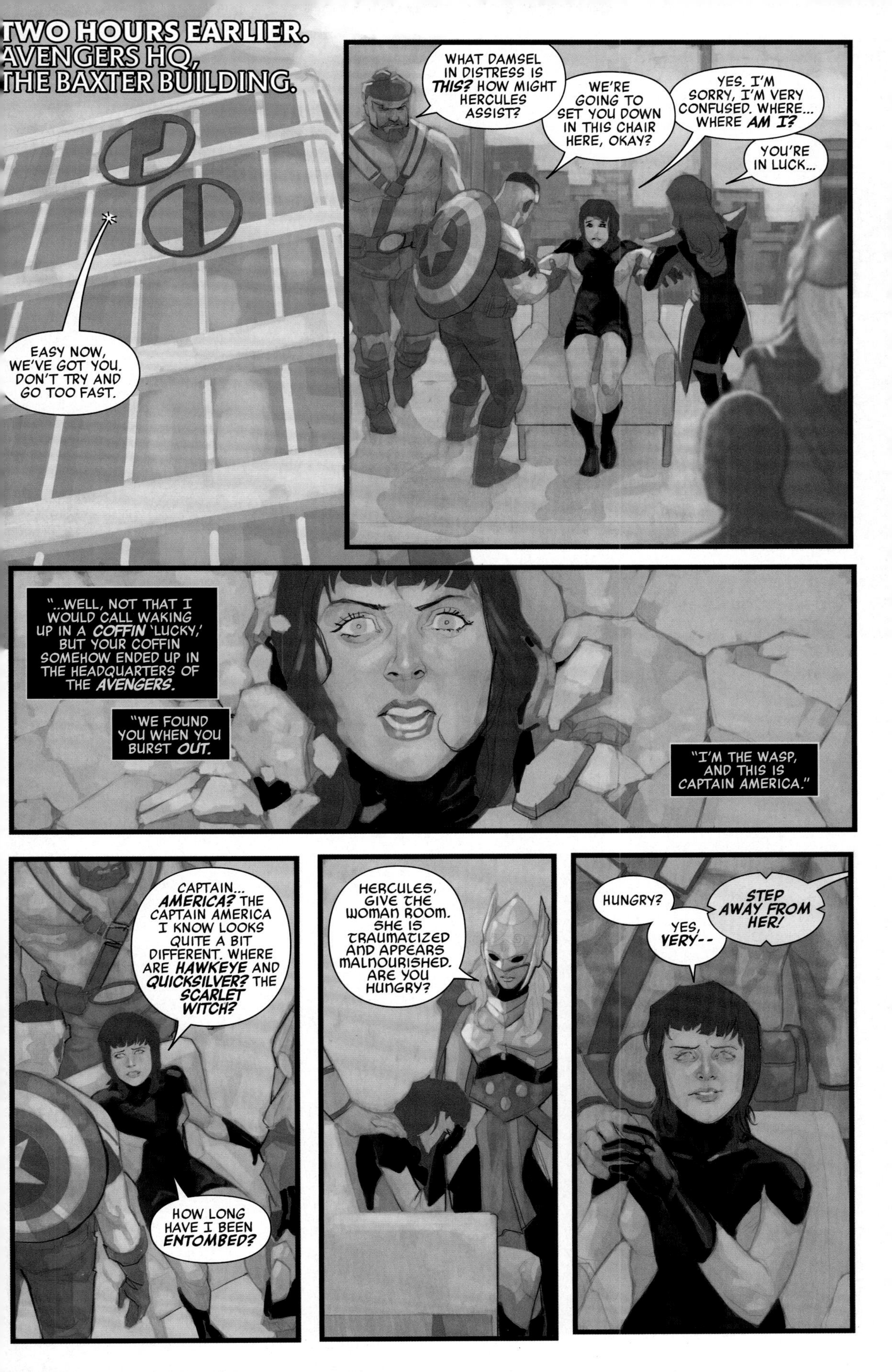

TWO HOURS EARLIER. AVENGERS HQ, THE BAXTER BUILDING.
EASY NOW, WE'VE GOT YOU. DON'T TRY AND GO TOO FAST.
WHAT DAMSEL IN DISTRESS IS THIS? HOW MIGHT HERCULES ASSIST?
WE'RE GOING TO SET YOU DOWN IN THIS CHAIR HERE, OKAY?
YES. I'M SORRY, I'M VERY CONFUSED. WHERE... WHERE AM I?
YOU'RE IN LUCK...
"...WELL, NOT THAT I WOULD CALL WAKING UP IN A COFFIN 'LUCKY,' BUT YOUR COFFIN SOMEHOW ENDED UP IN THE HEADQUARTERS OF THE AVENGERS.
"WE FOUND YOU WHEN YOU BURST OUT.
"I'M THE WASP, AND THIS IS CAPTAIN AMERICA."
CAPTAIN... AMERICA? THE CAPTAIN AMERICA I KNOW LOOKS QUITE A BIT DIFFERENT. WHERE ARE HAWKEYE AND QUICKSILVER? THE SCARLET WITCH?
HOW LONG HAVE I BEEN ENTOMBED?
HERCULES, GIVE THE WOMAN ROOM. SHE IS TRAUMATIZED AND APPEARS MALNOURISHED. ARE YOU HUNGRY?
HUNGRY?
YES, VERY--
STEP AWAY FROM HER!

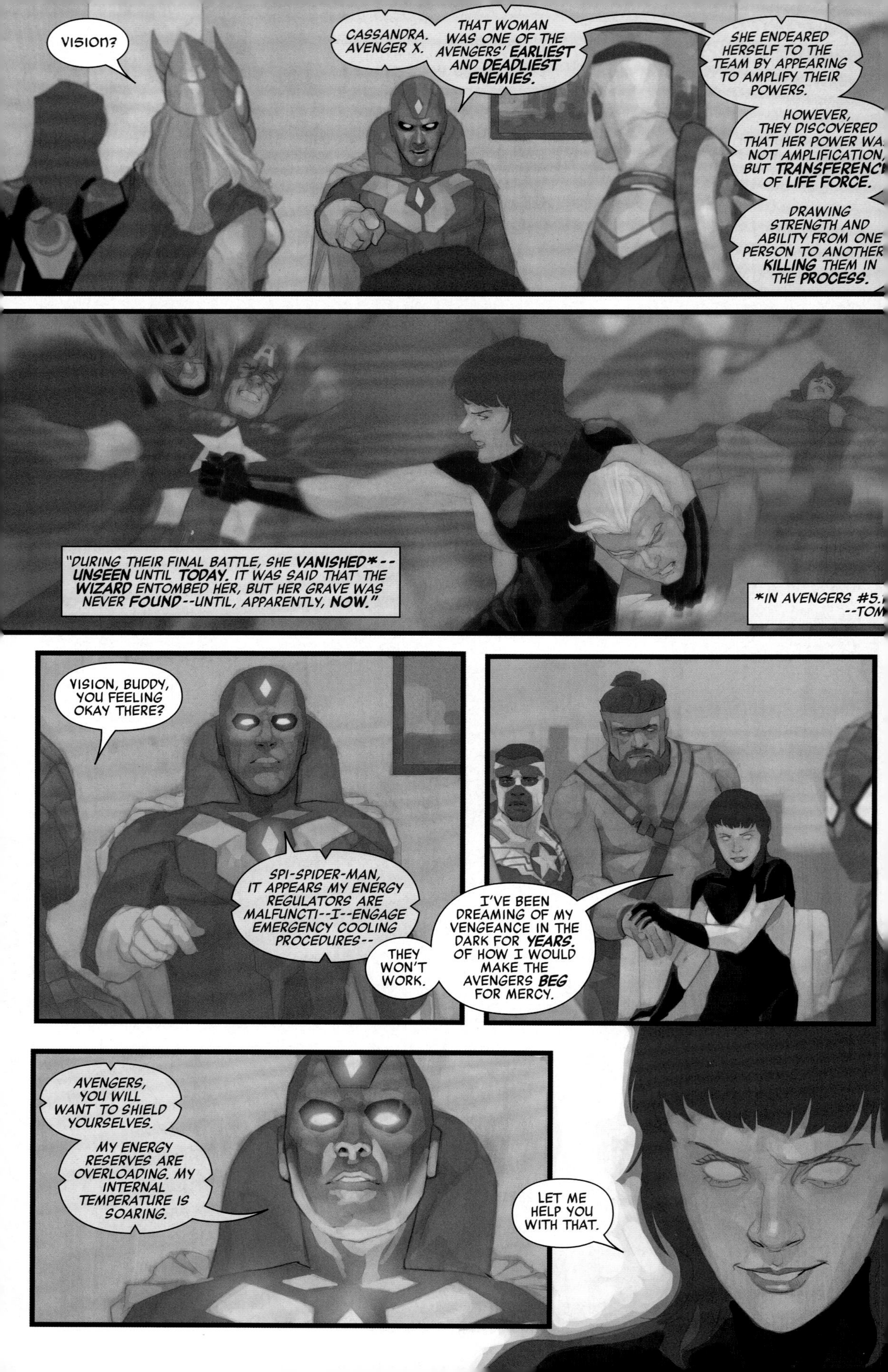
VISION?
CASSANDRA. AVENGER X.
THAT WOMAN WAS ONE OF THE AVENGERS' EARLIEST AND DEADLIEST ENEMIES.
SHE ENDEARED HERSELF TO THE TEAM BY APPEARING TO AMPLIFY THEIR POWERS.
HOWEVER, THEY DISCOVERED THAT HER POWER WA NOT AMPLIFICATION, BUT TRANSFERENC OF LIFE FORCE.
DRAWING STRENGTH AND ABILITY FROM ONE PERSON TO ANOTHER KILLING THEM IN THE PROCESS.
"DURING THEIR FINAL BATTLE, SHE VANISHED*--UNSEEN UNTIL TODAY. IT WAS SAID THAT THE WIZARD ENTOMBED HER, BUT HER GRAVE WAS NEVER FOUND--UNTIL, APPARENTLY, NOW."
*IN AVENGERS #5. --TOM
VISION, BUDDY, YOU FEELING OKAY THERE?
SPI-SPIDER-MAN, IT APPEARS MY ENERGY REGULATORS ARE MALFUNCTI--I--ENGAGE EMERGENCY COOLING PROCEDURES--
THEY WON'T WORK.
I'VE BEEN DREAMING OF MY VENGEANCE IN THE DARK FOR YEARS. OF HOW I WOULD MAKE THE AVENGERS BEG FOR MERCY.
AVENGERS, YOU WILL WANT TO SHIELD YOURSELVES.
MY ENERGY RESERVES ARE OVERLOADING. MY INTERNAL TEMPERATURE IS SOARING.
LET ME HELP YOU WITH THAT.

SHOOOM!

THIS WAS A *TRAP!* SHE WILL *PAY* FOR THIS!

WAIT! SHE WAS IN A *COFFIN* FOR *YEARS!* SHE'S OBVIOUSLY GOING THROUGH SOMETHING *TRAUMATIC!*

WELL, SHE HAD BETTER *HURRY* AND GET OVER IT.

HERCULES STILL LIVES, BUT HE IS GREATLY WEAKENED.

LOOKS LIKE VISION CRASHED. HE'S GOING TO NEED TO RECHARGE AND REBOOT.

I KNEW IT. I KNEW "AVENGER X" WAS BAD NEWS.

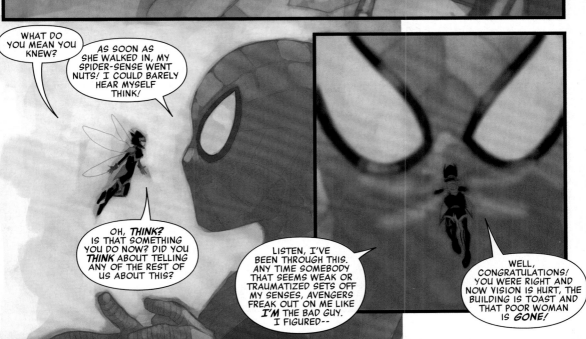

WHAT DO YOU MEAN YOU KNEW?

AS SOON AS SHE WALKED IN, MY SPIDER-SENSE WENT NUTS! I COULD BARELY HEAR MYSELF THINK!

OH, *THINK?* IS THAT SOMETHING YOU DO NOW? DID YOU *THINK* ABOUT TELLING ANY OF THE REST OF US ABOUT THIS?

LISTEN, I'VE BEEN THROUGH THIS. ANY TIME SOMEBODY THAT SEEMS WEAK OR TRAUMATIZED SETS OFF MY SENSES, AVENGERS FREAK OUT ON ME LIKE *I'M* THE BAD GUY. I FIGURED--

WELL, CONGRATULATIONS! YOU WERE RIGHT AND NOW VISION IS HURT, THE BUILDING IS TOAST AND THAT POOR WOMAN IS *GONE!*

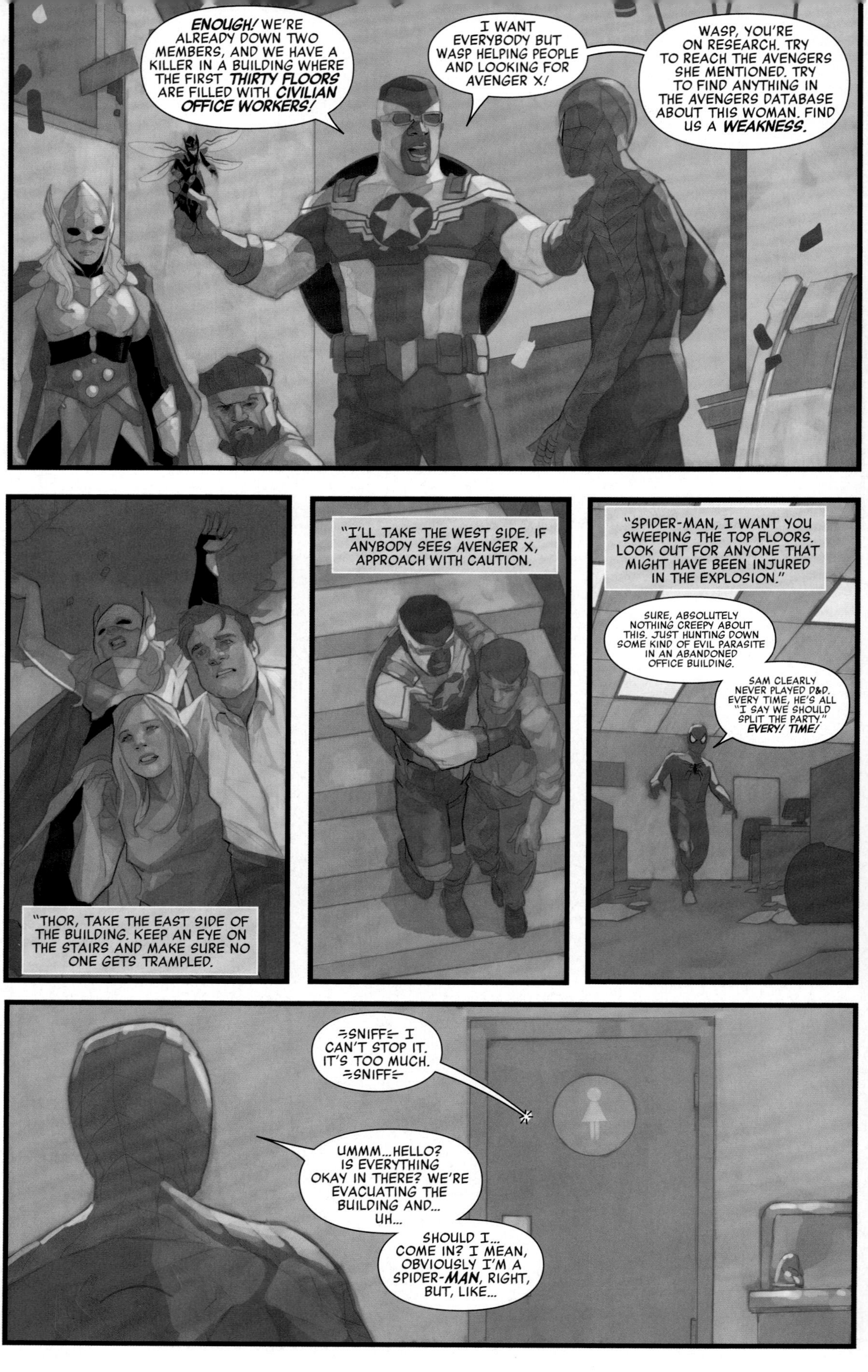
ENOUGH! WE'RE ALREADY DOWN TWO MEMBERS, AND WE HAVE A KILLER IN A BUILDING WHERE THE FIRST THIRTY FLOORS ARE FILLED WITH CIVILIAN OFFICE WORKERS!
I WANT EVERYBODY BUT WASP HELPING PEOPLE AND LOOKING FOR AVENGER X!
WASP, YOU'RE ON RESEARCH. TRY TO REACH THE AVENGERS SHE MENTIONED. TRY TO FIND ANYTHING IN THE AVENGERS DATABASE ABOUT THIS WOMAN. FIND US A WEAKNESS.
"THOR, TAKE THE EAST SIDE OF THE BUILDING. KEEP AN EYE ON THE STAIRS AND MAKE SURE NO ONE GETS TRAMPLED.
"I'LL TAKE THE WEST SIDE. IF ANYBODY SEES AVENGER X, APPROACH WITH CAUTION.
"SPIDER-MAN, I WANT YOU SWEEPING THE TOP FLOORS. LOOK OUT FOR ANYONE THAT MIGHT HAVE BEEN INJURED IN THE EXPLOSION."
SURE, ABSOLUTELY NOTHING CREEPY ABOUT THIS. JUST HUNTING DOWN SOME KIND OF EVIL PARASITE IN AN ABANDONED OFFICE BUILDING.
SAM CLEARLY NEVER PLAYED D&D. EVERY TIME, HE'S ALL "I SAY WE SHOULD SPLIT THE PARTY." EVERY! TIME!
=SNIFF= I CAN'T STOP IT. IT'S TOO MUCH. =SNIFF=
UMMM...HELLO? IS EVERYTHING OKAY IN THERE? WE'RE EVACUATING THE BUILDING AND... UH...
SHOULD I... COME IN? I MEAN, OBVIOUSLY I'M A SPIDER-MAN, RIGHT, BUT, LIKE...

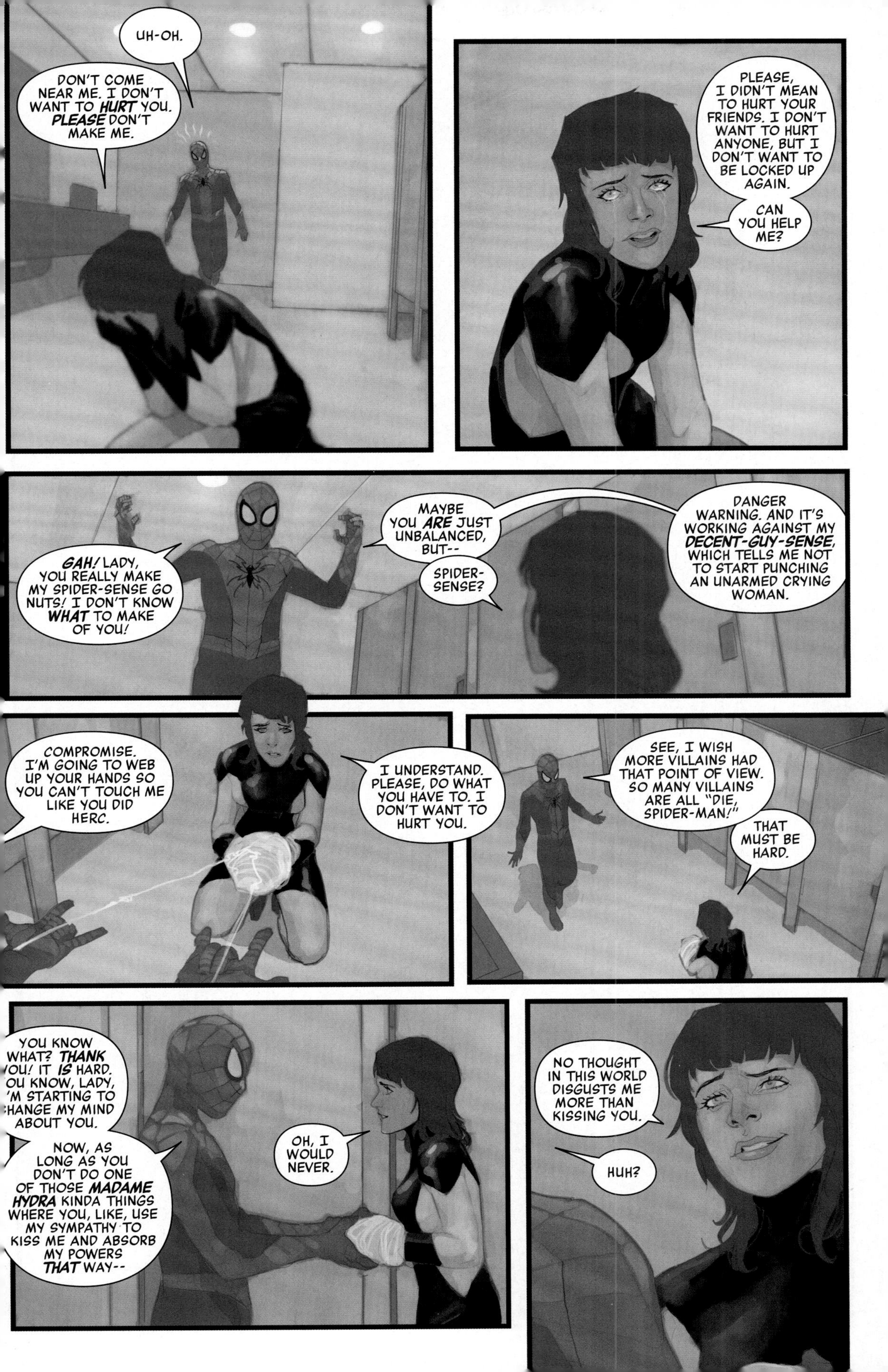
UH-OH.
DON'T COME NEAR ME. I DON'T WANT TO HURT YOU. PLEASE DON'T MAKE ME.
PLEASE, I DIDN'T MEAN TO HURT YOUR FRIENDS. I DON'T WANT TO HURT ANYONE, BUT I DON'T WANT TO BE LOCKED UP AGAIN.
CAN YOU HELP ME?
GAH! LADY, YOU REALLY MAKE MY SPIDER-SENSE GO NUTS! I DON'T KNOW WHAT TO MAKE OF YOU!
SPIDER-SENSE?
MAYBE YOU ARE JUST UNBALANCED, BUT--
DANGER WARNING. AND IT'S WORKING AGAINST MY DECENT-GUY-SENSE, WHICH TELLS ME NOT TO START PUNCHING AN UNARMED CRYING WOMAN.
COMPROMISE. I'M GOING TO WEB UP YOUR HANDS SO YOU CAN'T TOUCH ME LIKE YOU DID HERC.
I UNDERSTAND. PLEASE, DO WHAT YOU HAVE TO. I DON'T WANT TO HURT YOU.
SEE, I WISH MORE VILLAINS HAD THAT POINT OF VIEW. SO MANY VILLAINS ARE ALL "DIE, SPIDER-MAN!"
THAT MUST BE HARD.
YOU KNOW WHAT? THANK YOU! IT IS HARD. YOU KNOW, LADY, I'M STARTING TO CHANGE MY MIND ABOUT YOU.
NOW, AS LONG AS YOU DON'T DO ONE OF THOSE MADAME HYDRA KINDA THINGS WHERE YOU, LIKE, USE MY SYMPATHY TO KISS ME AND ABSORB MY POWERS THAT WAY--
OH, I WOULD NEVER.
NO THOUGHT IN THIS WORLD DISGUSTS ME MORE THAN KISSING YOU.
HUH?

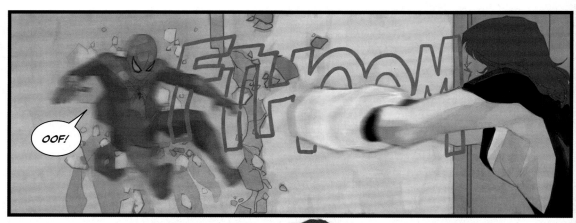

OOF!

I HAVE TO SAY, IT'S A RELIEF TO SEE THAT SUPER HEROES HAVEN'T GOTTEN ANY SMARTER SINCE I'VE BEEN LOCKED UP.

YOUR FRIEND HERCULES WAS SO NICE TO LEND ME HIS STRENGTH.

DON'T GO ANYWHERE YET, SPIDER. TELL ME MORE ABOUT THIS "SPIDER-SENSE."

BETTER YET--

--LET ME LEARN FOR MYSELF!

AAAAAAAHH!

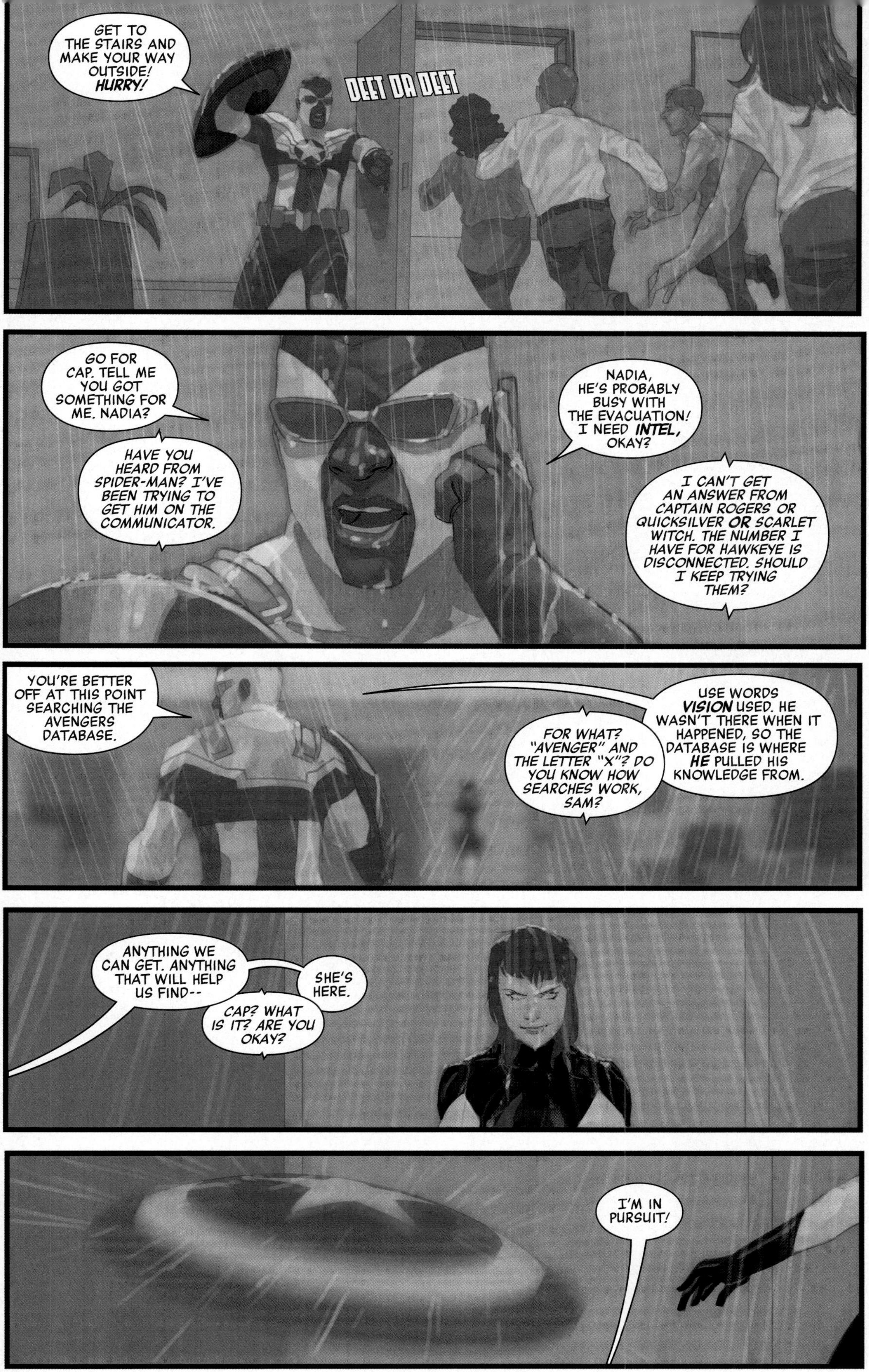
GET TO THE STAIRS AND MAKE YOUR WAY OUTSIDE! HURRY!
DEET DA DEET
GO FOR CAP. TELL ME YOU GOT SOMETHING FOR ME. NADIA?
HAVE YOU HEARD FROM SPIDER-MAN? I'VE BEEN TRYING TO GET HIM ON THE COMMUNICATOR.
NADIA, HE'S PROBABLY BUSY WITH THE EVACUATION! I NEED INTEL, OKAY?
I CAN'T GET AN ANSWER FROM CAPTAIN ROGERS OR QUICKSILVER OR SCARLET WITCH. THE NUMBER I HAVE FOR HAWKEYE IS DISCONNECTED. SHOULD I KEEP TRYING THEM?
YOU'RE BETTER OFF AT THIS POINT SEARCHING THE AVENGERS DATABASE.
FOR WHAT? "AVENGER" AND THE LETTER "X"? DO YOU KNOW HOW SEARCHES WORK, SAM?
USE WORDS VISION USED. HE WASN'T THERE WHEN IT HAPPENED, SO THE DATABASE IS WHERE HE PULLED HIS KNOWLEDGE FROM.
ANYTHING WE CAN GET. ANYTHING THAT WILL HELP US FIND--
SHE'S HERE.
CAP? WHAT IS IT? ARE YOU OKAY?
I'M IN PURSUIT!

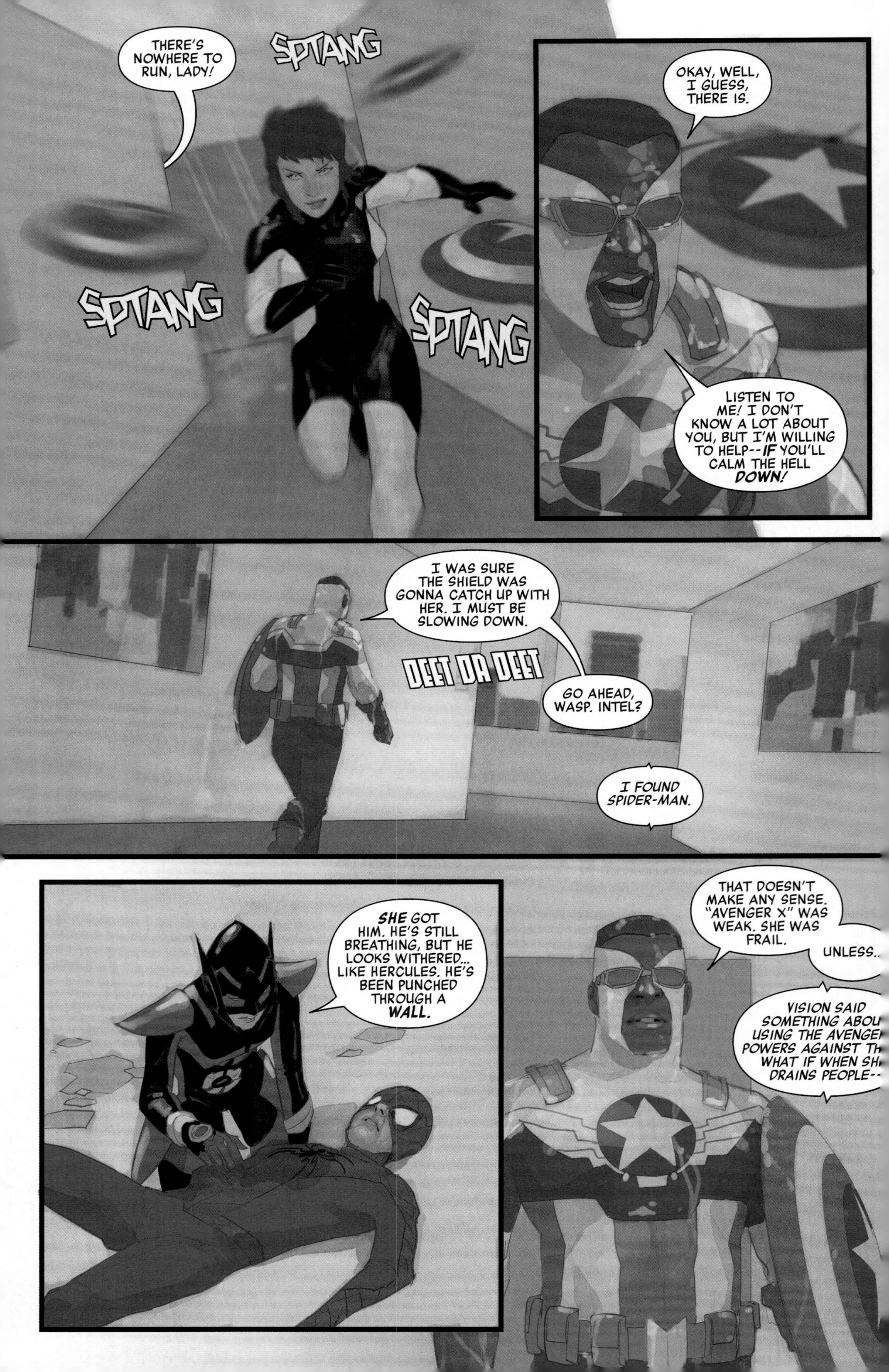
THERE'S NOWHERE TO RUN, LADY!
SPTANG
SPTANG
SPTANG
OKAY, WELL, I GUESS, THERE IS.
LISTEN TO ME! I DON'T KNOW A LOT ABOUT YOU, BUT I'M WILLING TO HELP--IF YOU'LL CALM THE HELL DOWN!
I WAS SURE THE SHIELD WAS GONNA CATCH UP WITH HER. I MUST BE SLOWING DOWN.
DEET DA DEET
GO AHEAD, WASP. INTEL?
I FOUND SPIDER-MAN.
SHE GOT HIM. HE'S STILL BREATHING, BUT HE LOOKS WITHERED... LIKE HERCULES. HE'S BEEN PUNCHED THROUGH A WALL.
THAT DOESN'T MAKE ANY SENSE. "AVENGER X" WAS WEAK. SHE WAS FRAIL.
UNLESS..
VISION SAID SOMETHING ABOU USING THE AVENGE POWERS AGAINST TH WHAT IF WHEN SH DRAINS PEOPLE--

--SHE GETS THEIR POWERS, TOO?

THUD
KSSSSH!

CAP? CAP, ARE YOU *THERE?* SAM?

SAM'S NOT AVAILABLE TO *TALK*, BABY WASP. IT'S JUST US GIRLS NOW.

AVENGER X, *PLEASE!* WHATEVER'S WRONG WITH YOU, LET US--

HELP? YOU'RE GOING TO HELP ME GET MY LIFE BACK?

YOU SEEM LIKE A SWEET GIRL. MY GRUDGE ISN'T WITH YOU. JUST RUN AWAY. AS FOR ME...

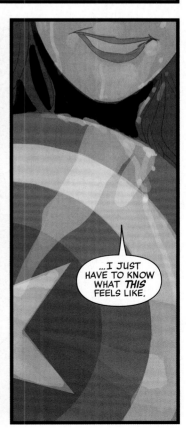

...I JUST HAVE TO KNOW WHAT *THIS* FEELS LIKE.

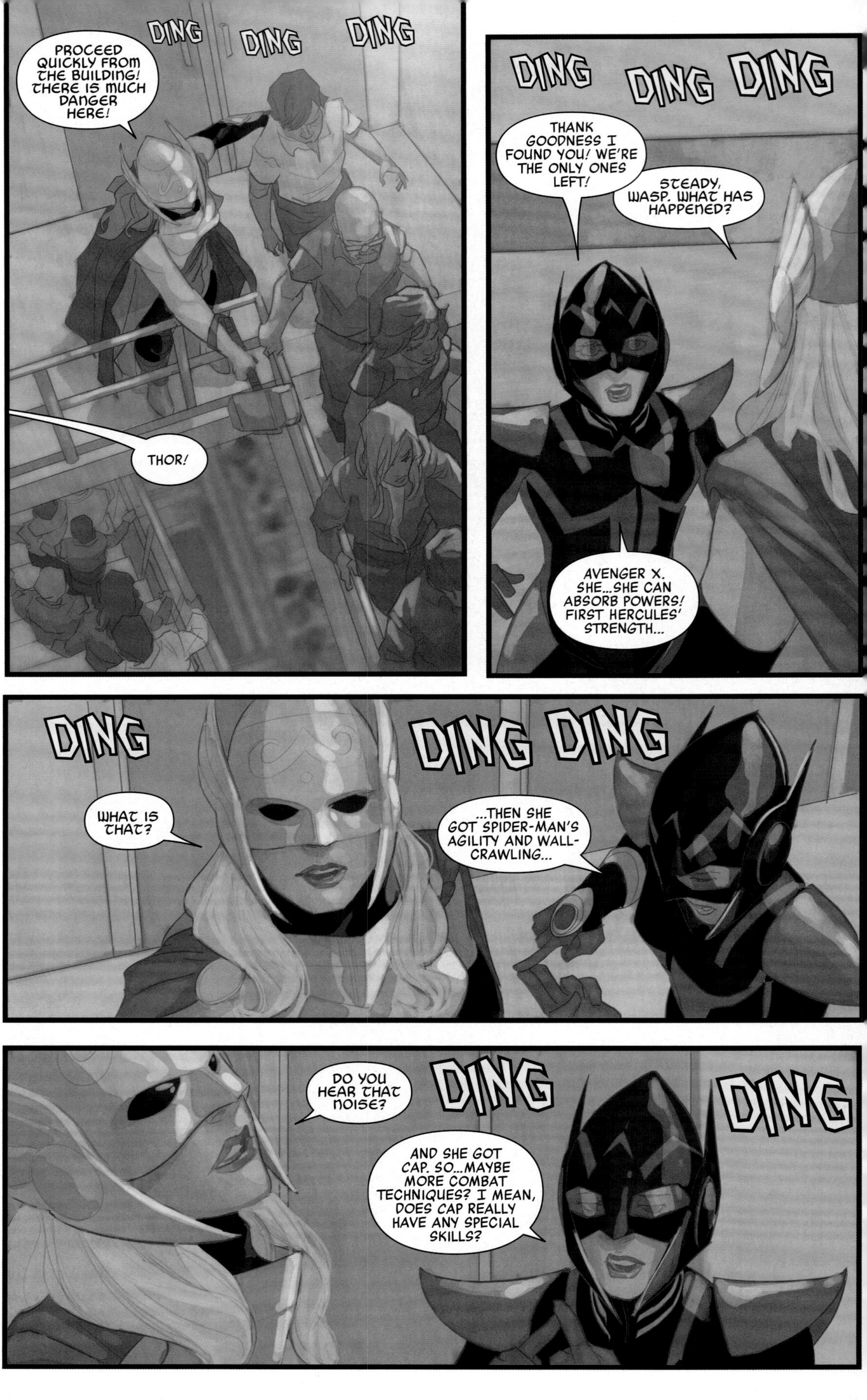
DING
DING
DING
PROCEED QUICKLY FROM THE BUILDING! THERE IS MUCH DANGER HERE!
THOR!
DING
DING
DING
THANK GOODNESS I FOUND YOU! WE'RE THE ONLY ONES LEFT!
STEADY, WASP. WHAT HAS HAPPENED?
AVENGER X. SHE...SHE CAN ABSORB POWERS! FIRST HERCULES' STRENGTH...
DING
DING
DING
WHAT IS THAT?
...THEN SHE GOT SPIDER-MAN'S AGILITY AND WALL-CRAWLING...
DO YOU HEAR THAT NOISE?
DING
DING
AND SHE GOT CAP. SO...MAYBE MORE COMBAT TECHNIQUES? I MEAN, DOES CAP REALLY HAVE ANY SPECIAL SKILLS?

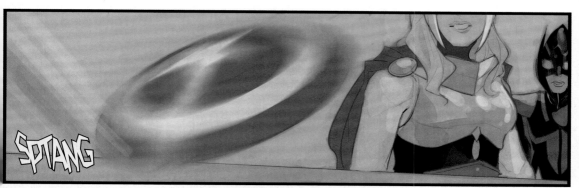

SPTANG

SPTANG

NNNHF--!

CLANG

THOR!

THOR?
ARE YOU--

I'M FINE.
WHERE IS MY
HELMET?

IT FELL
DOWN THE
STAIRS. THOR,
YOU DON'T LOOK
OKAY. THAT
SHIELD HIT
YOU HARD.

GO, NADIA!
I WILL STOP
HER.

THOR, NO!
WE NEED TO
GET YOU--

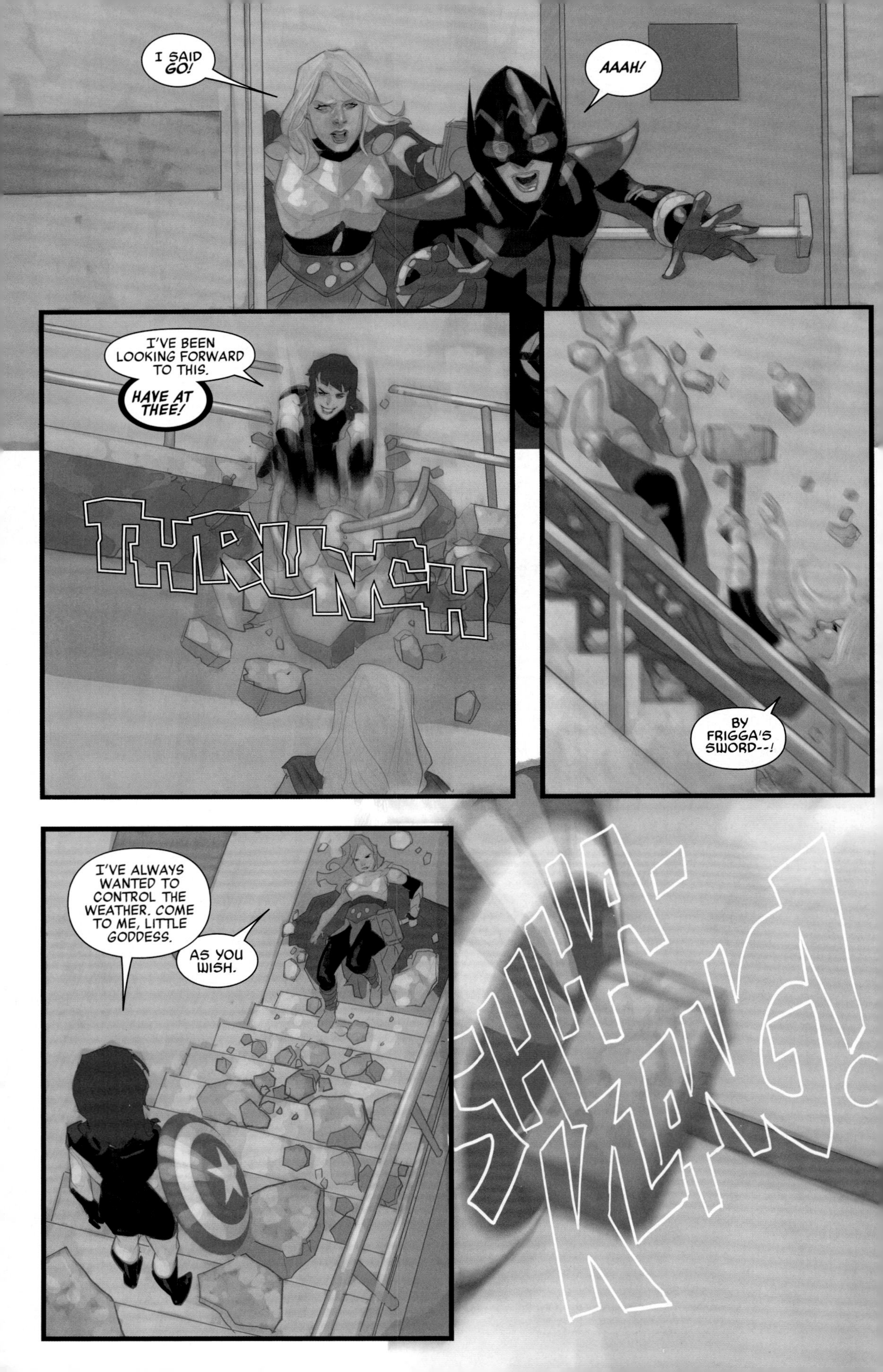

I SAID GO!
AAAH!
I'VE BEEN LOOKING FORWARD TO THIS.
HAVE AT THEE!
THRUNCH
BY FRIGGA'S SWORD--!
I'VE ALWAYS WANTED TO CONTROL THE WEATHER. COME TO ME, LITTLE GODDESS.
AS YOU WISH.
SHHA-KLANG!

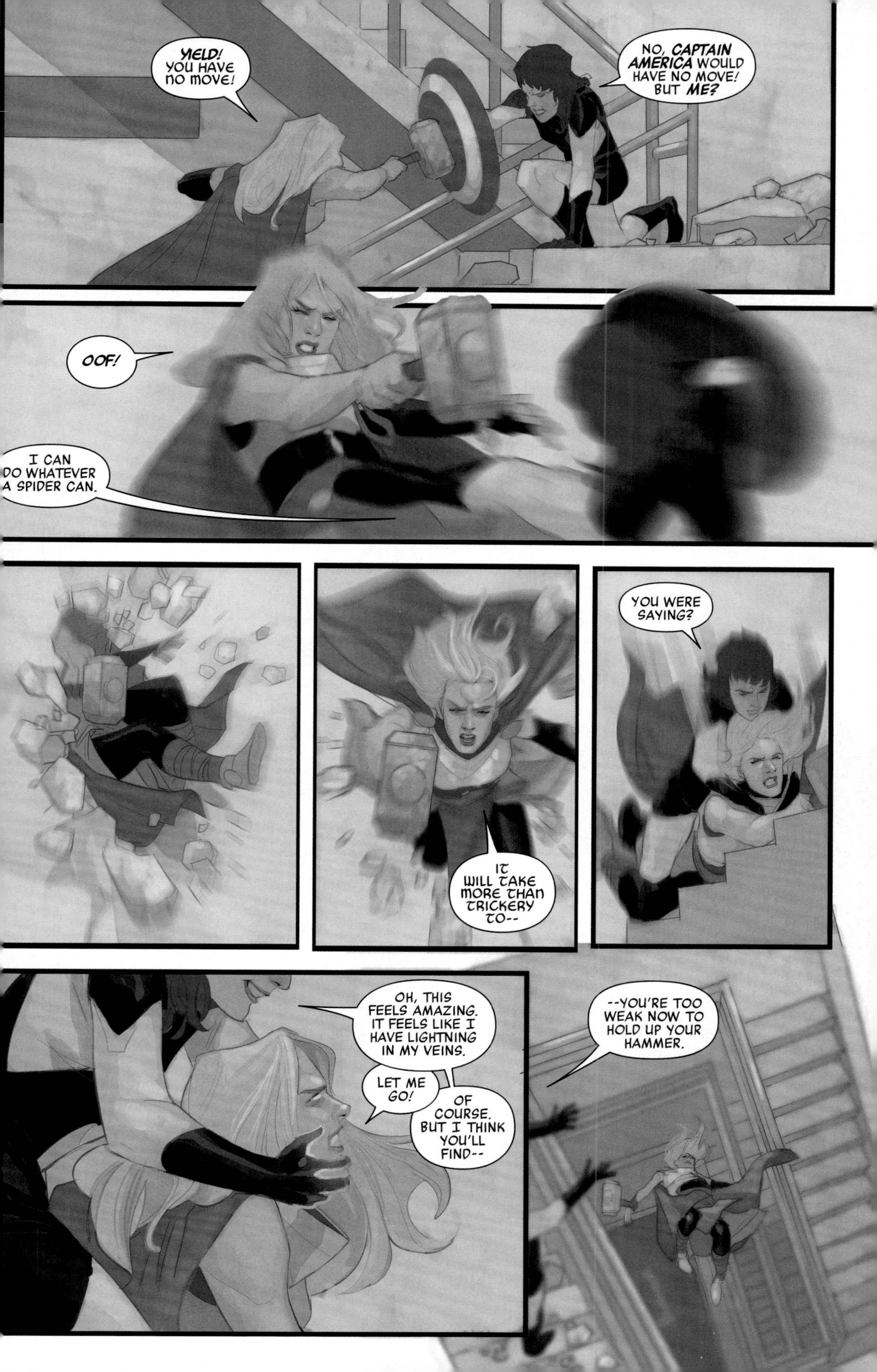
YIELD! YOU HAVE NO MOVE!
NO, CAPTAIN AMERICA WOULD HAVE NO MOVE! BUT ME?
OOF!
I CAN DO WHATEVER A SPIDER CAN.
IT WILL TAKE MORE THAN TRICKERY TO--
YOU WERE SAYING?
OH, THIS FEELS AMAZING. IT FEELS LIKE I HAVE LIGHTNING IN MY VEINS.
LET ME GO!
OF COURSE. BUT I THINK YOU'LL FIND--
--YOU'RE TOO WEAK NOW TO HOLD UP YOUR HAMMER.

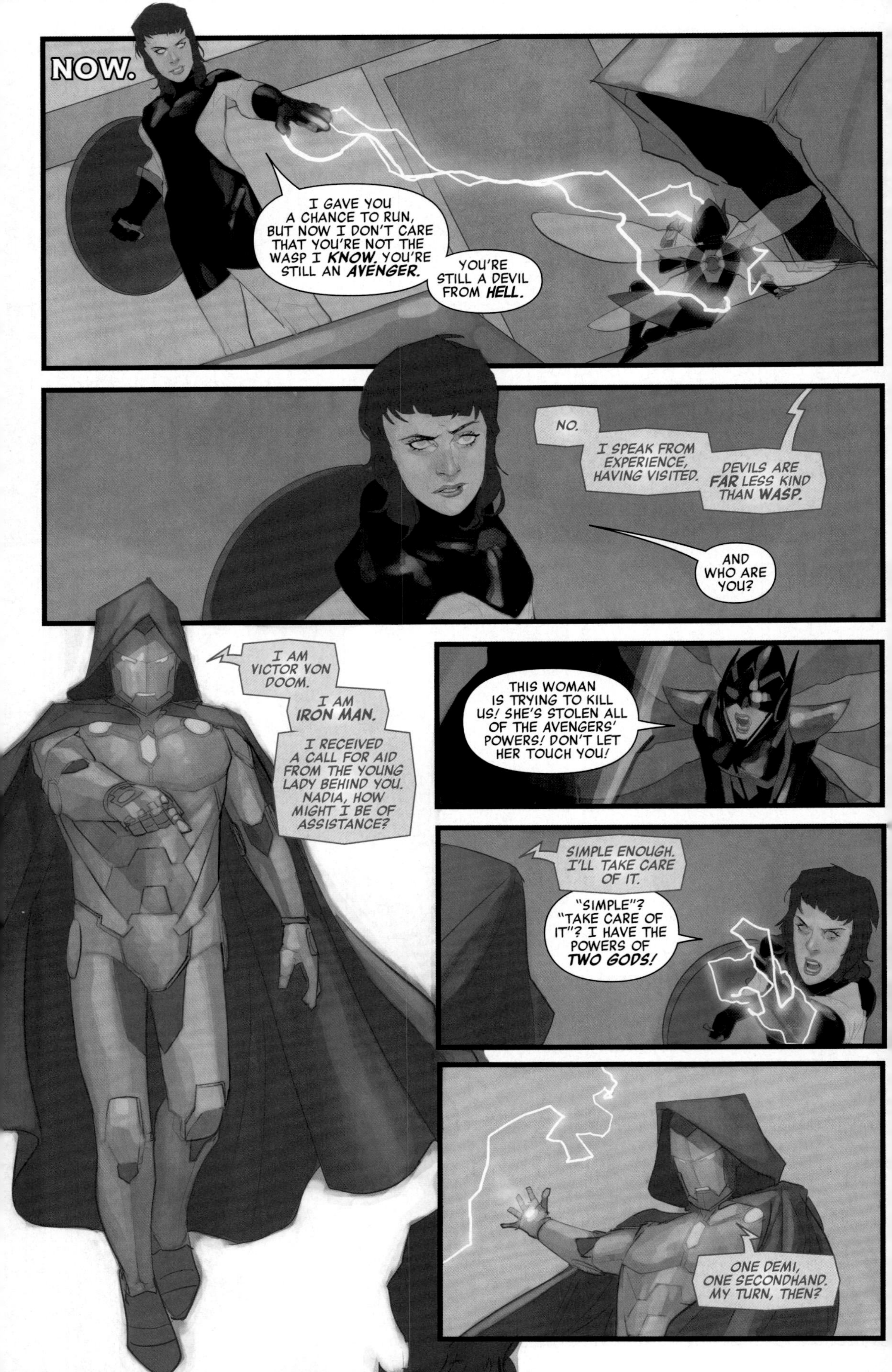
NOW.
I GAVE YOU A CHANCE TO RUN, BUT NOW I DON'T CARE THAT YOU'RE NOT THE WASP I KNOW. YOU'RE STILL AN AVENGER.
YOU'RE STILL A DEVIL FROM HELL.
NO.
I SPEAK FROM EXPERIENCE, HAVING VISITED.
DEVILS ARE FAR LESS KIND THAN WASP.
AND WHO ARE YOU?
I AM VICTOR VON DOOM.
I AM IRON MAN.
I RECEIVED A CALL FOR AID FROM THE YOUNG LADY BEHIND YOU. NADIA, HOW MIGHT I BE OF ASSISTANCE?
THIS WOMAN IS TRYING TO KILL US! SHE'S STOLEN ALL OF THE AVENGERS' POWERS! DON'T LET HER TOUCH YOU!
SIMPLE ENOUGH. I'LL TAKE CARE OF IT.
"SIMPLE"? "TAKE CARE OF IT"? I HAVE THE POWERS OF TWO GODS!
ONE DEMI, ONE SECONDHAND. MY TURN, THEN?

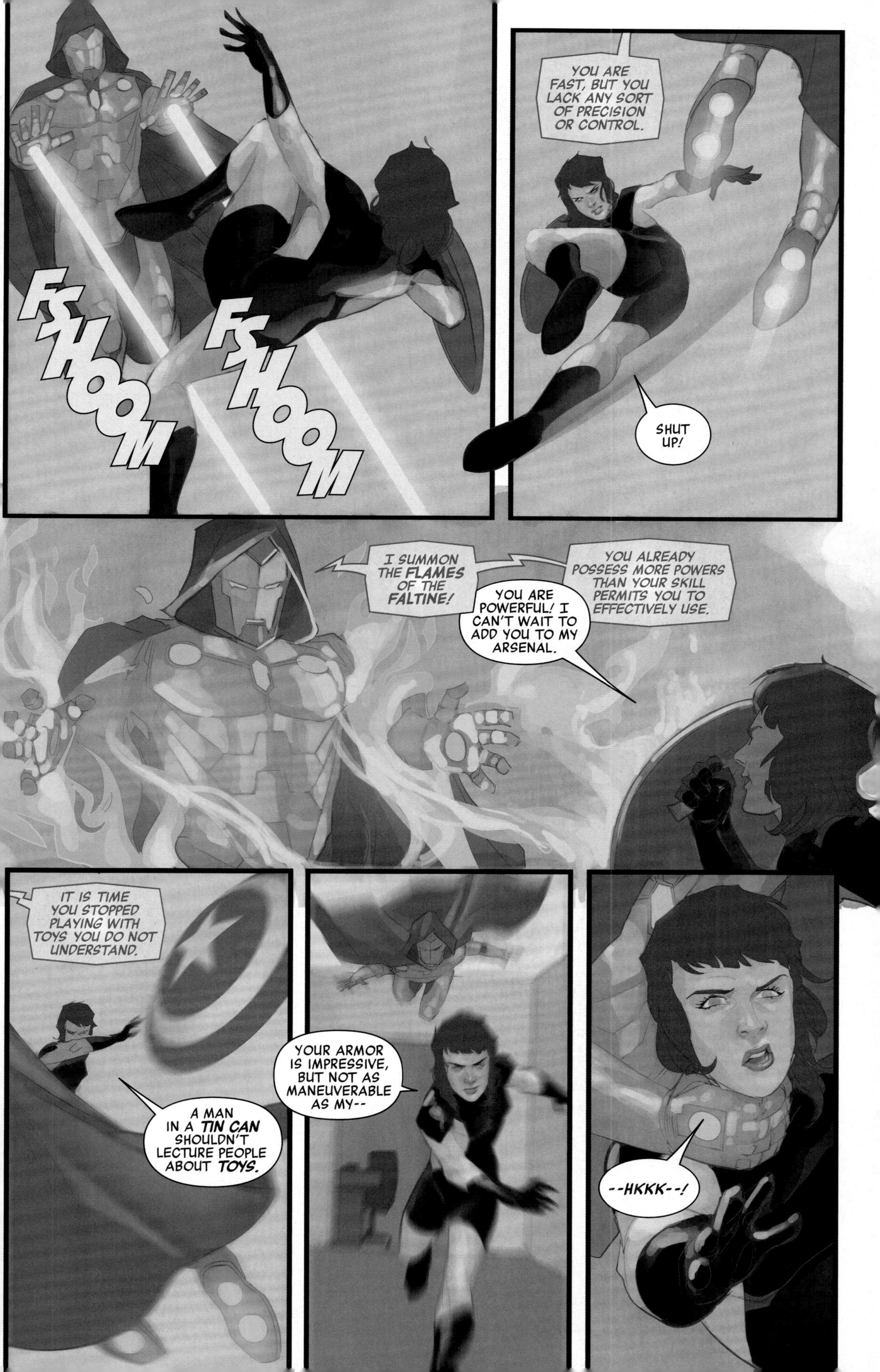
FSHOOM
FSHOOM
YOU ARE FAST, BUT YOU LACK ANY SORT OF PRECISION OR CONTROL.
SHUT UP!
I SUMMON THE FLAMES OF THE FALTINE!
YOU ALREADY POSSESS MORE POWERS THAN YOUR SKILL PERMITS YOU TO EFFECTIVELY USE.
YOU ARE POWERFUL! I CAN'T WAIT TO ADD YOU TO MY ARSENAL.
IT IS TIME YOU STOPPED PLAYING WITH TOYS YOU DO NOT UNDERSTAND.
A MAN IN A TIN CAN SHOULDN'T LECTURE PEOPLE ABOUT TOYS.
YOUR ARMOR IS IMPRESSIVE, BUT NOT AS MANEUVERABLE AS MY--
--HKKK--!

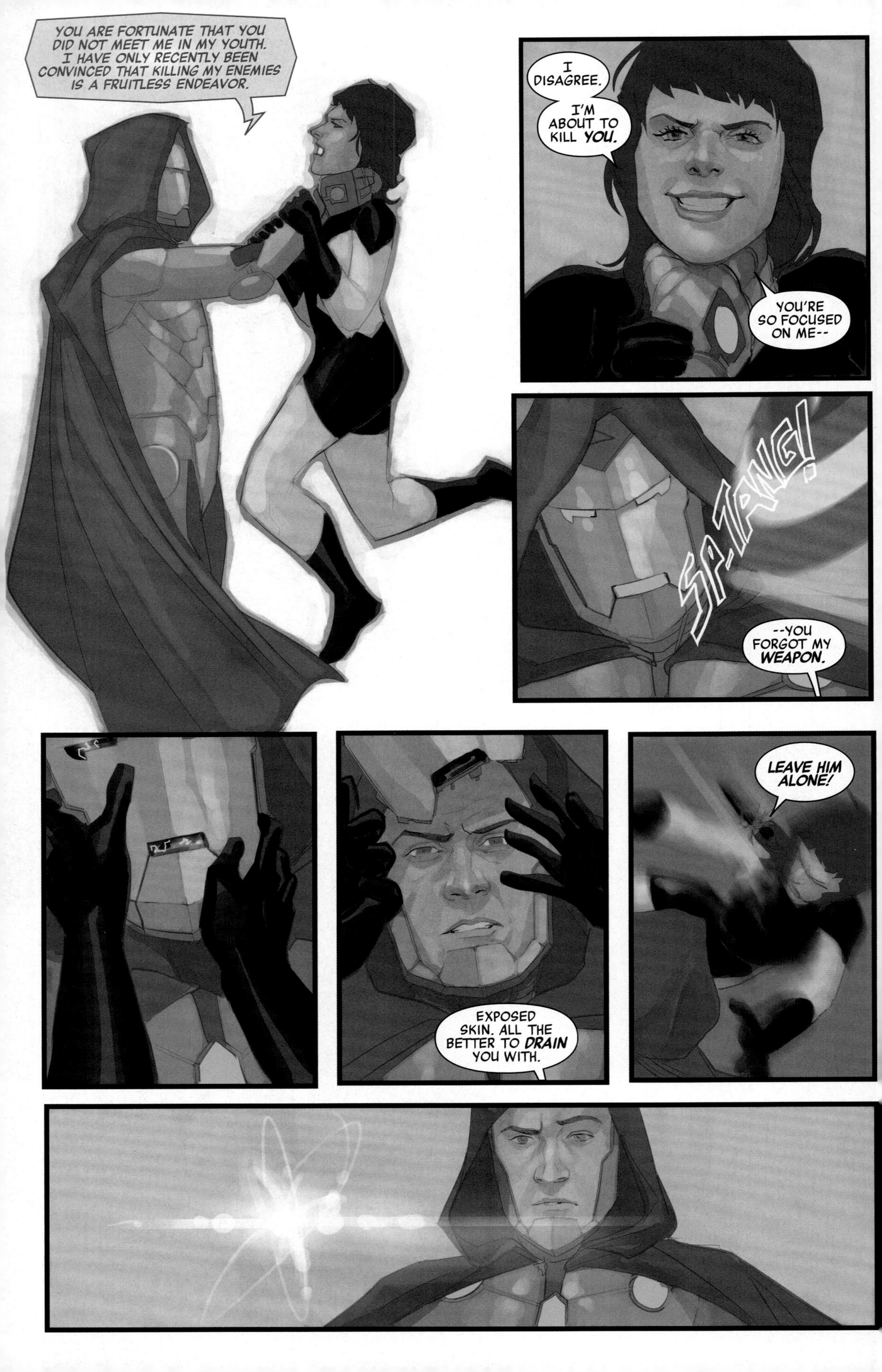
YOU ARE FORTUNATE THAT YOU DID NOT MEET ME IN MY YOUTH. I HAVE ONLY RECENTLY BEEN CONVINCED THAT KILLING MY ENEMIES IS A FRUITLESS ENDEAVOR.
I DISAGREE.
I'M ABOUT TO KILL YOU.
YOU'RE SO FOCUSED ON ME--
SPTANG!
--YOU FORGOT MY WEAPON.
EXPOSED SKIN. ALL THE BETTER TO DRAIN YOU WITH.
LEAVE HIM ALONE!

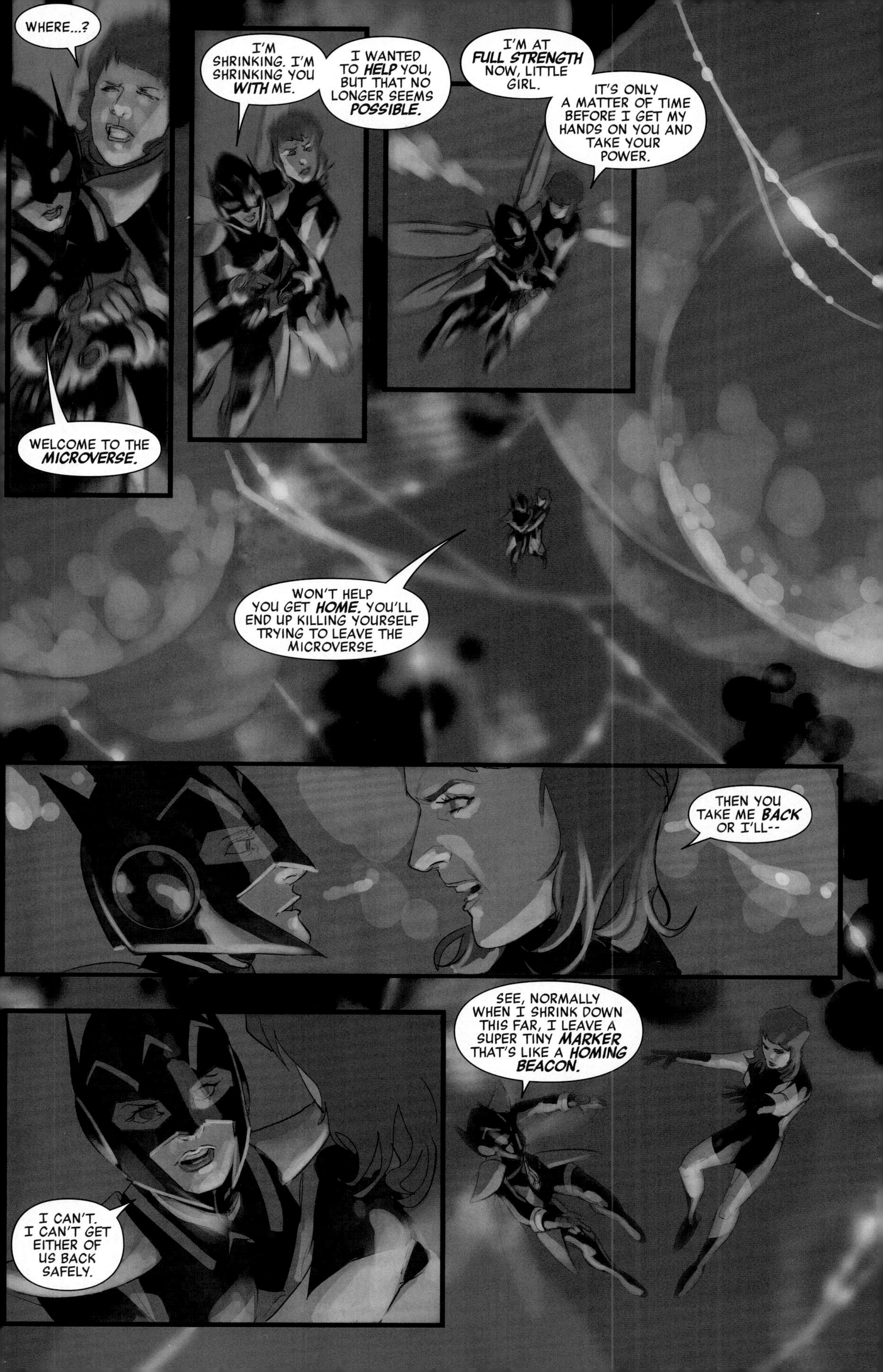
WHERE...?
WELCOME TO THE MICROVERSE.
I'M SHRINKING. I'M SHRINKING YOU WITH ME.
I WANTED TO HELP YOU, BUT THAT NO LONGER SEEMS POSSIBLE.
I'M AT FULL STRENGTH NOW, LITTLE GIRL.
IT'S ONLY A MATTER OF TIME BEFORE I GET MY HANDS ON YOU AND TAKE YOUR POWER.
WON'T HELP YOU GET HOME. YOU'LL END UP KILLING YOURSELF TRYING TO LEAVE THE MICROVERSE.
THEN YOU TAKE ME BACK OR I'LL--
SEE, NORMALLY WHEN I SHRINK DOWN THIS FAR, I LEAVE A SUPER TINY MARKER THAT'S LIKE A HOMING BEACON.
I CAN'T. I CAN'T GET EITHER OF US BACK SAFELY.

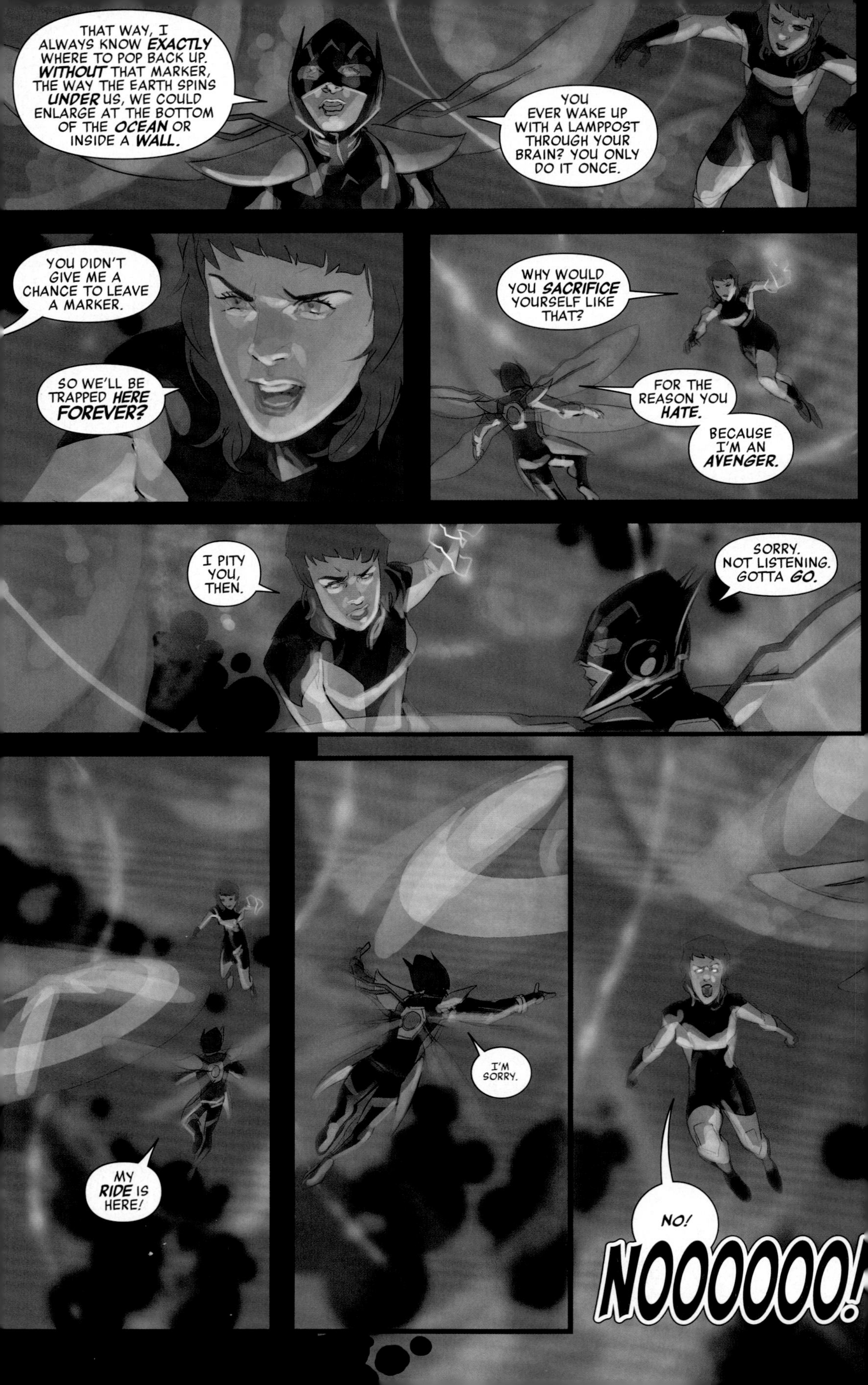
THAT WAY, I ALWAYS KNOW EXACTLY WHERE TO POP BACK UP. WITHOUT THAT MARKER, THE WAY THE EARTH SPINS UNDER US, WE COULD ENLARGE AT THE BOTTOM OF THE OCEAN OR INSIDE A WALL.
YOU EVER WAKE UP WITH A LAMPPOST THROUGH YOUR BRAIN? YOU ONLY DO IT ONCE.
YOU DIDN'T GIVE ME A CHANCE TO LEAVE A MARKER.
SO WE'LL BE TRAPPED HERE FOREVER?
WHY WOULD YOU SACRIFICE YOURSELF LIKE THAT?
FOR THE REASON YOU HATE.
BECAUSE I'M AN AVENGER.
I PITY YOU, THEN.
SORRY. NOT LISTENING. GOTTA GO.
MY RIDE IS HERE!
I'M SORRY.
NO!
NOOOOOO!

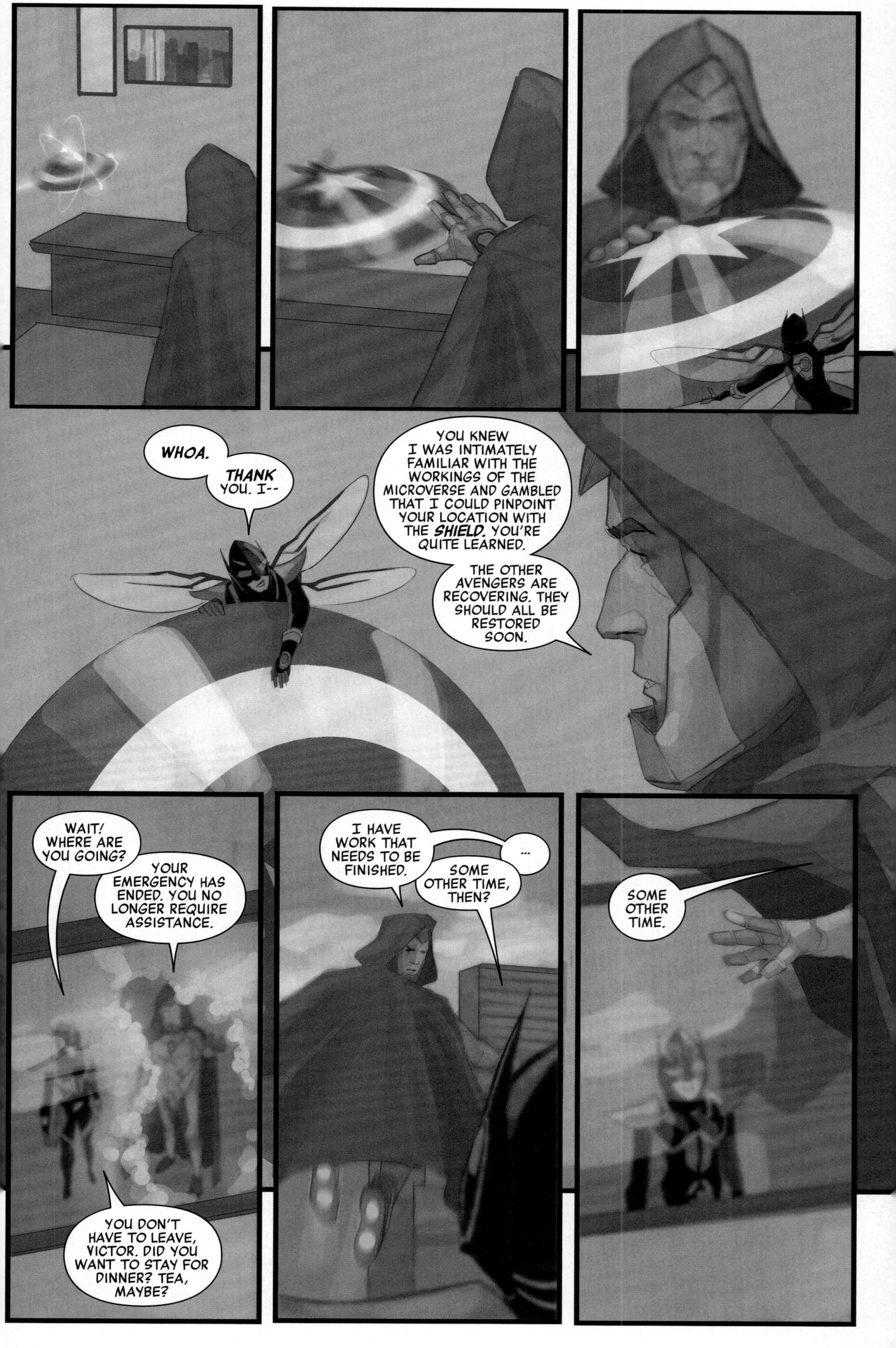
WHOA.
THANK YOU. I--
YOU KNEW I WAS INTIMATELY FAMILIAR WITH THE WORKINGS OF THE MICROVERSE AND GAMBLED THAT I COULD PINPOINT YOUR LOCATION WITH THE SHIELD. YOU'RE QUITE LEARNED.
THE OTHER AVENGERS ARE RECOVERING. THEY SHOULD ALL BE RESTORED SOON.
WAIT! WHERE ARE YOU GOING?
YOUR EMERGENCY HAS ENDED. YOU NO LONGER REQUIRE ASSISTANCE.
YOU DON'T HAVE TO LEAVE, VICTOR. DID YOU WANT TO STAY FOR DINNER? TEA, MAYBE?
I HAVE WORK THAT NEEDS TO BE FINISHED.
...
SOME OTHER TIME, THEN?
SOME OTHER TIME.

[9]

WHERE IS THOR?

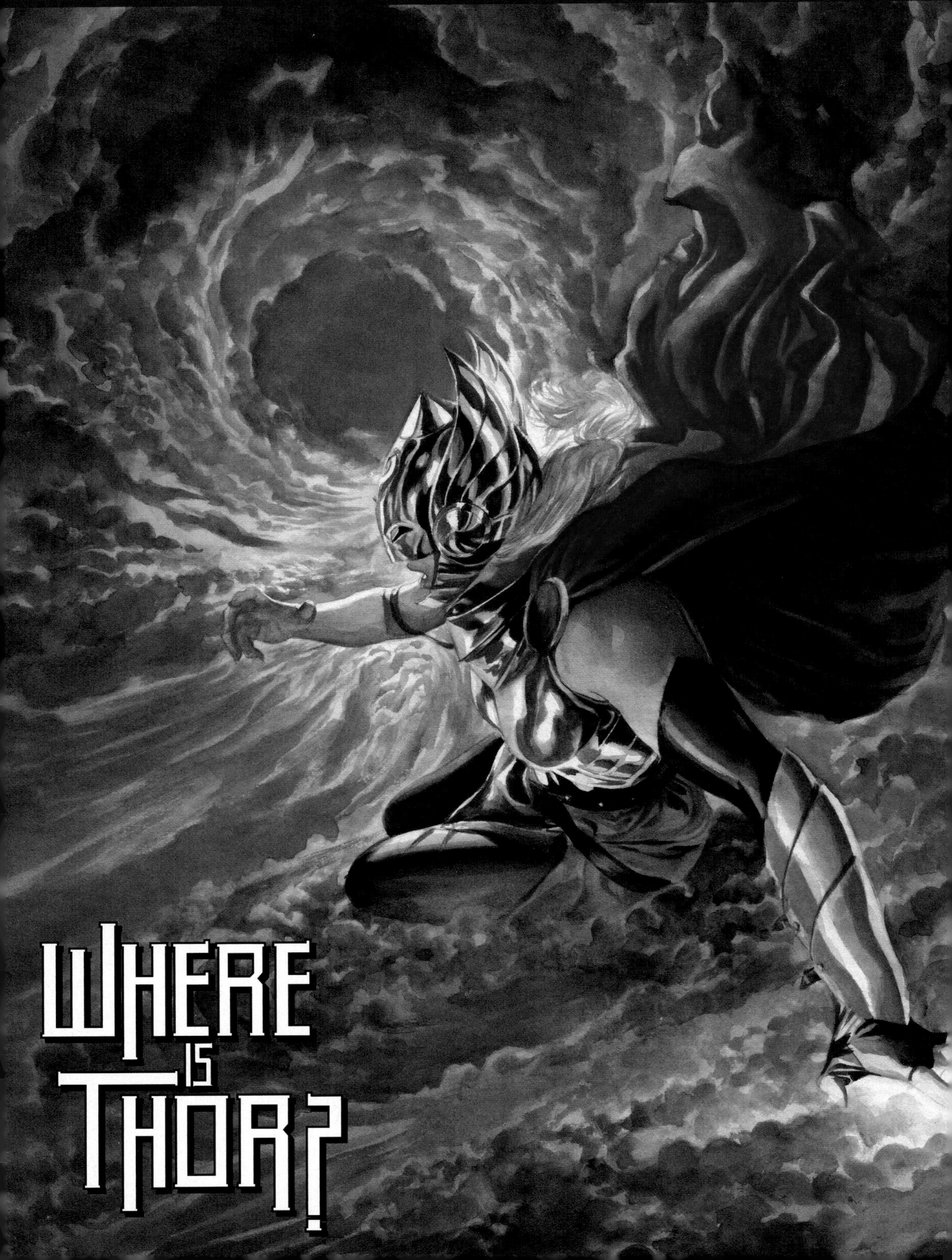

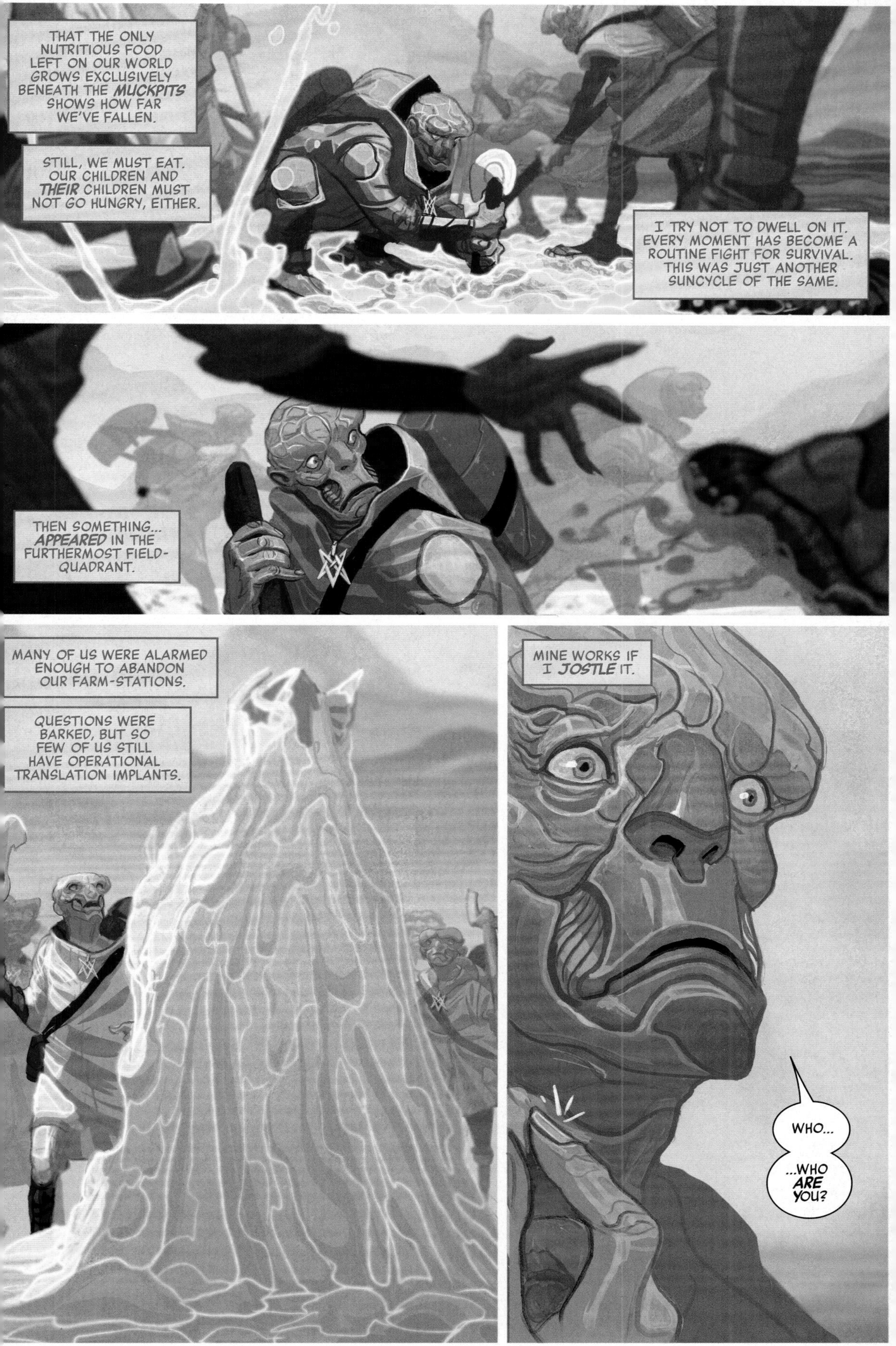

THAT THE ONLY NUTRITIOUS FOOD LEFT ON OUR WORLD GROWS EXCLUSIVELY BENEATH THE ***MUCKPITS*** SHOWS HOW FAR WE'VE FALLEN.
STILL, WE MUST EAT. OUR CHILDREN AND ***THEIR*** CHILDREN MUST NOT GO HUNGRY, EITHER.
I TRY NOT TO DWELL ON IT. EVERY MOMENT HAS BECOME A ROUTINE FIGHT FOR SURVIVAL. THIS WAS JUST ANOTHER SUNCYCLE OF THE SAME.
THEN SOMETHING... ***APPEARED*** IN THE FURTHERMOST FIELD-QUADRANT.
MANY OF US WERE ALARMED ENOUGH TO ABANDON OUR FARM-STATIONS.
QUESTIONS WERE BARKED, BUT SO FEW OF US STILL HAVE OPERATIONAL TRANSLATION IMPLANTS.
MINE WORKS IF I ***JOSTLE*** IT.
WHO...
...WHO ***ARE*** YOU?

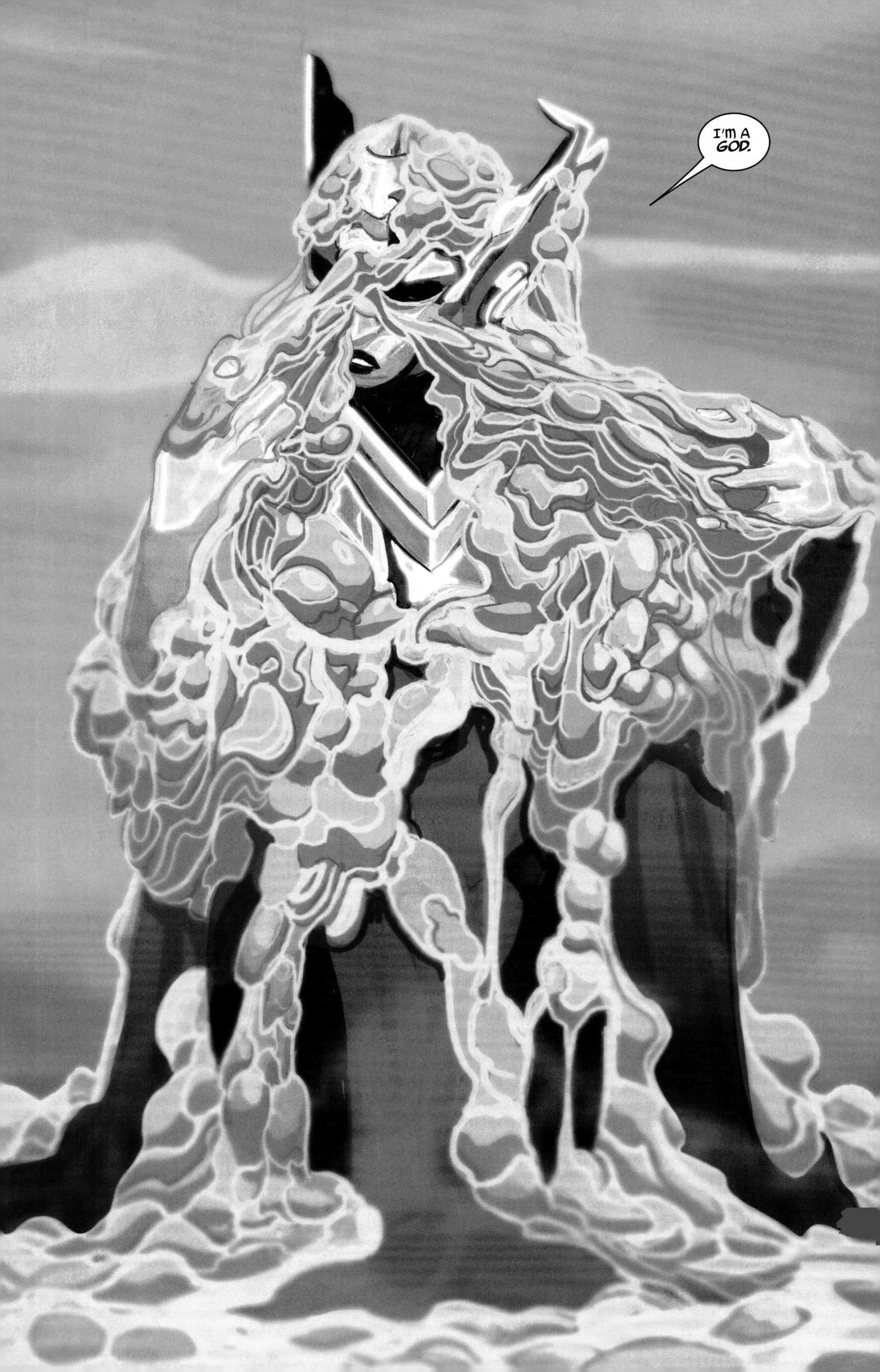
I'M A GOD.

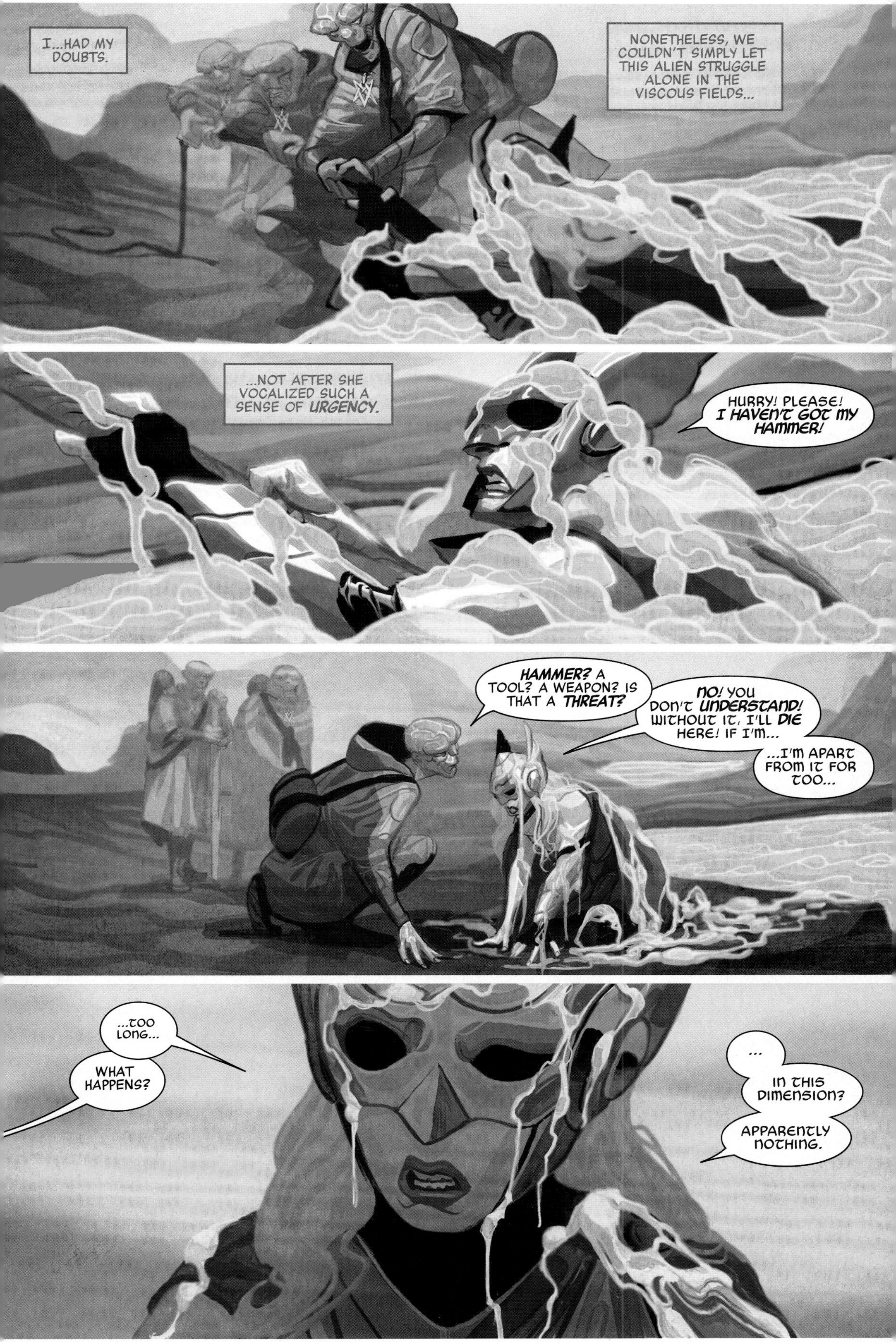
I...HAD MY DOUBTS.
NONETHELESS, WE COULDN'T SIMPLY LET THIS ALIEN STRUGGLE ALONE IN THE VISCOUS FIELDS...
...NOT AFTER SHE VOCALIZED SUCH A SENSE OF URGENCY.
HURRY! PLEASE! I HAVEN'T GOT MY HAMMER!
HAMMER? A TOOL? A WEAPON? IS THAT A THREAT?
NO! YOU DON'T UNDERSTAND! WITHOUT IT, I'LL DIE HERE! IF I'M...
...I'M APART FROM IT FOR TOO...
...TOO LONG...
WHAT HAPPENS?
...
IN THIS DIMENSION?
APPARENTLY NOTHING.

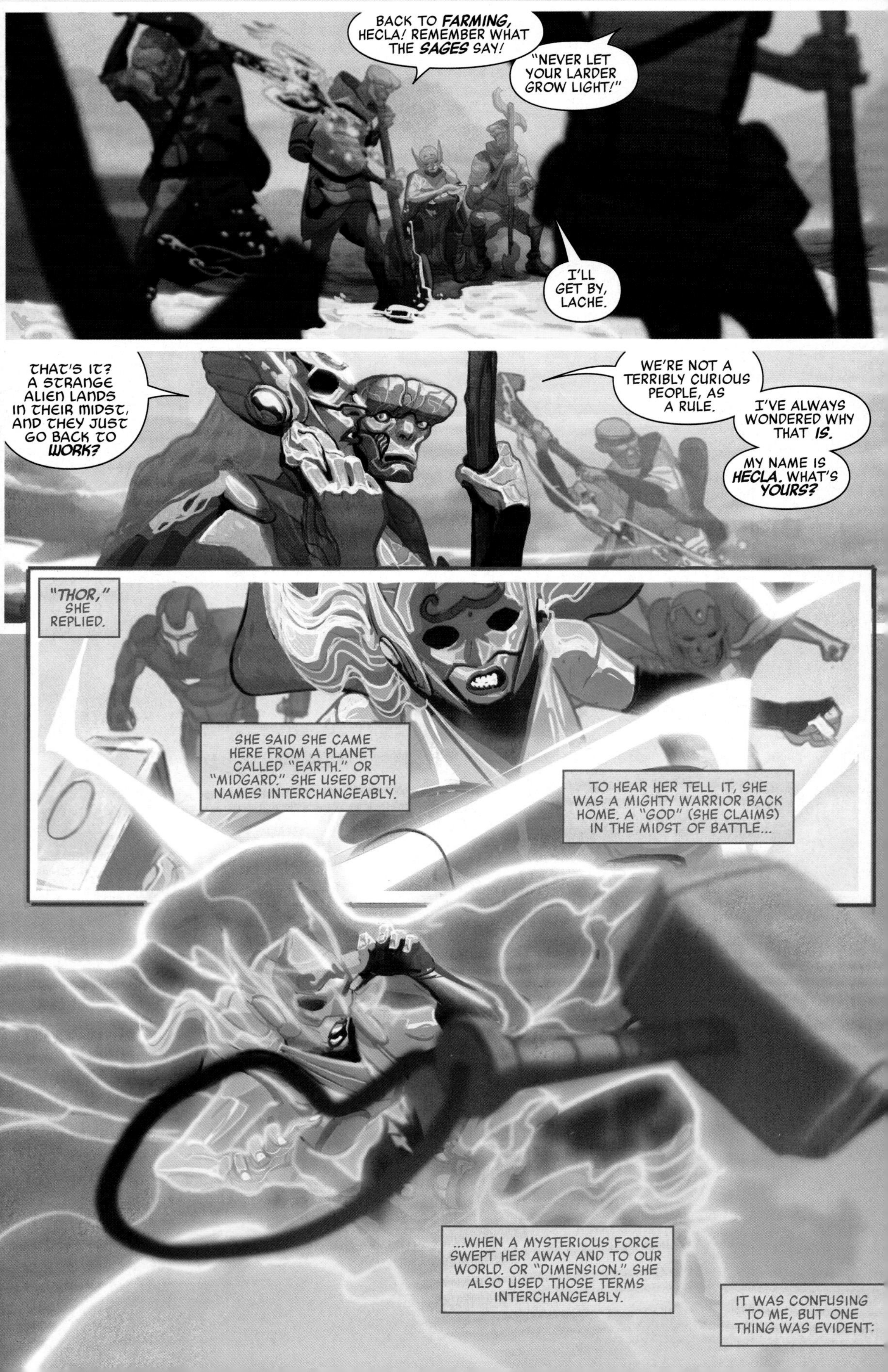

BACK TO **FARMING,** HECLA! REMEMBER WHAT THE **SAGES** SAY!
"NEVER LET YOUR LARDER GROW LIGHT!"
I'LL GET BY, LACHE.
THAT'S IT? A STRANGE ALIEN LANDS IN THEIR MIDST, AND THEY JUST GO BACK TO **WORK?**
WE'RE NOT A TERRIBLY CURIOUS PEOPLE, AS A RULE.
I'VE ALWAYS WONDERED WHY THAT **IS.**
MY NAME IS **HECLA.** WHAT'S **YOURS?**
"**THOR,**" SHE REPLIED.
SHE SAID SHE CAME HERE FROM A PLANET CALLED "EARTH." OR "MIDGARD." SHE USED BOTH NAMES INTERCHANGEABLY.
TO HEAR HER TELL IT, SHE WAS A MIGHTY WARRIOR BACK HOME. A "GOD" (SHE CLAIMS) IN THE MIDST OF BATTLE...
...WHEN A MYSTERIOUS FORCE SWEPT HER AWAY AND TO OUR WORLD. OR "DIMENSION." SHE ALSO USED THOSE TERMS INTERCHANGEABLY.
IT WAS CONFUSING TO ME, BUT ONE THING WAS EVIDENT:

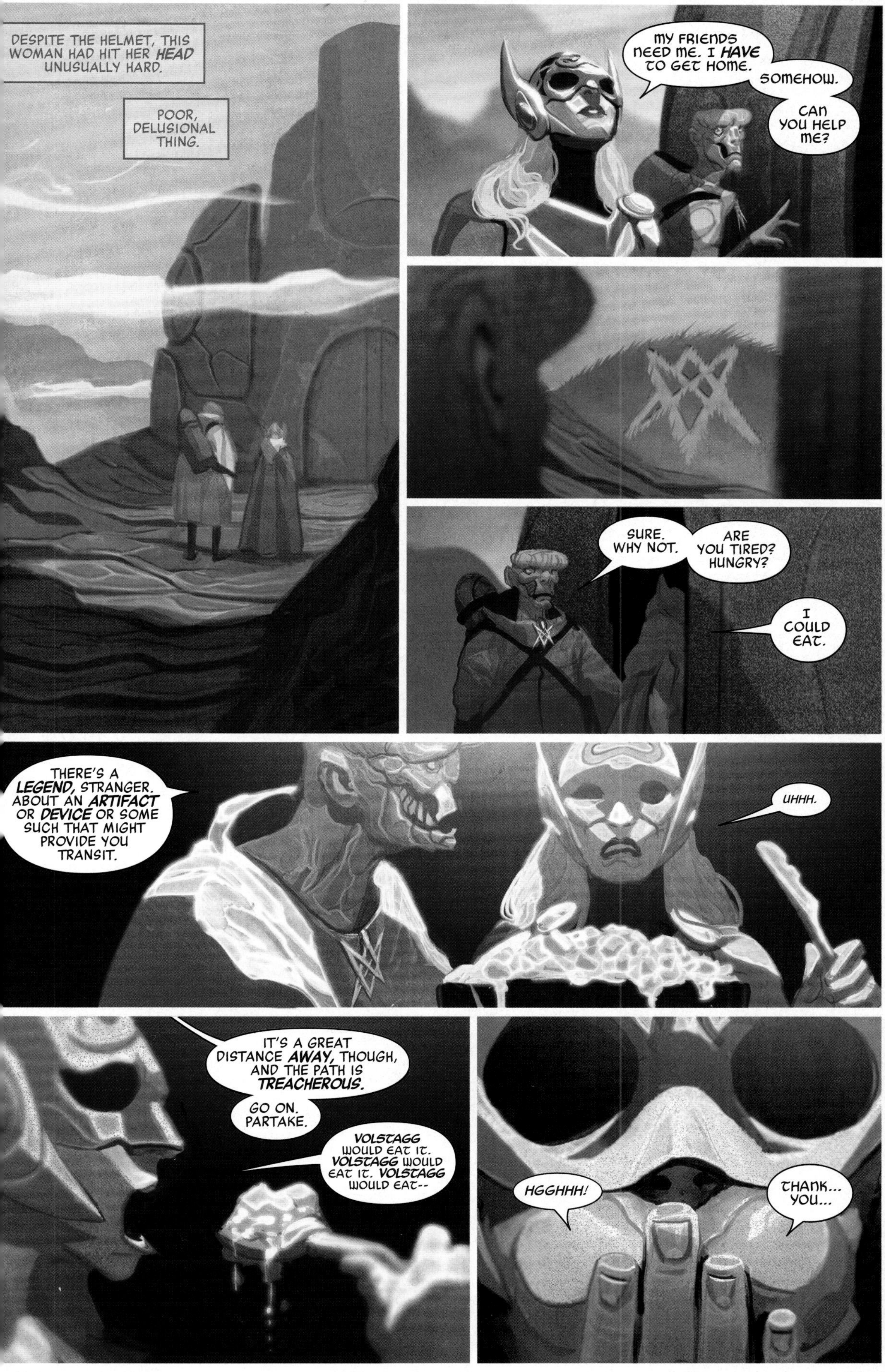

DESPITE THE HELMET, THIS WOMAN HAD HIT HER HEAD UNUSUALLY HARD.
POOR, DELUSIONAL THING.
MY FRIENDS NEED ME. I HAVE TO GET HOME.
SOMEHOW.
CAN YOU HELP ME?
SURE. WHY NOT.
ARE YOU TIRED? HUNGRY?
I COULD EAT.
THERE'S A LEGEND, STRANGER. ABOUT AN ARTIFACT OR DEVICE OR SOME SUCH THAT MIGHT PROVIDE YOU TRANSIT.
UHHH.
IT'S A GREAT DISTANCE AWAY, THOUGH, AND THE PATH IS TREACHEROUS.
GO ON. PARTAKE.
VOLSTAGG WOULD EAT IT. VOLSTAGG WOULD EAT IT. VOLSTAGG WOULD EAT--
HGGHHH!
THANK... YOU...

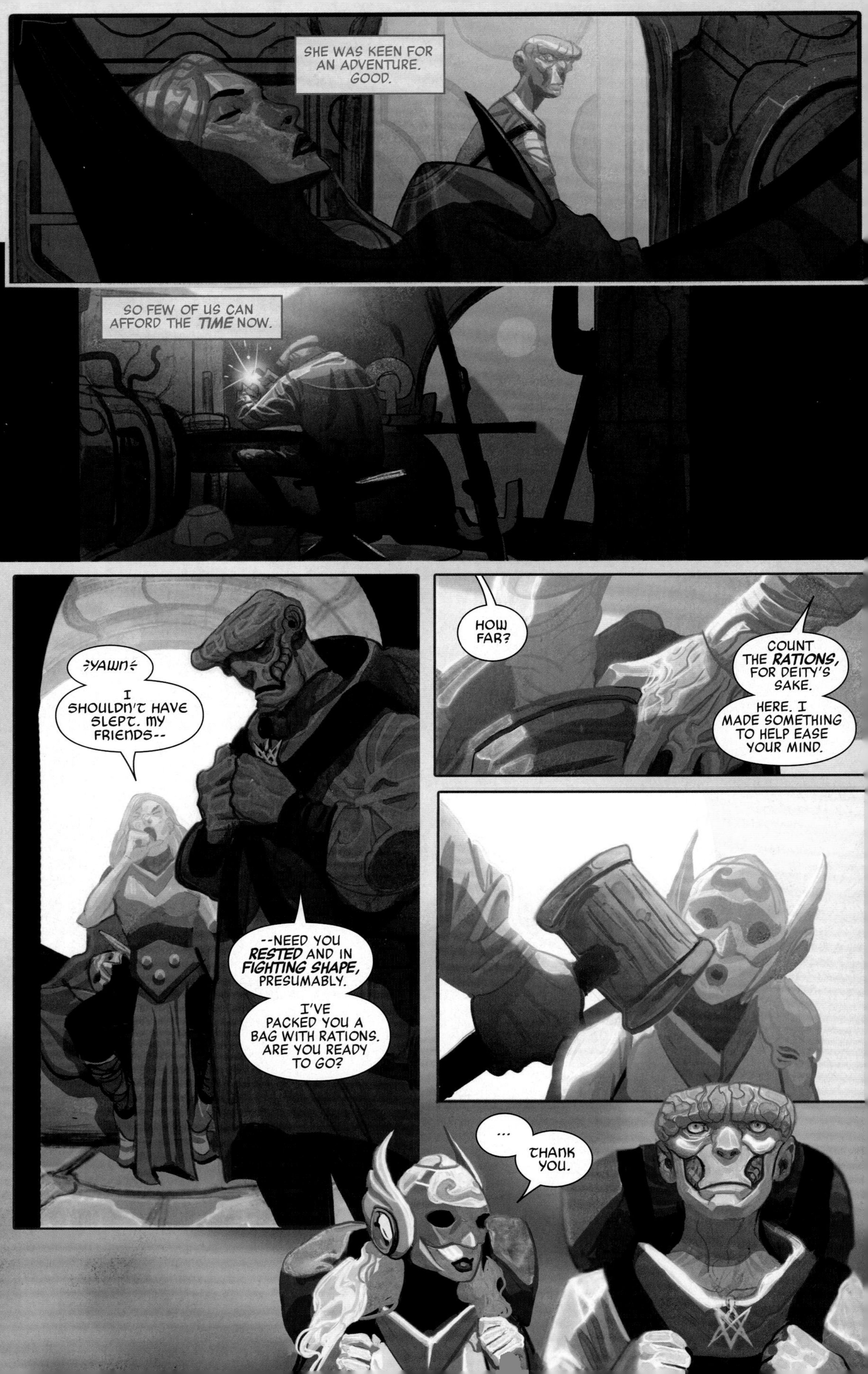
SHE WAS KEEN FOR AN ADVENTURE. GOOD.
SO FEW OF US CAN AFFORD THE TIME NOW.
=YAWN=
I SHOULDN'T HAVE SLEPT. MY FRIENDS--
--NEED YOU RESTED AND IN FIGHTING SHAPE, PRESUMABLY.
I'VE PACKED YOU A BAG WITH RATIONS. ARE YOU READY TO GO?
HOW FAR?
COUNT THE RATIONS, FOR DEITY'S SAKE.
HERE. I MADE SOMETHING TO HELP EASE YOUR MIND.
...
THANK YOU.

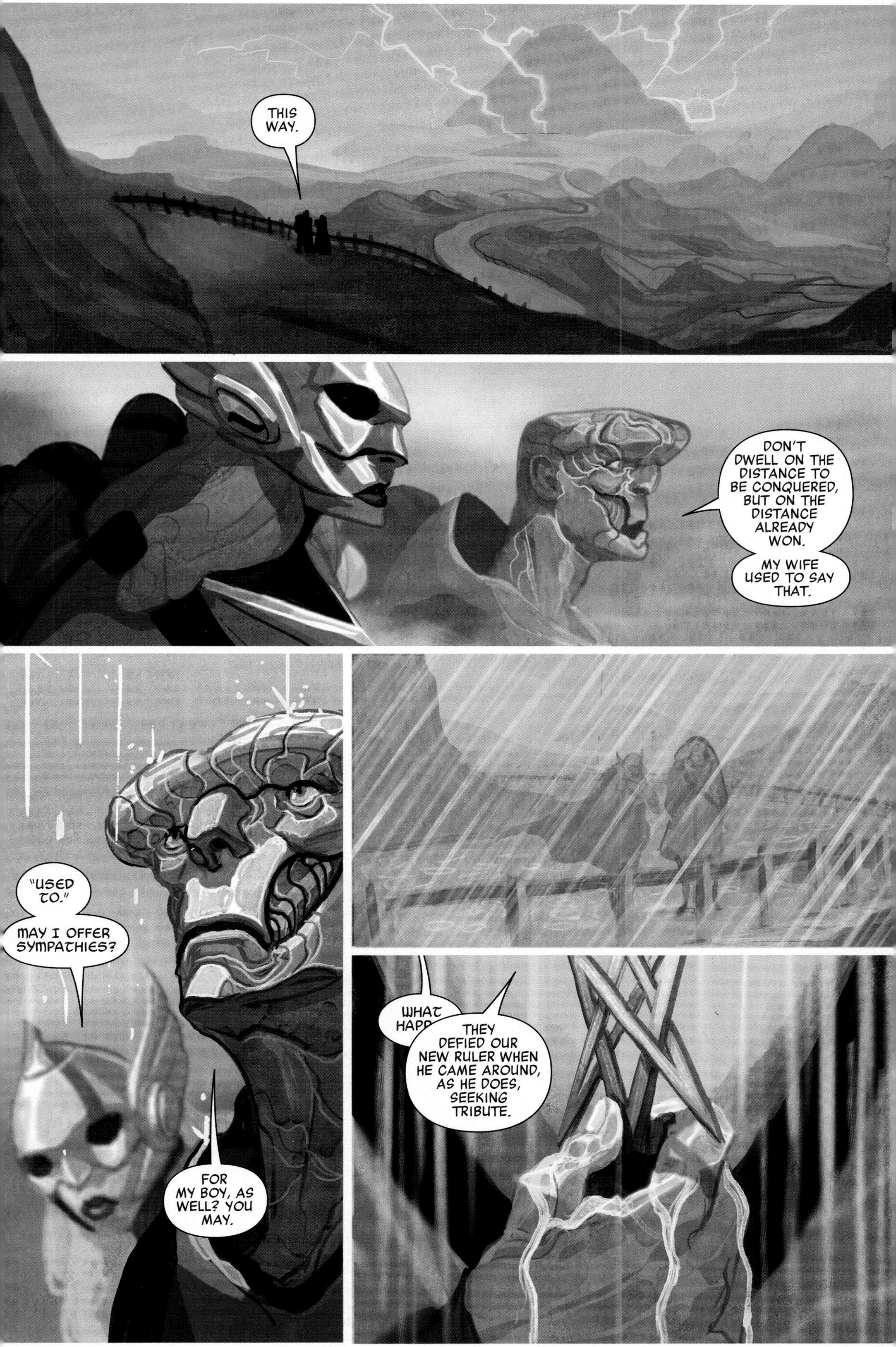
THIS WAY.
DON'T DWELL ON THE DISTANCE TO BE CONQUERED, BUT ON THE DISTANCE ALREADY WON.
MY WIFE USED TO SAY THAT.
"USED TO."
MAY I OFFER SYMPATHIES?
FOR MY BOY, AS WELL? YOU MAY.
THEY DEFIED OUR NEW RULER WHEN HE CAME AROUND, AS HE DOES, SEEKING TRIBUTE.

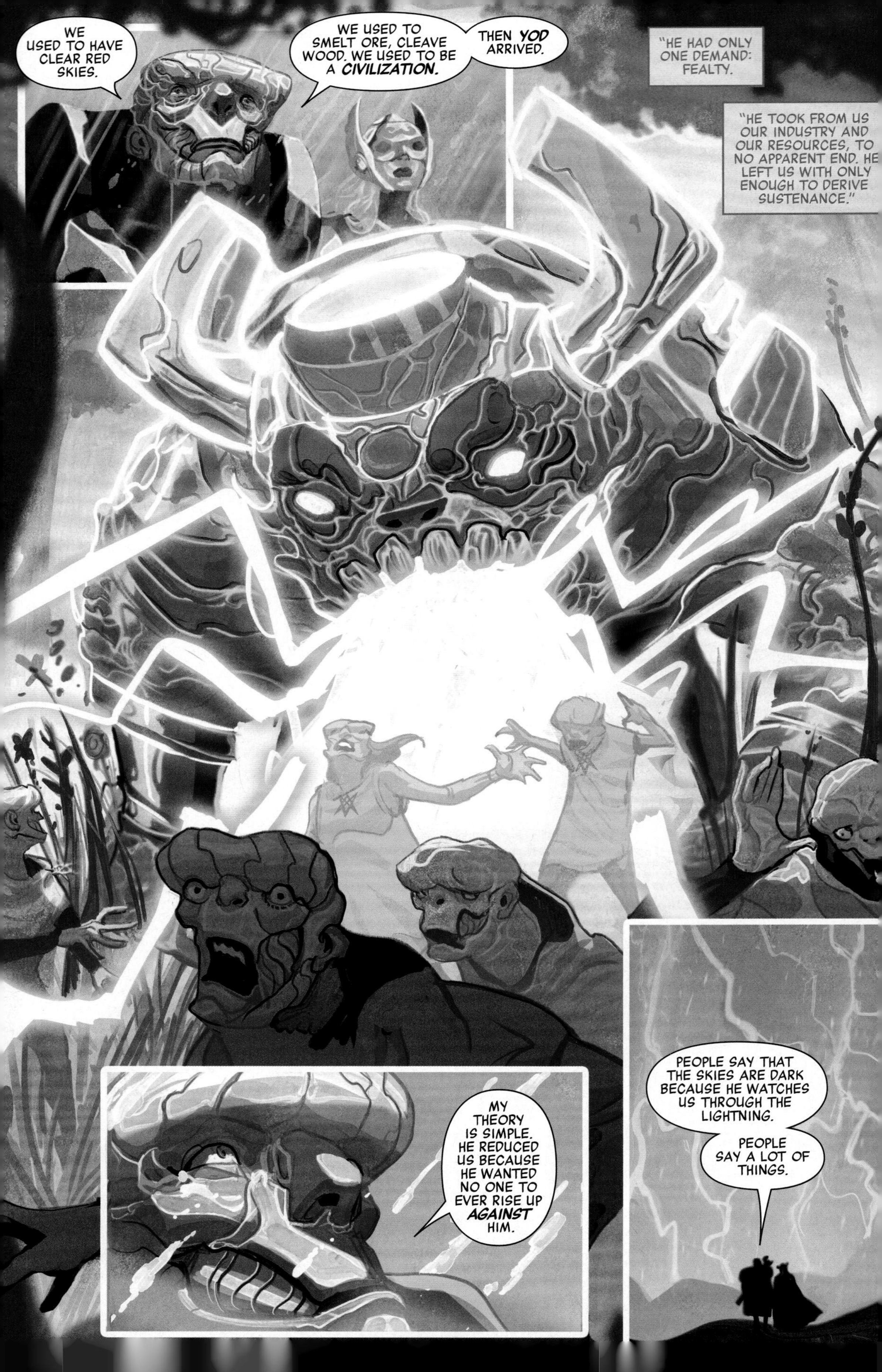
WE USED TO HAVE CLEAR RED SKIES.
WE USED TO SMELT ORE, CLEAVE WOOD. WE USED TO BE A **CIVILIZATION.**
THEN **YOD** ARRIVED.
"HE HAD ONLY ONE DEMAND: FEALTY.
"HE TOOK FROM US OUR INDUSTRY AND OUR RESOURCES, TO NO APPARENT END. HE LEFT US WITH ONLY ENOUGH TO DERIVE SUSTENANCE."
MY THEORY IS SIMPLE. HE REDUCED US BECAUSE HE WANTED NO ONE TO EVER RISE UP **AGAINST** HIM.
PEOPLE SAY THAT THE SKIES ARE DARK BECAUSE HE WATCHES US THROUGH THE LIGHTNING.
PEOPLE SAY A LOT OF THINGS.

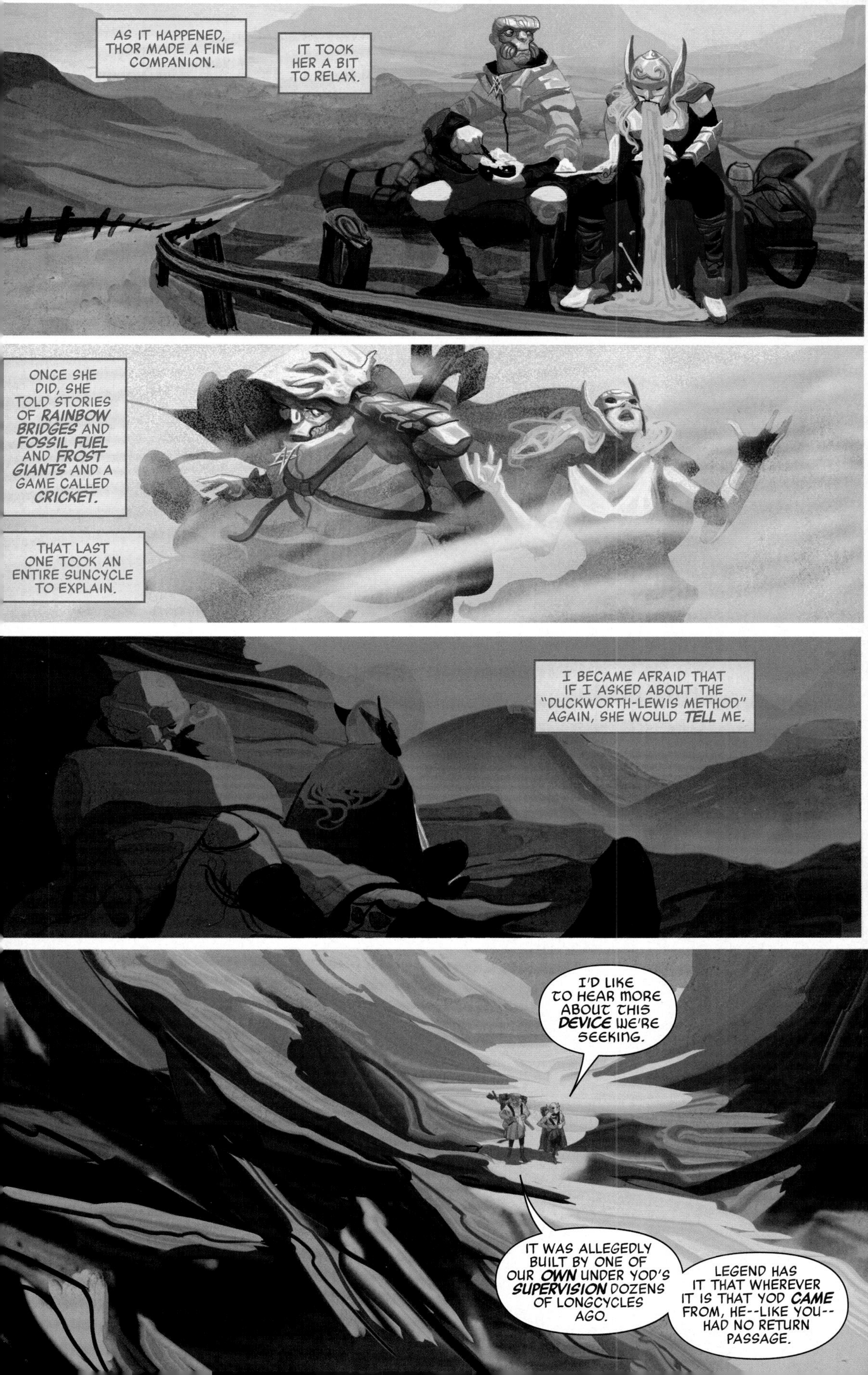
AS IT HAPPENED, THOR MADE A FINE COMPANION.
IT TOOK HER A BIT TO RELAX.
ONCE SHE DID, SHE TOLD STORIES OF RAINBOW BRIDGES AND FOSSIL FUEL AND FROST GIANTS AND A GAME CALLED CRICKET.
THAT LAST ONE TOOK AN ENTIRE SUNCYCLE TO EXPLAIN.
I BECAME AFRAID THAT IF I ASKED ABOUT THE "DUCKWORTH-LEWIS METHOD" AGAIN, SHE WOULD TELL ME.
I'D LIKE TO HEAR MORE ABOUT THIS DEVICE WE'RE SEEKING.
IT WAS ALLEGEDLY BUILT BY ONE OF OUR OWN UNDER YOD'S SUPERVISION DOZENS OF LONGCYCLES AGO.
LEGEND HAS IT THAT WHEREVER IT IS THAT YOD CAME FROM, HE--LIKE YOU--HAD NO RETURN PASSAGE.

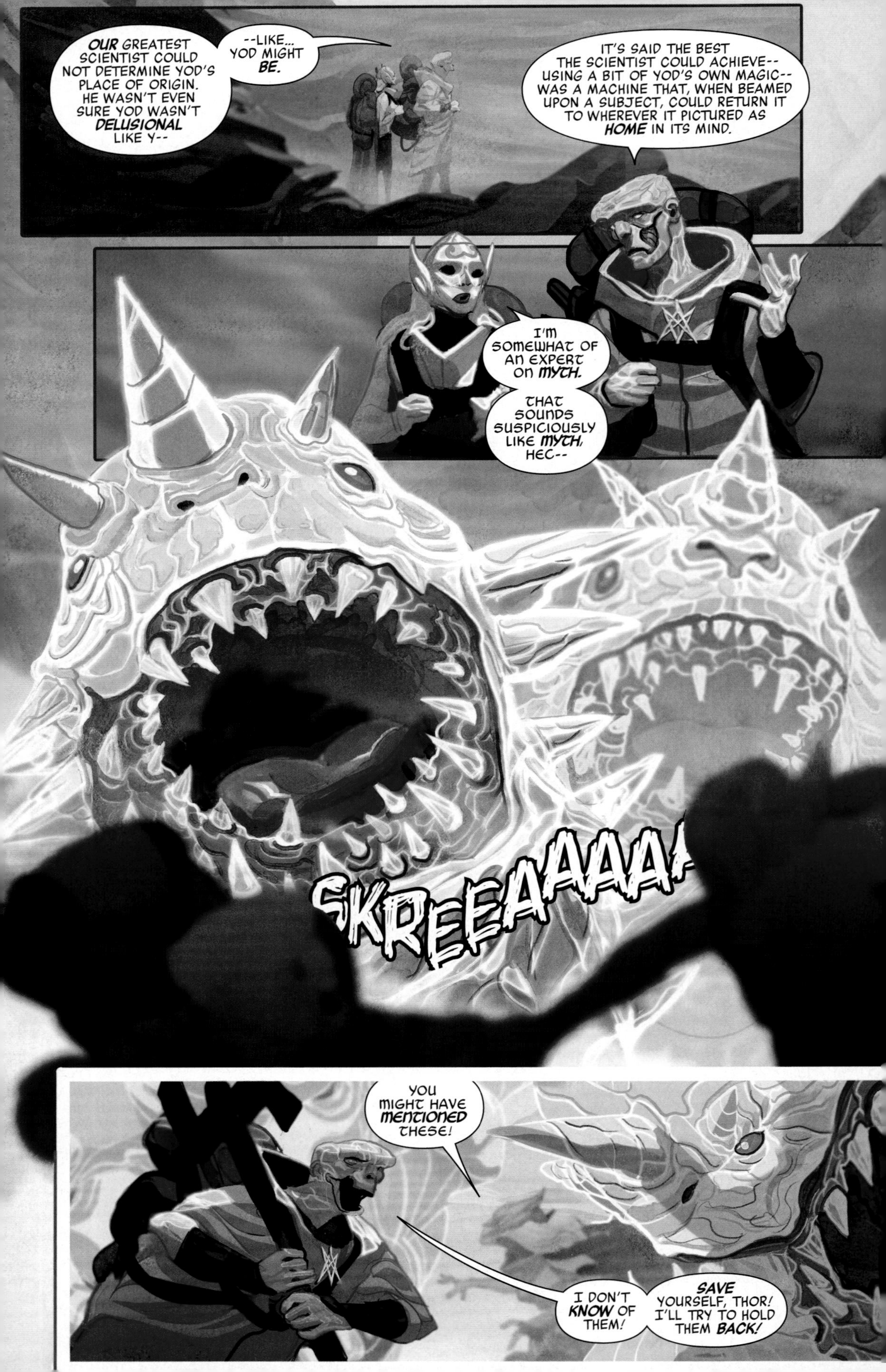
OUR GREATEST SCIENTIST COULD NOT DETERMINE YOD'S PLACE OF ORIGIN. HE WASN'T EVEN SURE YOD WASN'T DELUSIONAL LIKE Y--
--LIKE... YOD MIGHT BE.
IT'S SAID THE BEST THE SCIENTIST COULD ACHIEVE-- USING A BIT OF YOD'S OWN MAGIC-- WAS A MACHINE THAT, WHEN BEAMED UPON A SUBJECT, COULD RETURN IT TO WHEREVER IT PICTURED AS HOME IN ITS MIND.
I'M SOMEWHAT OF AN EXPERT ON MYTH.
THAT SOUNDS SUSPICIOUSLY LIKE MYTH, HEC--
SKREEAAAAA
YOU MIGHT HAVE MENTIONED THESE!
I DON'T KNOW OF THEM!
SAVE YOURSELF, THOR! I'LL TRY TO HOLD THEM BACK!

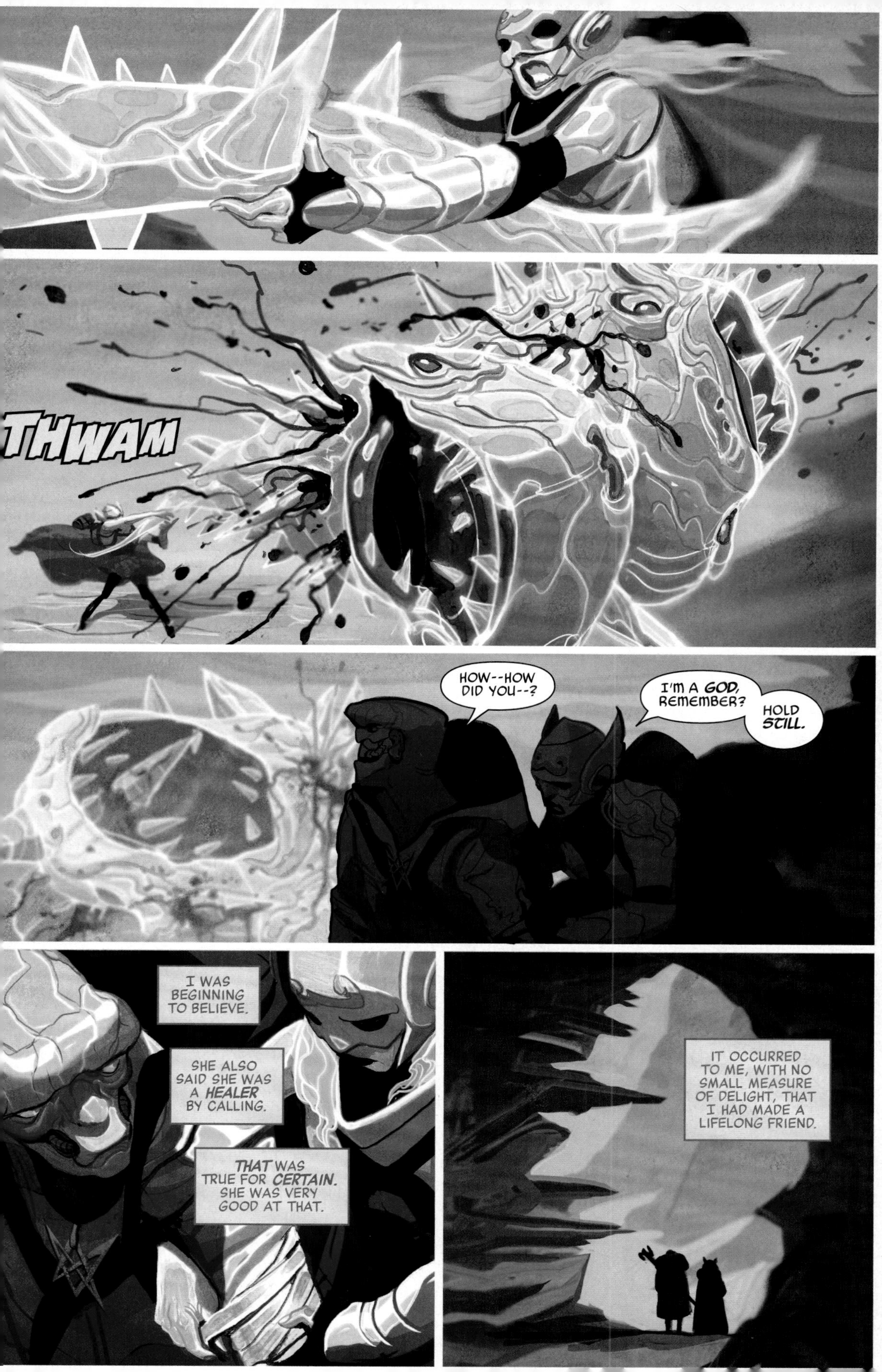
THWAM
HOW--HOW DID YOU--?
I'M A GOD, REMEMBER?
HOLD STILL.
I WAS BEGINNING TO BELIEVE.
SHE ALSO SAID SHE WAS A HEALER BY CALLING.
THAT WAS TRUE FOR CERTAIN. SHE WAS VERY GOOD AT THAT.
IT OCCURRED TO ME, WITH NO SMALL MEASURE OF DELIGHT, THAT I HAD MADE A LIFELONG FRIEND.

THERE. INSIDE THE MOUNTAIN. THE LAIR OF YOD.

I WILL LEAD THE WAY.

I WILL NOT ARGUE.

STAY CLOSE. YOU ARE SAFER WITH ME THAN ON YOUR OWN.

I SO WANTED TO LISTEN. I SO WANTED TO TRUST HER.

MARCHING INTO THE JAWS OF DEATH WASN'T FRIGHTENING, I TOLD MYSELF. AFTER ALL, WHAT DID I HAVE TO LOSE?

BUT I BROKE. INSTINCT OVERWHELMED THOUGHT, AND I RAN.

HECLA!

DEATH WAS QUICK.

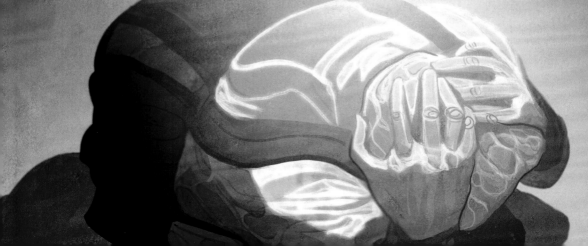

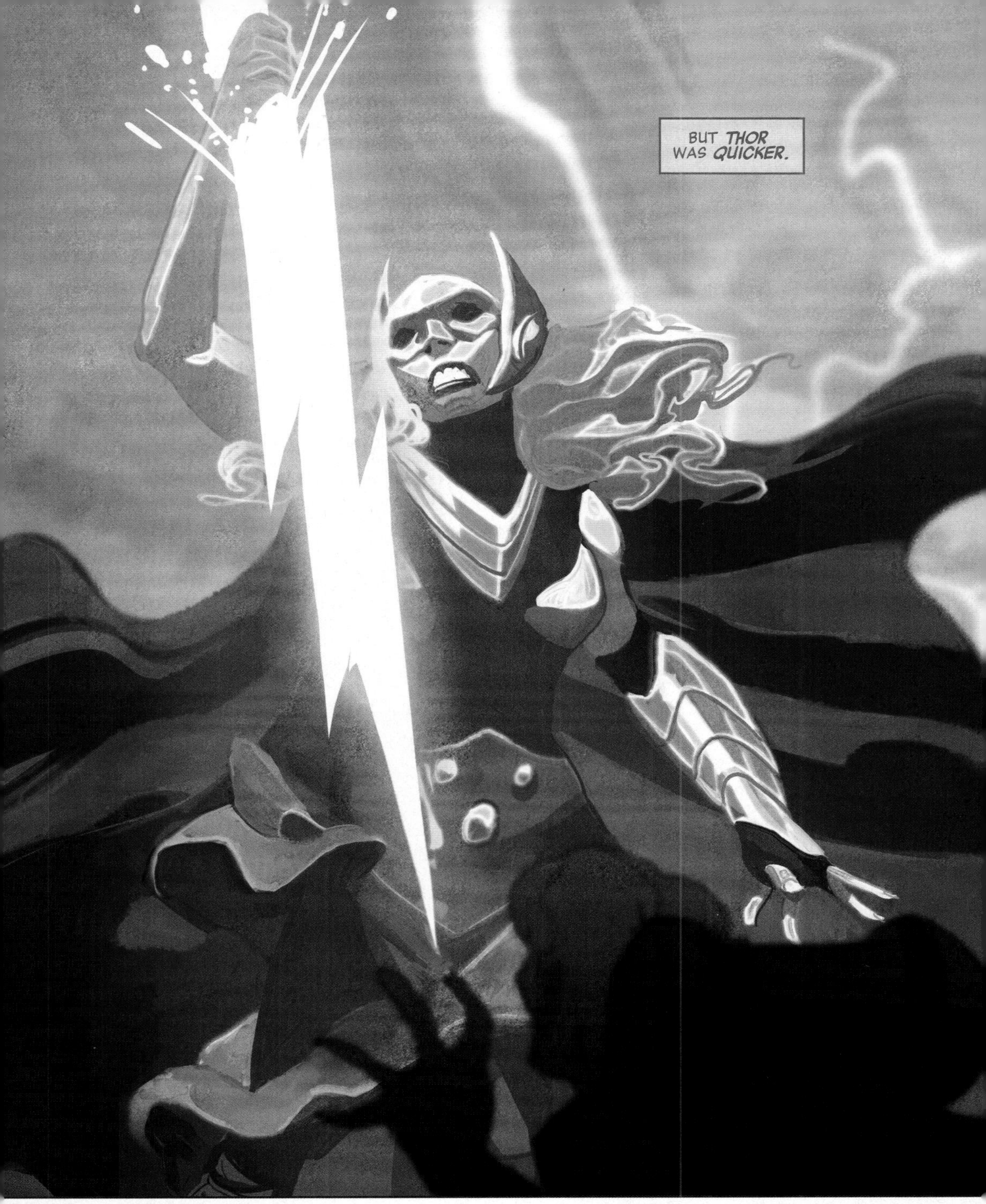
BUT THOR WAS QUICKER.

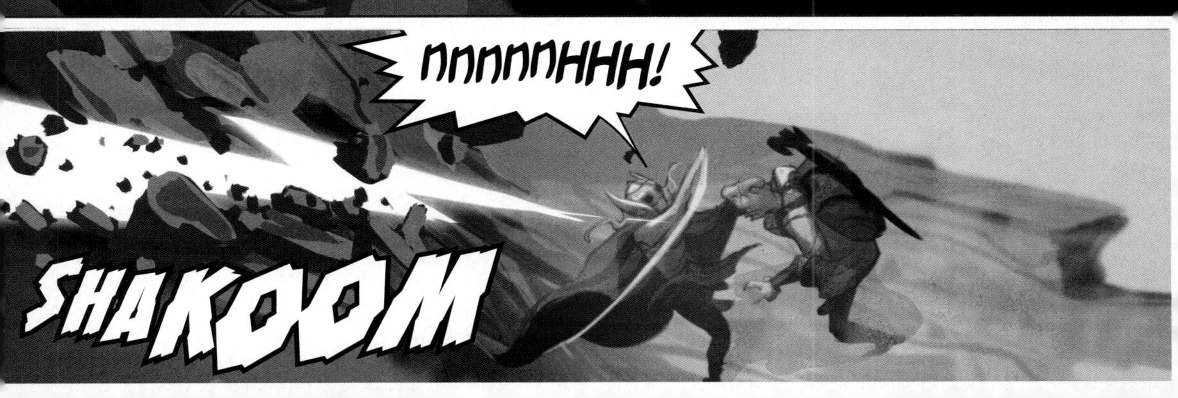
NNNNNHHH!
SHAKOOM

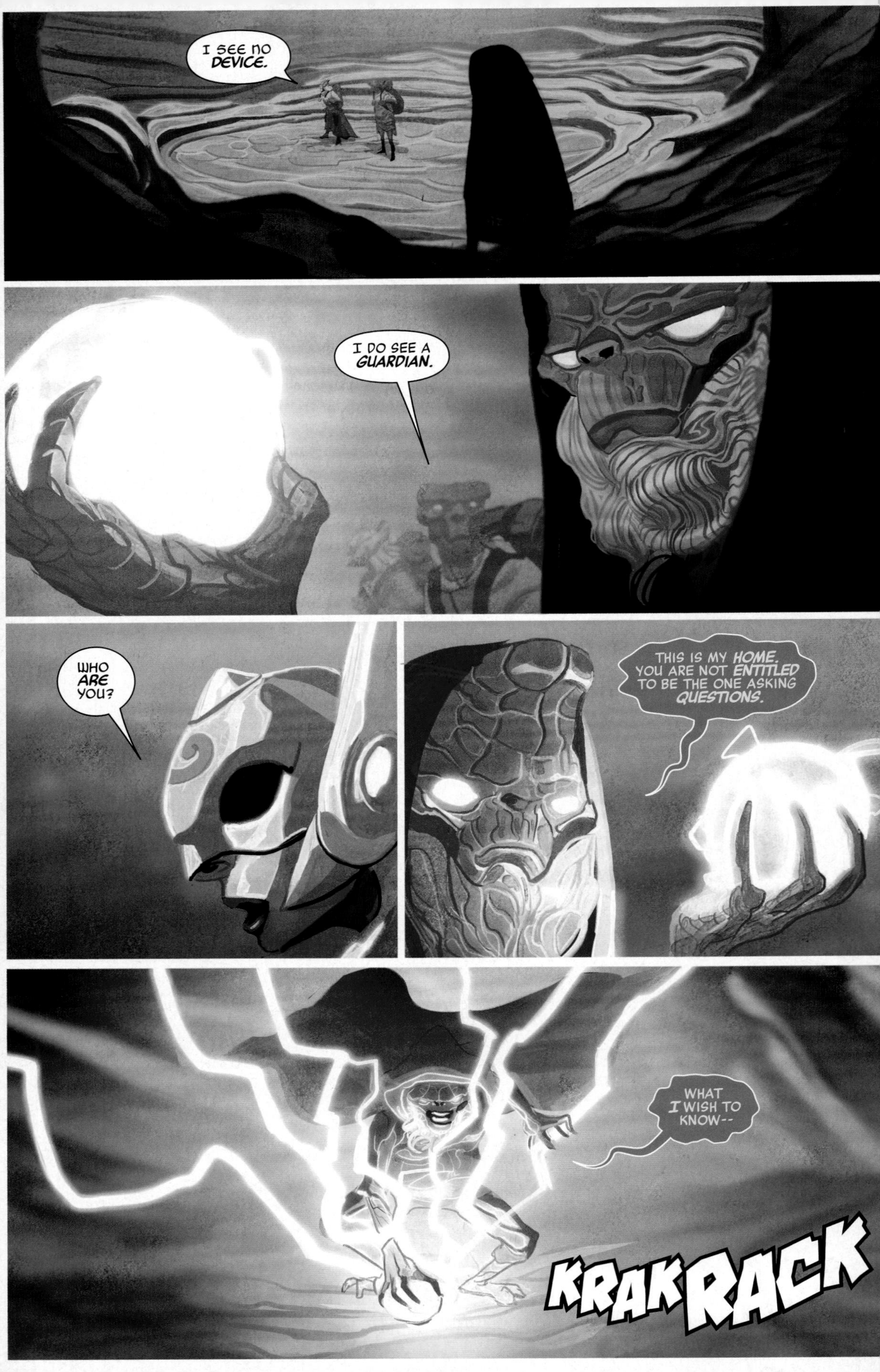
I SEE NO DEVICE.
I DO SEE A GUARDIAN.
WHO ARE YOU?
THIS IS MY HOME. YOU ARE NOT ENTITLED TO BE THE ONE ASKING QUESTIONS.
WHAT I WISH TO KNOW--
KRAKRACK

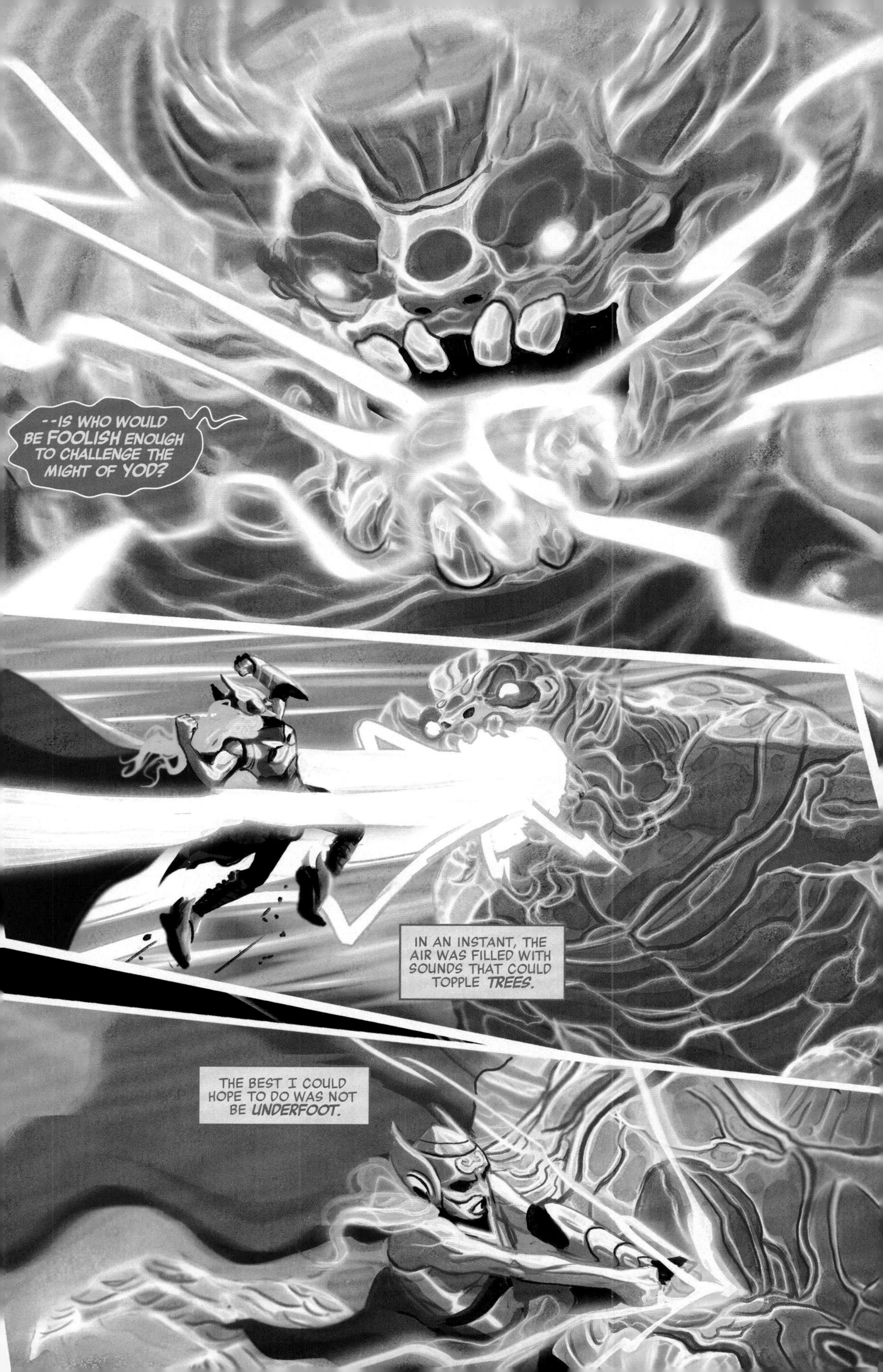
--IS WHO WOULD BE FOOLISH ENOUGH TO CHALLENGE THE MIGHT OF YOD?
IN AN INSTANT, THE AIR WAS FILLED WITH SOUNDS THAT COULD TOPPLE TREES.
THE BEST I COULD HOPE TO DO WAS NOT BE UNDERFOOT.

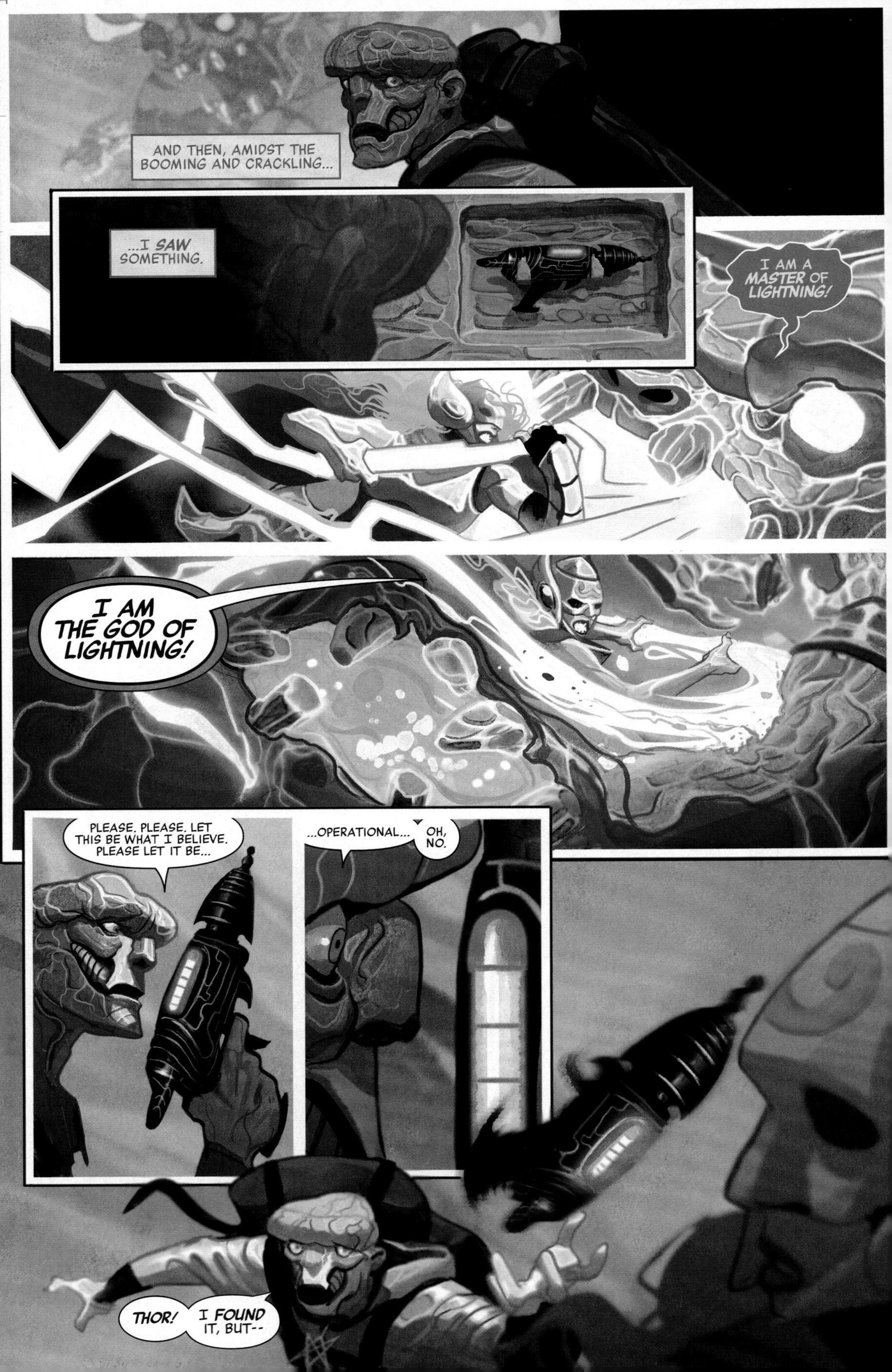
AND THEN, AMIDST THE BOOMING AND CRACKLING...
...I SAW SOMETHING.
I AM A MASTER OF LIGHTNING!
I AM THE GOD OF LIGHTNING!
PLEASE. PLEASE. LET THIS BE WHAT I BELIEVE. PLEASE LET IT BE...
...OPERATIONAL...
OH, NO.
THOR!
I FOUND IT, BUT--

EYAAAAAH!

KZAAAK

FORGET... YOD. SAVE... YOUR FRIENDS. SAVE YOUR... YOURSELF...

LET IT...TAKE YOU HOME... WHERE YOU'RE NEEDED...

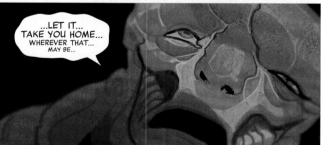

...LET IT... TAKE YOU HOME... WHEREVER THAT... MAY BE...

STAY STRONG, HECLA! STAY STRONG UNTIL I CAN BANISH YOD!

NO...! THOR, THERE WOULD SEEM...

...SEEM TO BE ONLY ONE CHARGE LEFT...IN THE DEVICE...

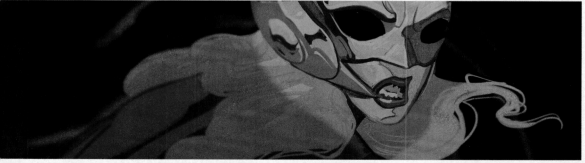

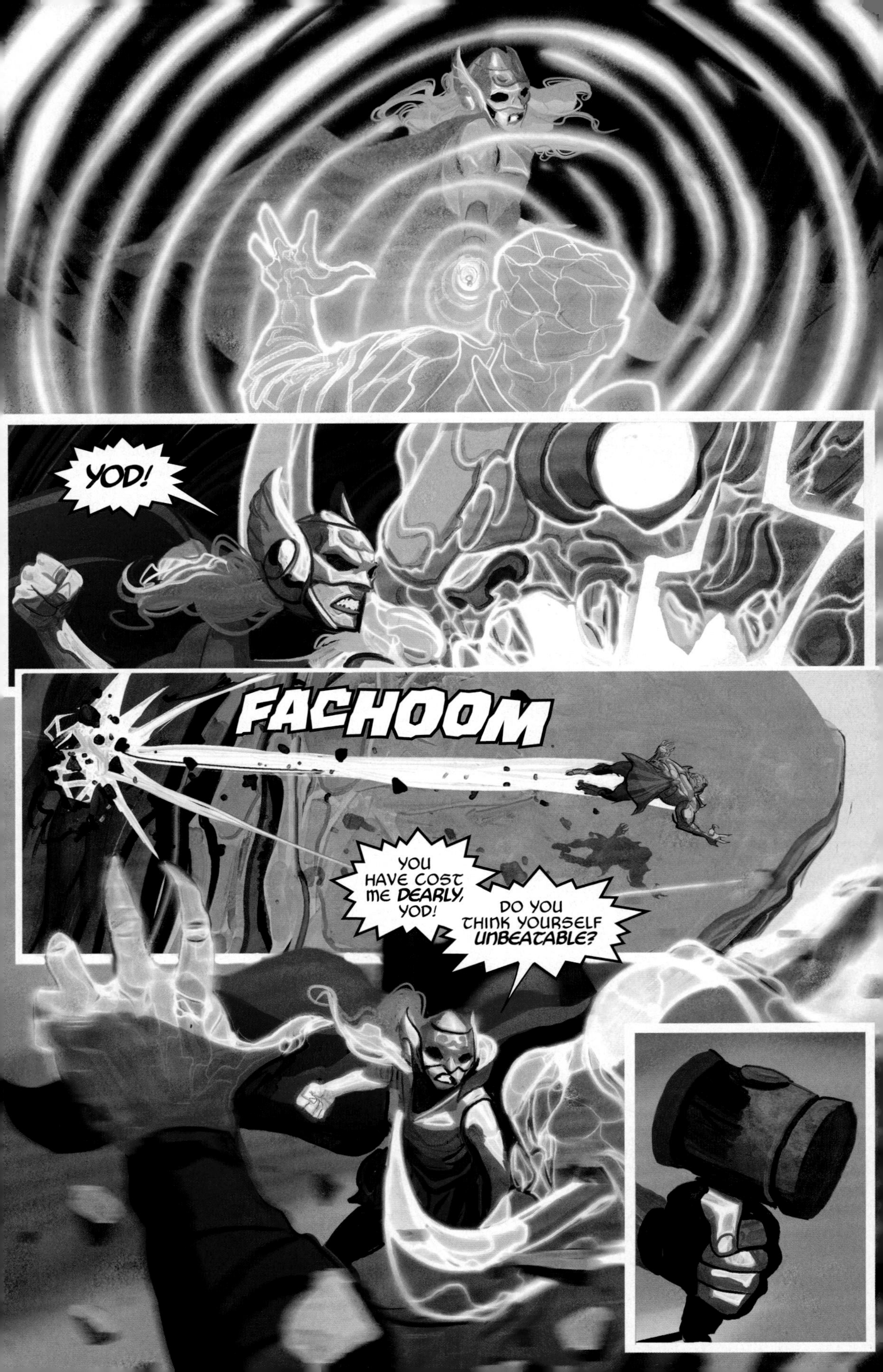

YOD!
FACHOOM
YOU HAVE COST ME DEARLY, YOD!
DO YOU THINK YOURSELF UNBEATABLE?

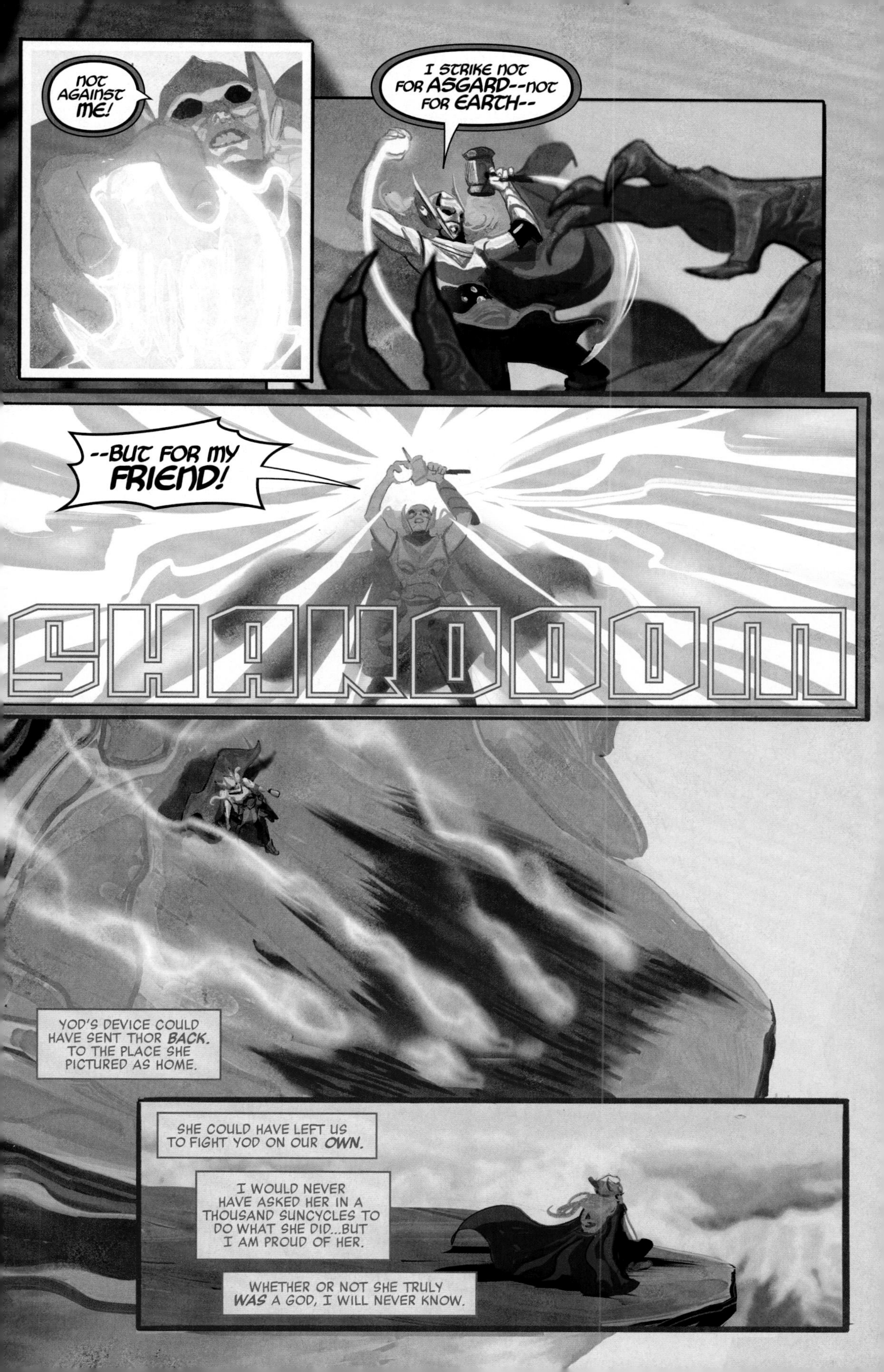
NOT AGAINST ME!
I STRIKE NOT FOR ASGARD--NOT FOR EARTH--
--BUT FOR MY FRIEND!
SHAKOOOM
YOD'S DEVICE COULD HAVE SENT THOR BACK. TO THE PLACE SHE PICTURED AS HOME.
SHE COULD HAVE LEFT US TO FIGHT YOD ON OUR OWN.
I WOULD NEVER HAVE ASKED HER IN A THOUSAND SUNCYCLES TO DO WHAT SHE DID...BUT I AM PROUD OF HER.
WHETHER OR NOT SHE TRULY WAS A GOD, I WILL NEVER KNOW.

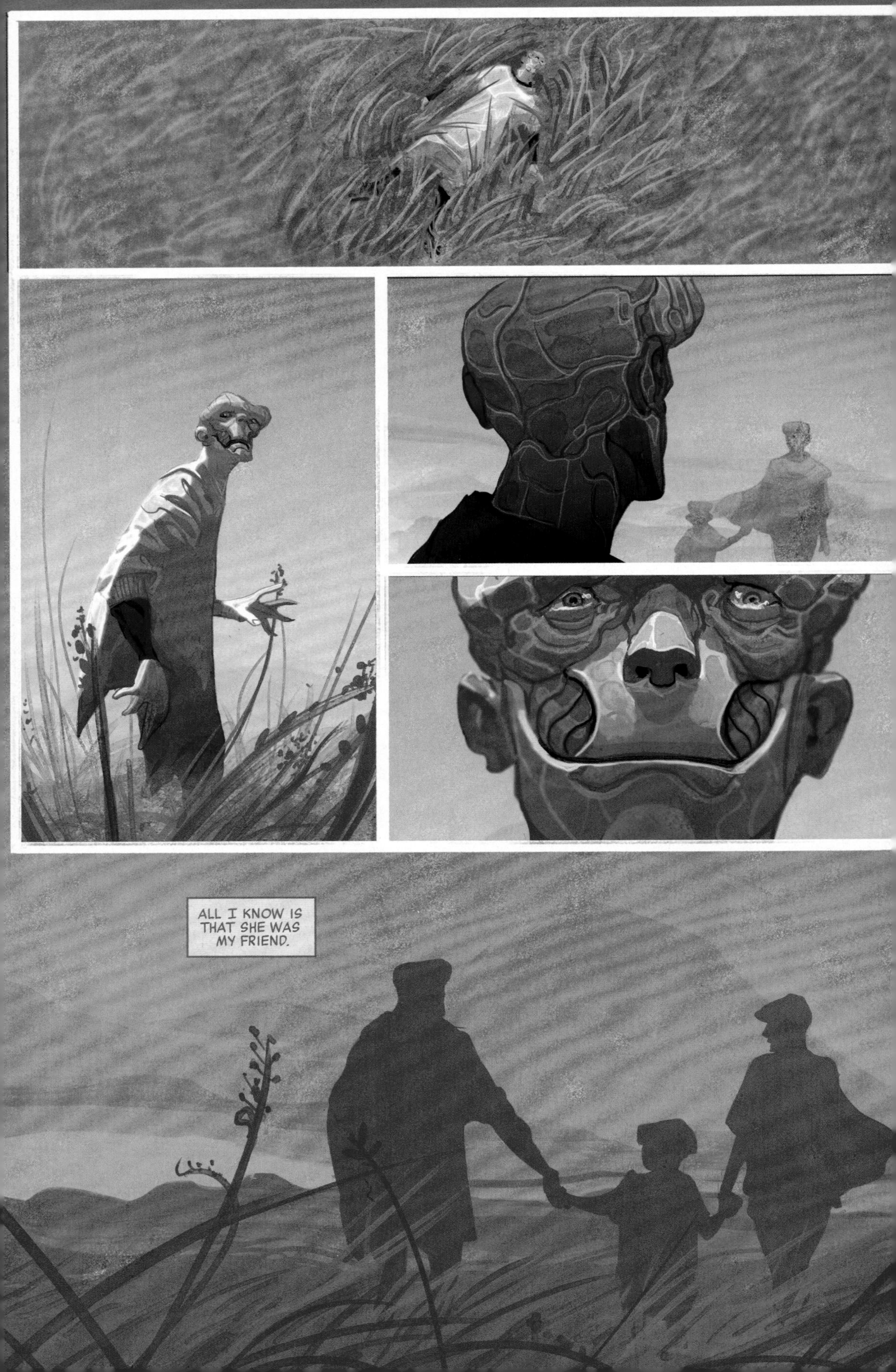
ALL I KNOW IS THAT SHE WAS MY FRIEND.

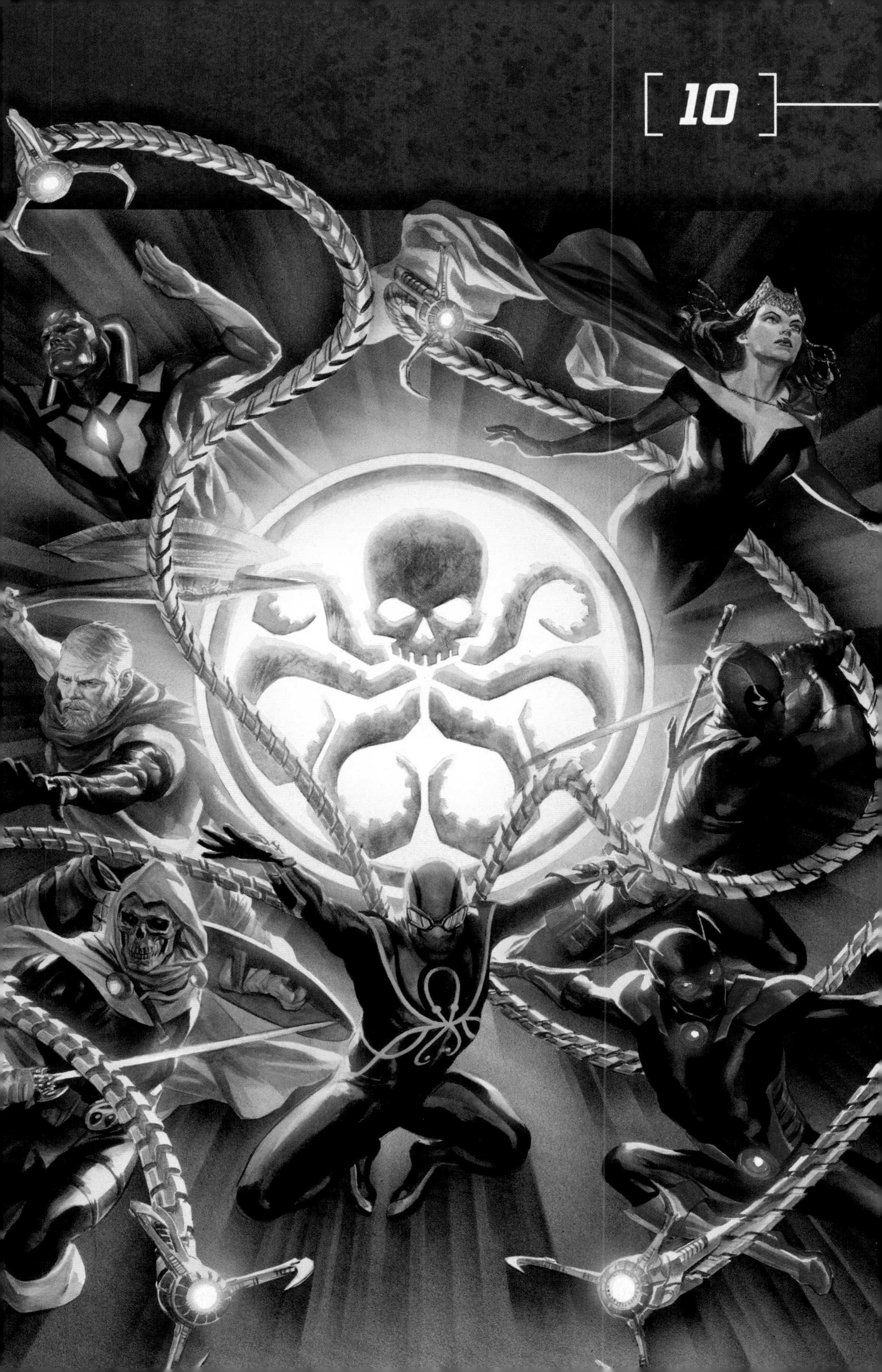

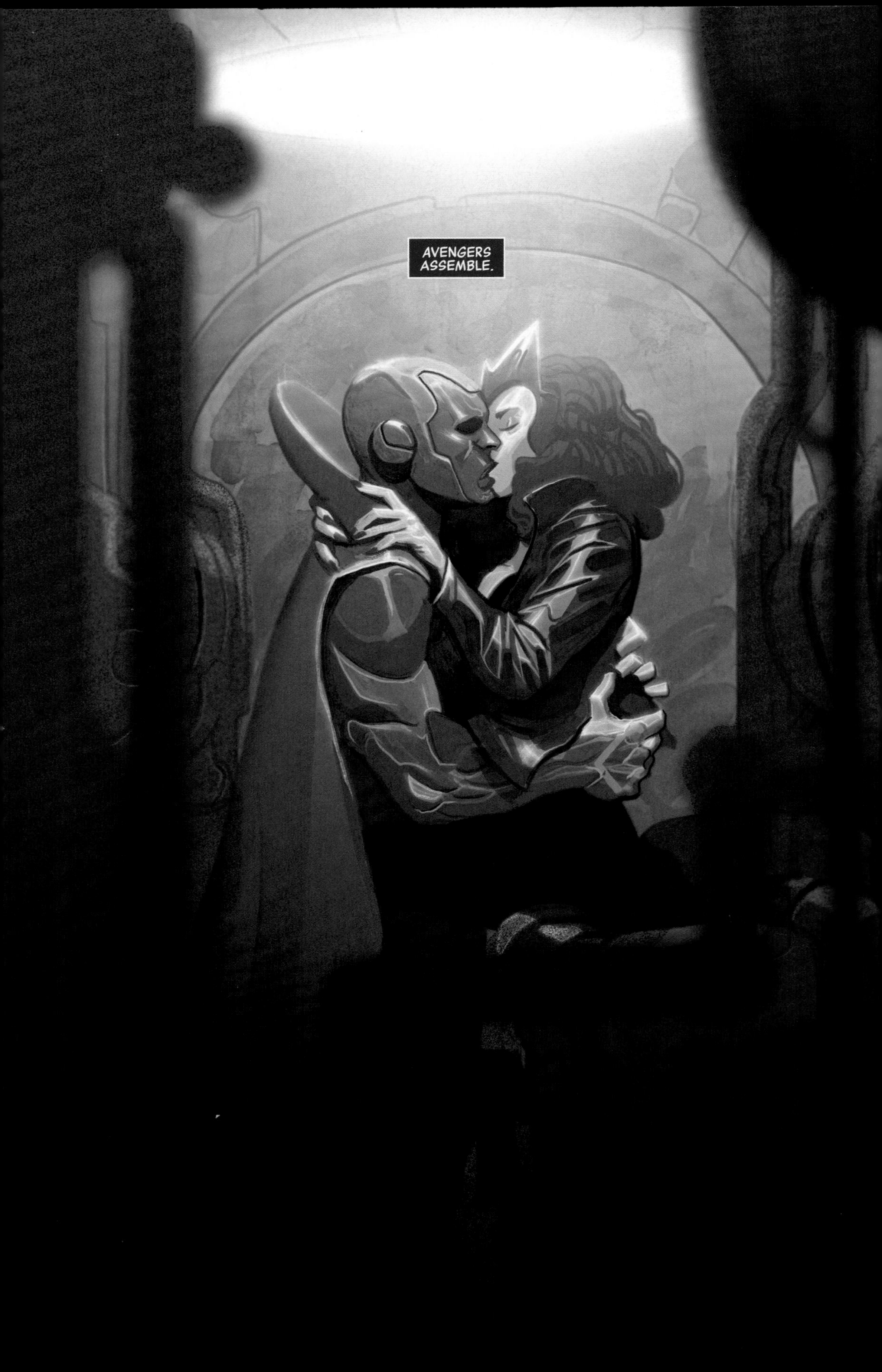
AVENGERS ASSEMBLE.

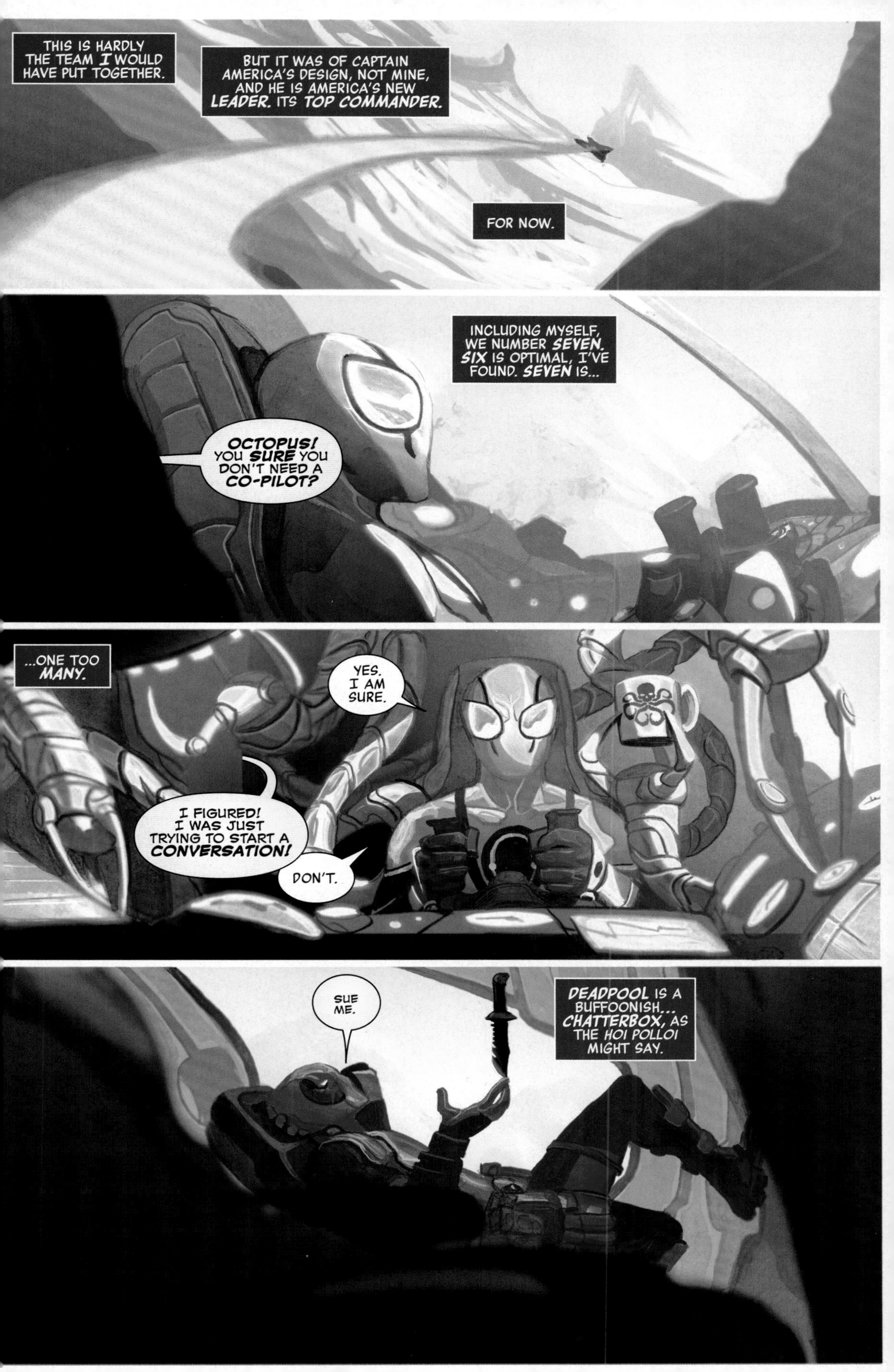
THIS IS HARDLY THE TEAM I WOULD HAVE PUT TOGETHER.
BUT IT WAS OF CAPTAIN AMERICA'S DESIGN, NOT MINE, AND HE IS AMERICA'S NEW LEADER. ITS TOP COMMANDER.
FOR NOW.
INCLUDING MYSELF, WE NUMBER SEVEN. SIX IS OPTIMAL, I'VE FOUND. SEVEN IS...
OCTOPUS! YOU SURE YOU DON'T NEED A CO-PILOT?
...ONE TOO MANY.
YES. I AM SURE.
I FIGURED! I WAS JUST TRYING TO START A CONVERSATION!
DON'T.
SUE ME.
DEADPOOL IS A BUFFOONISH... CHATTERBOX, AS THE HOI POLLOI MIGHT SAY.

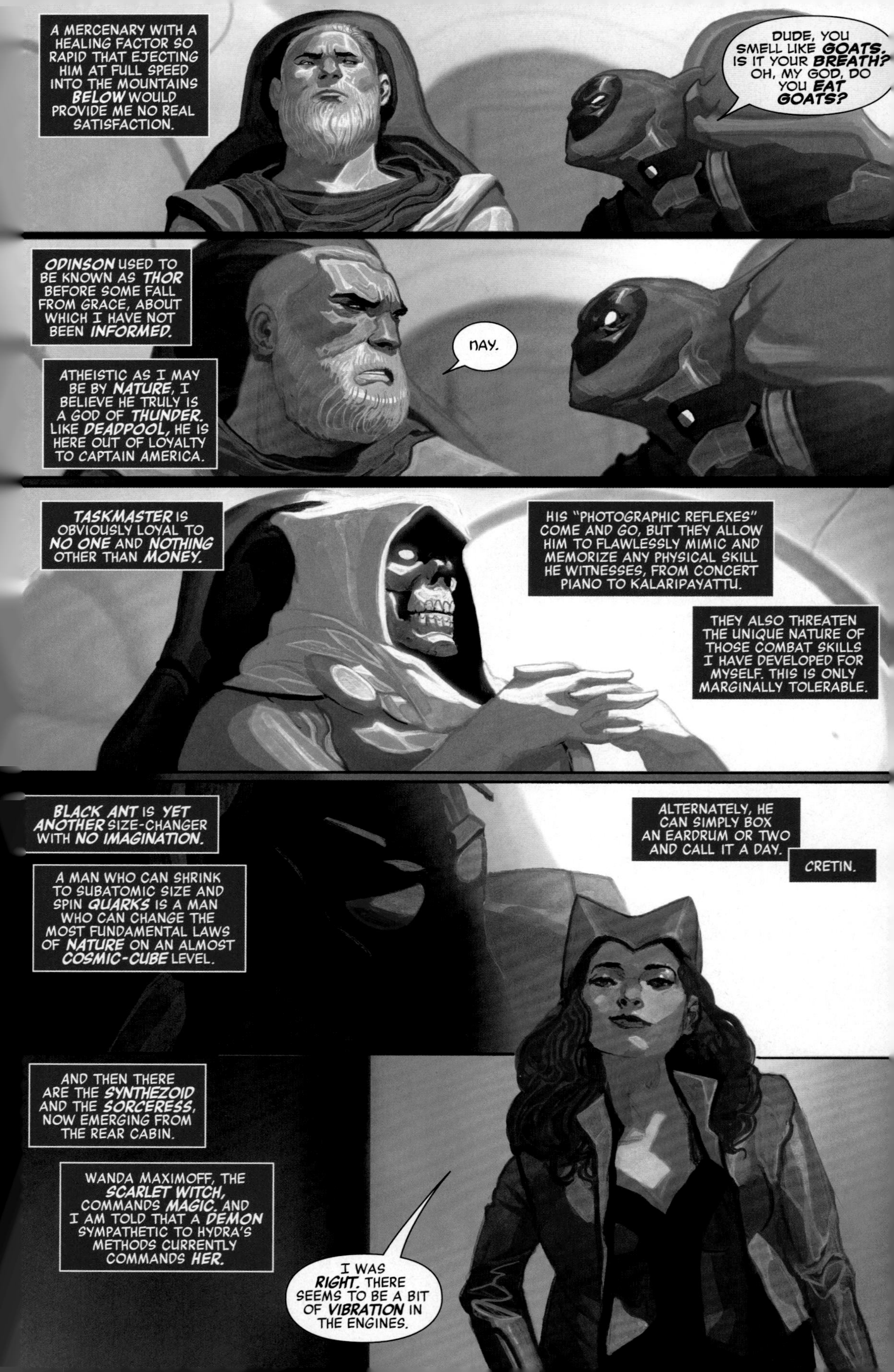
A MERCENARY WITH A HEALING FACTOR SO RAPID THAT EJECTING HIM AT FULL SPEED INTO THE MOUNTAINS BELOW WOULD PROVIDE ME NO REAL SATISFACTION.
DUDE, YOU SMELL LIKE GOATS. IS IT YOUR BREATH? OH, MY GOD, DO YOU EAT GOATS?
ODINSON USED TO BE KNOWN AS THOR BEFORE SOME FALL FROM GRACE, ABOUT WHICH I HAVE NOT BEEN INFORMED.
NAY.
ATHEISTIC AS I MAY BE BY NATURE, I BELIEVE HE TRULY IS A GOD OF THUNDER. LIKE DEADPOOL, HE IS HERE OUT OF LOYALTY TO CAPTAIN AMERICA.
TASKMASTER IS OBVIOUSLY LOYAL TO NO ONE AND NOTHING OTHER THAN MONEY.
HIS "PHOTOGRAPHIC REFLEXES" COME AND GO, BUT THEY ALLOW HIM TO FLAWLESSLY MIMIC AND MEMORIZE ANY PHYSICAL SKILL HE WITNESSES, FROM CONCERT PIANO TO KALARIPAYATTU.
THEY ALSO THREATEN THE UNIQUE NATURE OF THOSE COMBAT SKILLS I HAVE DEVELOPED FOR MYSELF. THIS IS ONLY MARGINALLY TOLERABLE.
BLACK ANT IS YET ANOTHER SIZE-CHANGER WITH NO IMAGINATION.
A MAN WHO CAN SHRINK TO SUBATOMIC SIZE AND SPIN QUARKS IS A MAN WHO CAN CHANGE THE MOST FUNDAMENTAL LAWS OF NATURE ON AN ALMOST COSMIC-CUBE LEVEL.
ALTERNATELY, HE CAN SIMPLY BOX AN EARDRUM OR TWO AND CALL IT A DAY.
CRETIN.
AND THEN THERE ARE THE SYNTHEZOID AND THE SORCERESS, NOW EMERGING FROM THE REAR CABIN.
WANDA MAXIMOFF, THE SCARLET WITCH, COMMANDS MAGIC. AND I AM TOLD THAT A DEMON SYMPATHETIC TO HYDRA'S METHODS CURRENTLY COMMANDS HER.
I WAS RIGHT. THERE SEEMS TO BE A BIT OF VIBRATION IN THE ENGINES.

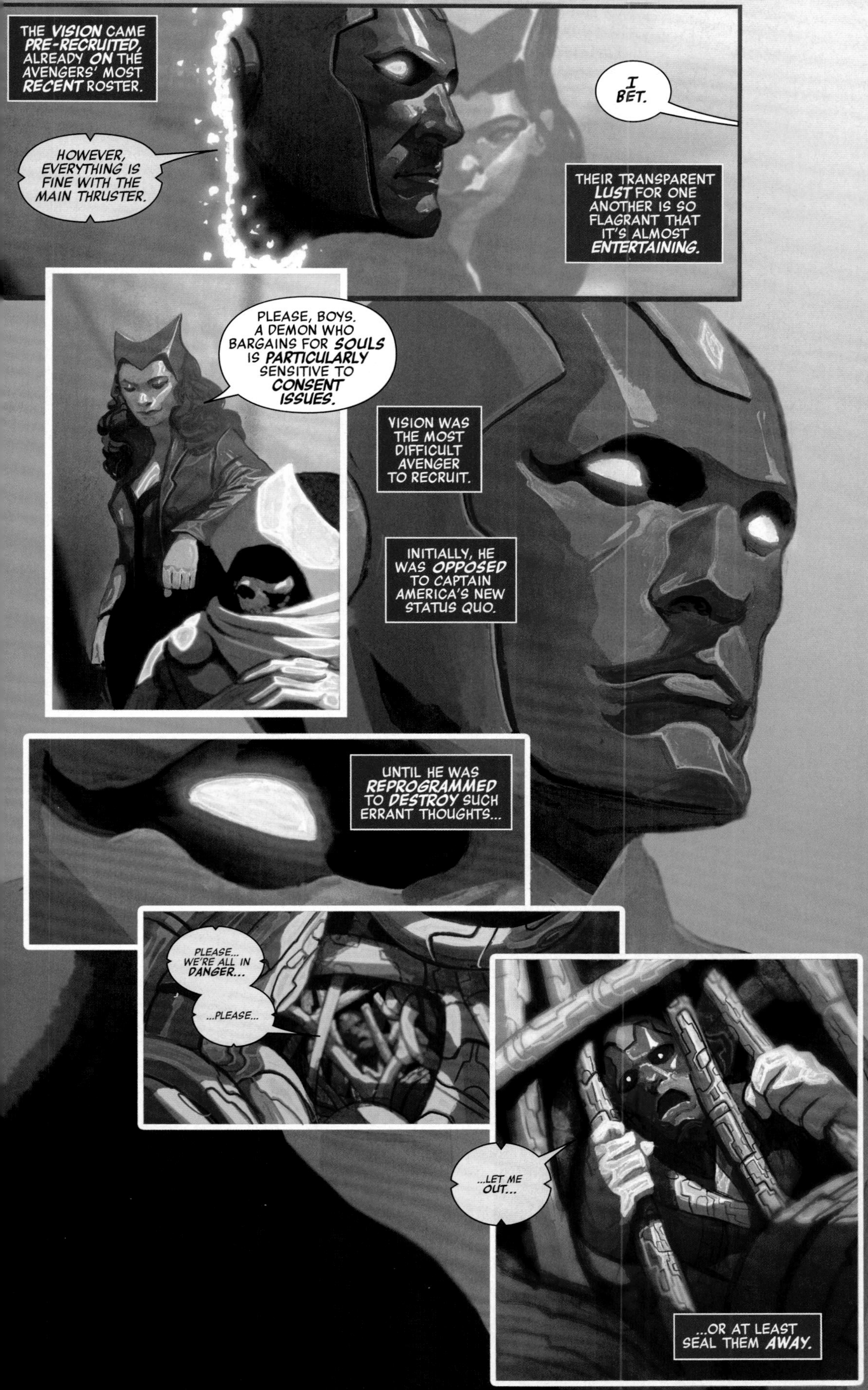
THE VISION CAME PRE-RECRUITED, ALREADY ON THE AVENGERS' MOST RECENT ROSTER.
HOWEVER, EVERYTHING IS FINE WITH THE MAIN THRUSTER.
I BET.
THEIR TRANSPARENT LUST FOR ONE ANOTHER IS SO FLAGRANT THAT IT'S ALMOST ENTERTAINING.
PLEASE, BOYS. A DEMON WHO BARGAINS FOR SOULS IS PARTICULARLY SENSITIVE TO CONSENT ISSUES.
VISION WAS THE MOST DIFFICULT AVENGER TO RECRUIT.
INITIALLY, HE WAS OPPOSED TO CAPTAIN AMERICA'S NEW STATUS QUO.
UNTIL HE WAS REPROGRAMMED TO DESTROY SUCH ERRANT THOUGHTS...
PLEASE... WE'RE ALL IN DANGER...
...PLEASE...
...LET ME OUT...
...OR AT LEAST SEAL THEM AWAY.

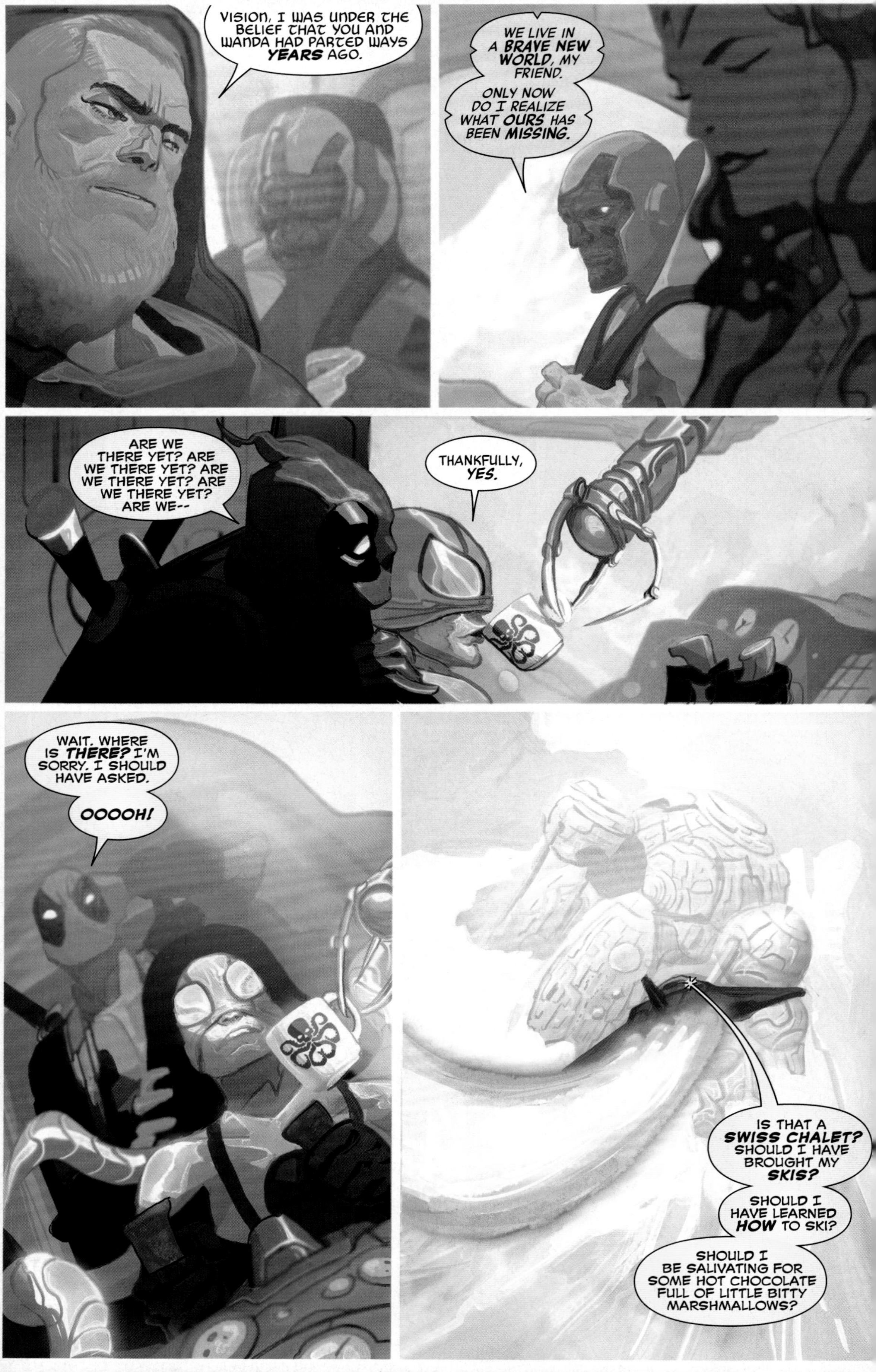
VISION, I WAS UNDER THE BELIEF THAT YOU AND WANDA HAD PARTED WAYS YEARS AGO.
WE LIVE IN A BRAVE NEW WORLD, MY FRIEND.
ONLY NOW DO I REALIZE WHAT OURS HAS BEEN MISSING.
ARE WE THERE YET? ARE WE THERE YET? ARE WE THERE YET? ARE WE THERE YET? ARE WE--
THANKFULLY, YES.
WAIT. WHERE IS THERE? I'M SORRY. I SHOULD HAVE ASKED.
OOOOH!
IS THAT A SWISS CHALET? SHOULD I HAVE BROUGHT MY SKIS?
SHOULD I HAVE LEARNED HOW TO SKI?
SHOULD I BE SALIVATING FOR SOME HOT CHOCOLATE FULL OF LITTLE BITTY MARSHMALLOWS?

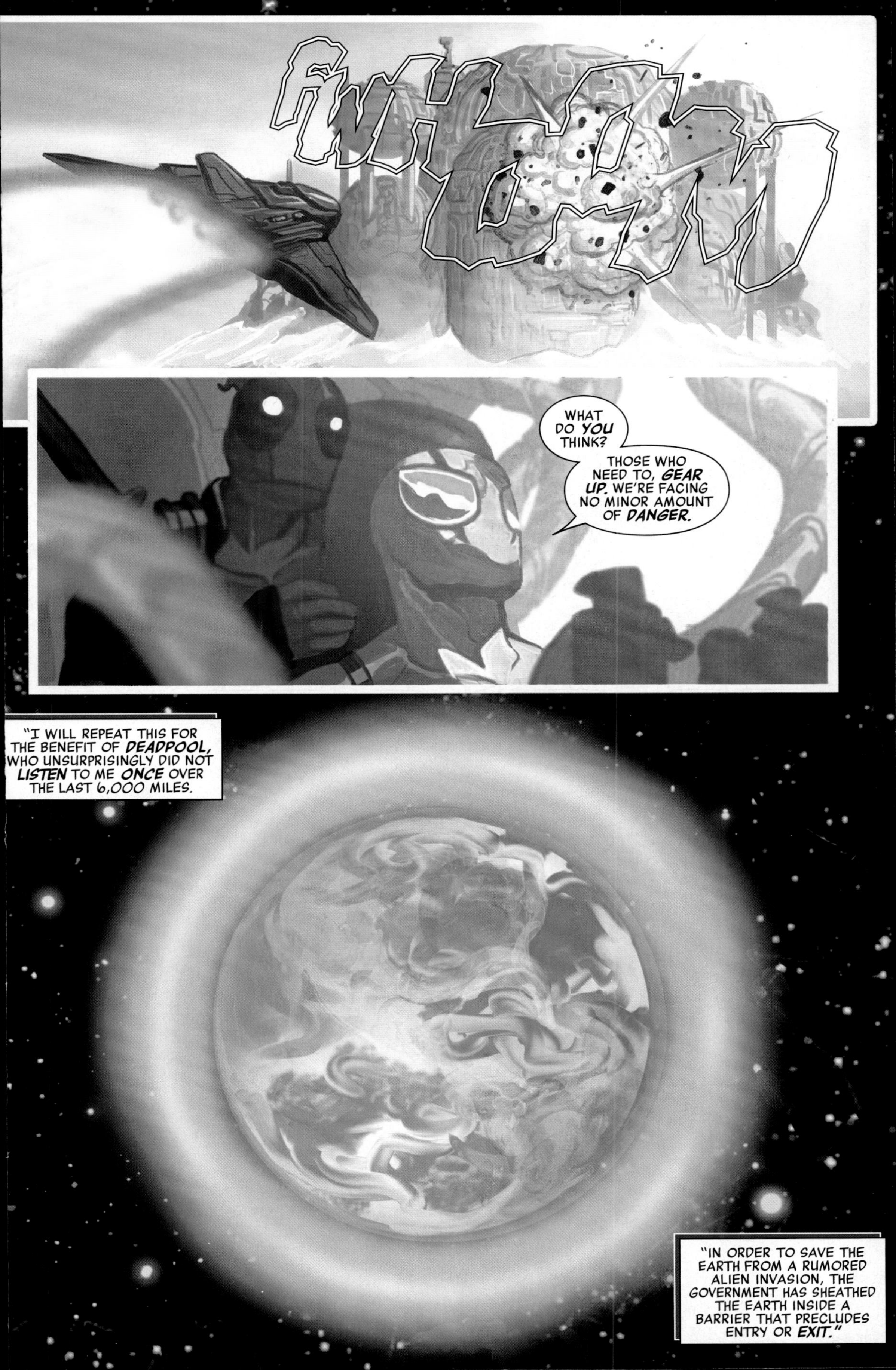
WHAT DO YOU THINK?
THOSE WHO NEED TO, GEAR UP. WE'RE FACING NO MINOR AMOUNT OF DANGER.
"I WILL REPEAT THIS FOR THE BENEFIT OF DEADPOOL, WHO UNSURPRISINGLY DID NOT LISTEN TO ME ONCE OVER THE LAST 6,000 MILES.
"IN ORDER TO SAVE THE EARTH FROM A RUMORED ALIEN INVASION, THE GOVERNMENT HAS SHEATHED THE EARTH INSIDE A BARRIER THAT PRECLUDES ENTRY OR EXIT."

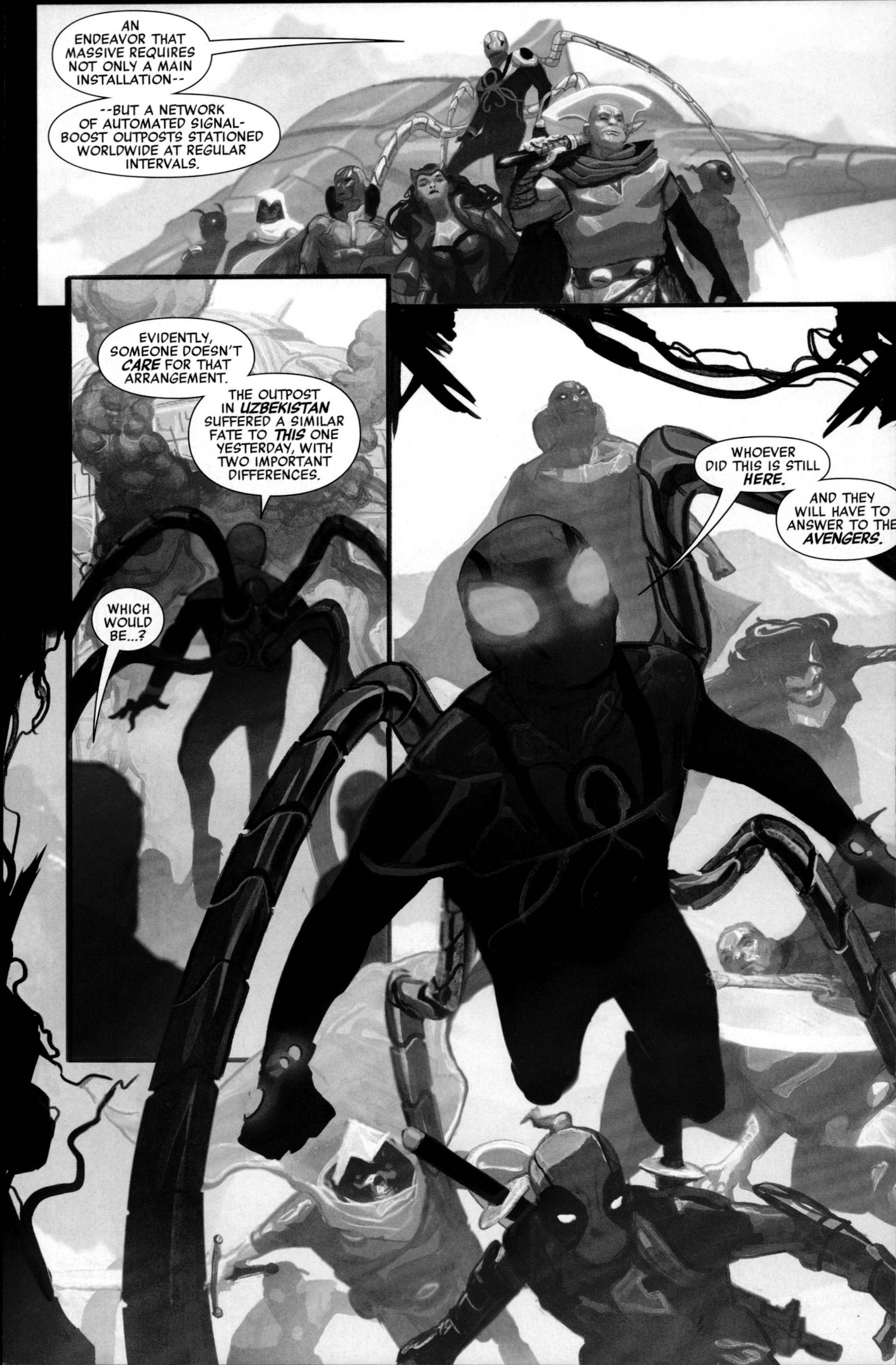
AN ENDEAVOR THAT MASSIVE REQUIRES NOT ONLY A MAIN INSTALLATION--
--BUT A NETWORK OF AUTOMATED SIGNAL-BOOST OUTPOSTS STATIONED WORLDWIDE AT REGULAR INTERVALS.
EVIDENTLY, SOMEONE DOESN'T CARE FOR THAT ARRANGEMENT.
THE OUTPOST IN UZBEKISTAN SUFFERED A SIMILAR FATE TO THIS ONE YESTERDAY, WITH TWO IMPORTANT DIFFERENCES.
WHICH WOULD BE...?
WHOEVER DID THIS IS STILL HERE.
AND THEY WILL HAVE TO ANSWER TO THE AVENGERS.

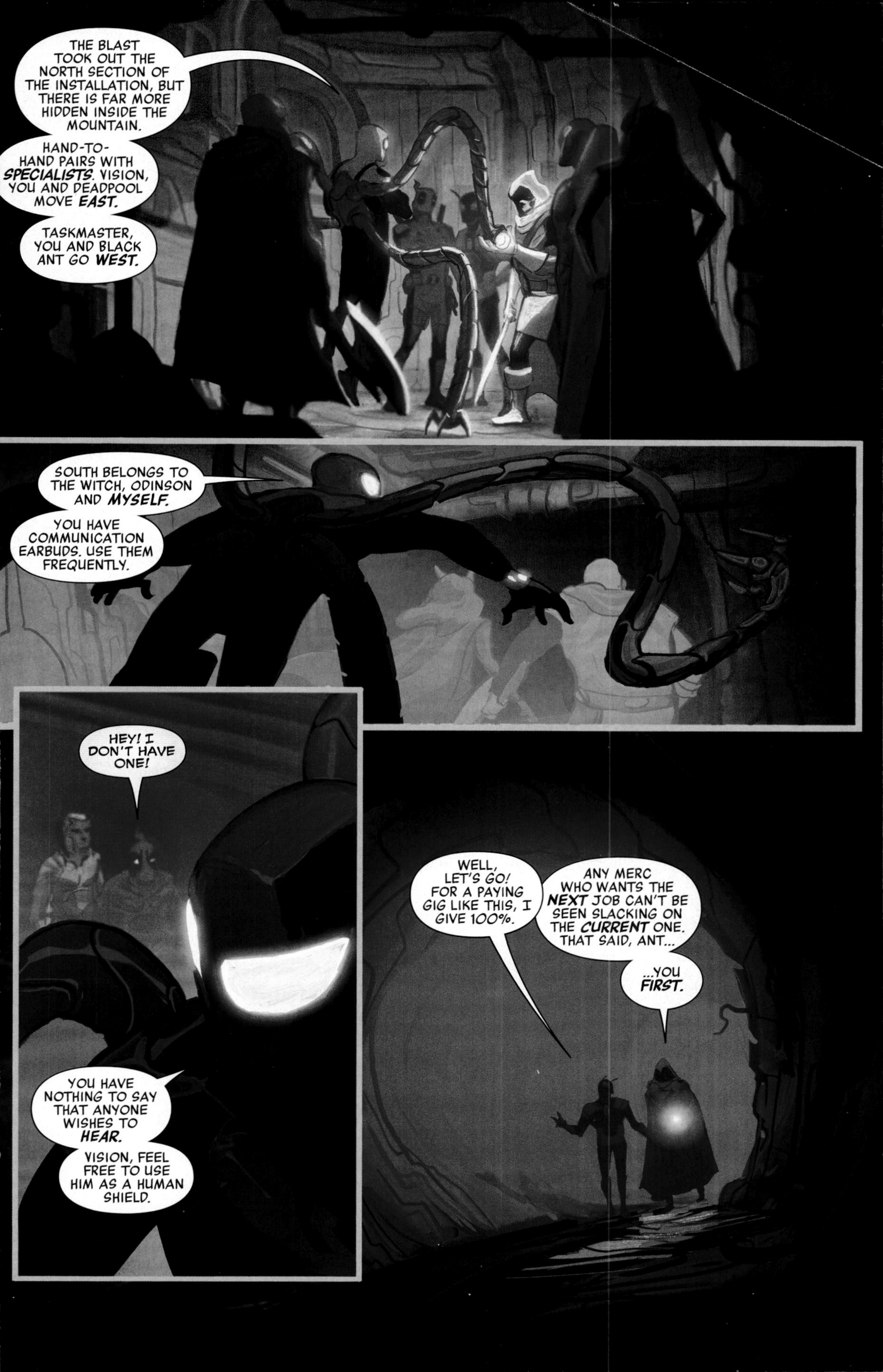
THE BLAST TOOK OUT THE NORTH SECTION OF THE INSTALLATION, BUT THERE IS FAR MORE HIDDEN INSIDE THE MOUNTAIN.
HAND-TO-HAND PAIRS WITH SPECIALISTS. VISION, YOU AND DEADPOOL MOVE EAST.
TASKMASTER, YOU AND BLACK ANT GO WEST.
SOUTH BELONGS TO THE WITCH, ODINSON AND MYSELF.
YOU HAVE COMMUNICATION EARBUDS. USE THEM FREQUENTLY.
HEY! I DON'T HAVE ONE!
YOU HAVE NOTHING TO SAY THAT ANYONE WISHES TO HEAR.
VISION, FEEL FREE TO USE HIM AS A HUMAN SHIELD.
WELL, LET'S GO! FOR A PAYING GIG LIKE THIS, I GIVE 100%.
ANY MERC WHO WANTS THE NEXT JOB CAN'T BE SEEN SLACKING ON THE CURRENT ONE. THAT SAID, ANT...
...YOU FIRST.

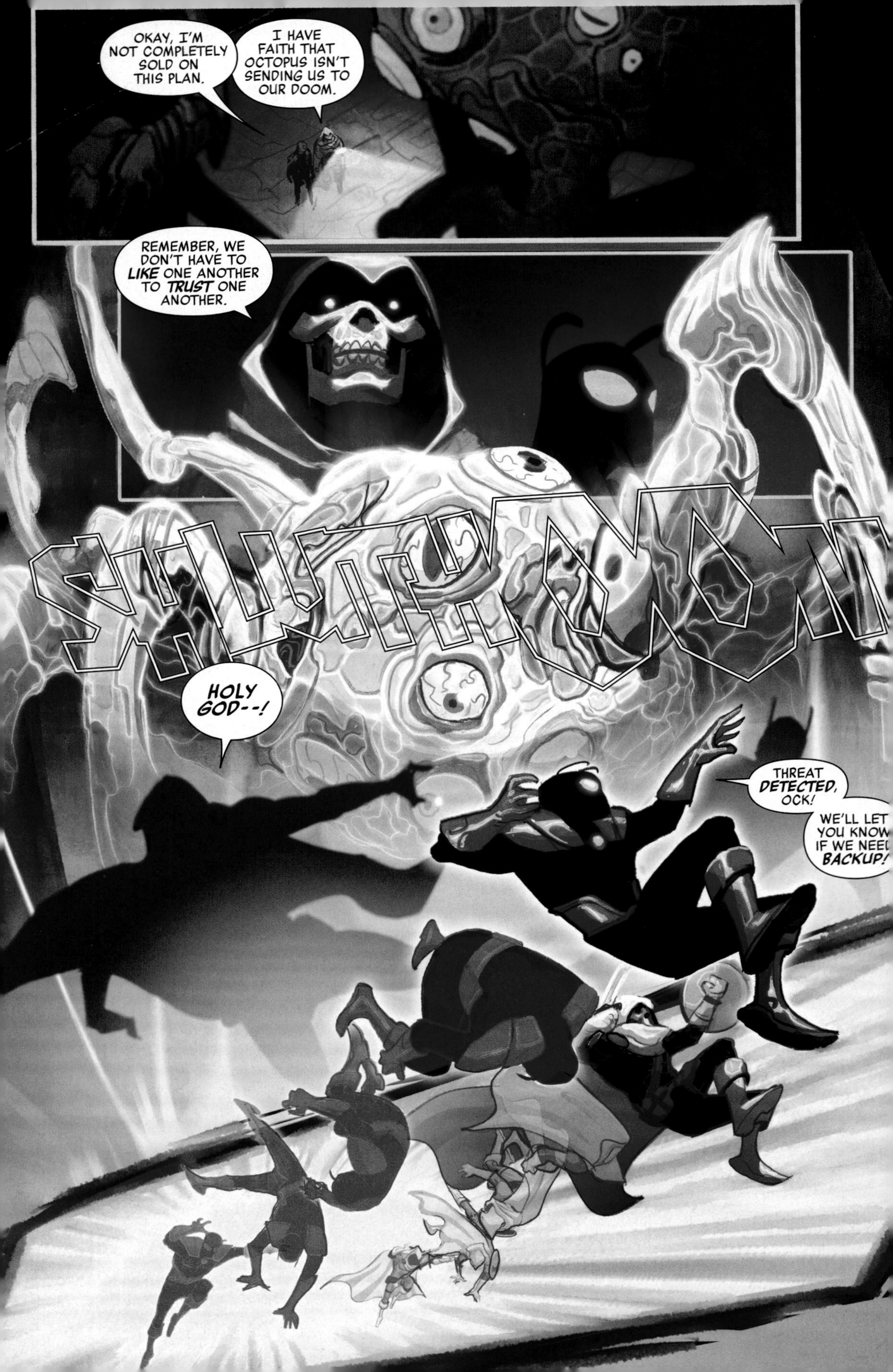
OKAY, I'M NOT COMPLETELY SOLD ON THIS PLAN.
I HAVE FAITH THAT OCTOPUS ISN'T SENDING US TO OUR DOOM.
REMEMBER, WE DON'T HAVE TO LIKE ONE ANOTHER TO TRUST ONE ANOTHER.
HOLY GOD--!
THREAT DETECTED, OCK!
WE'LL LET YOU KNOW IF WE NEED BACKUP!

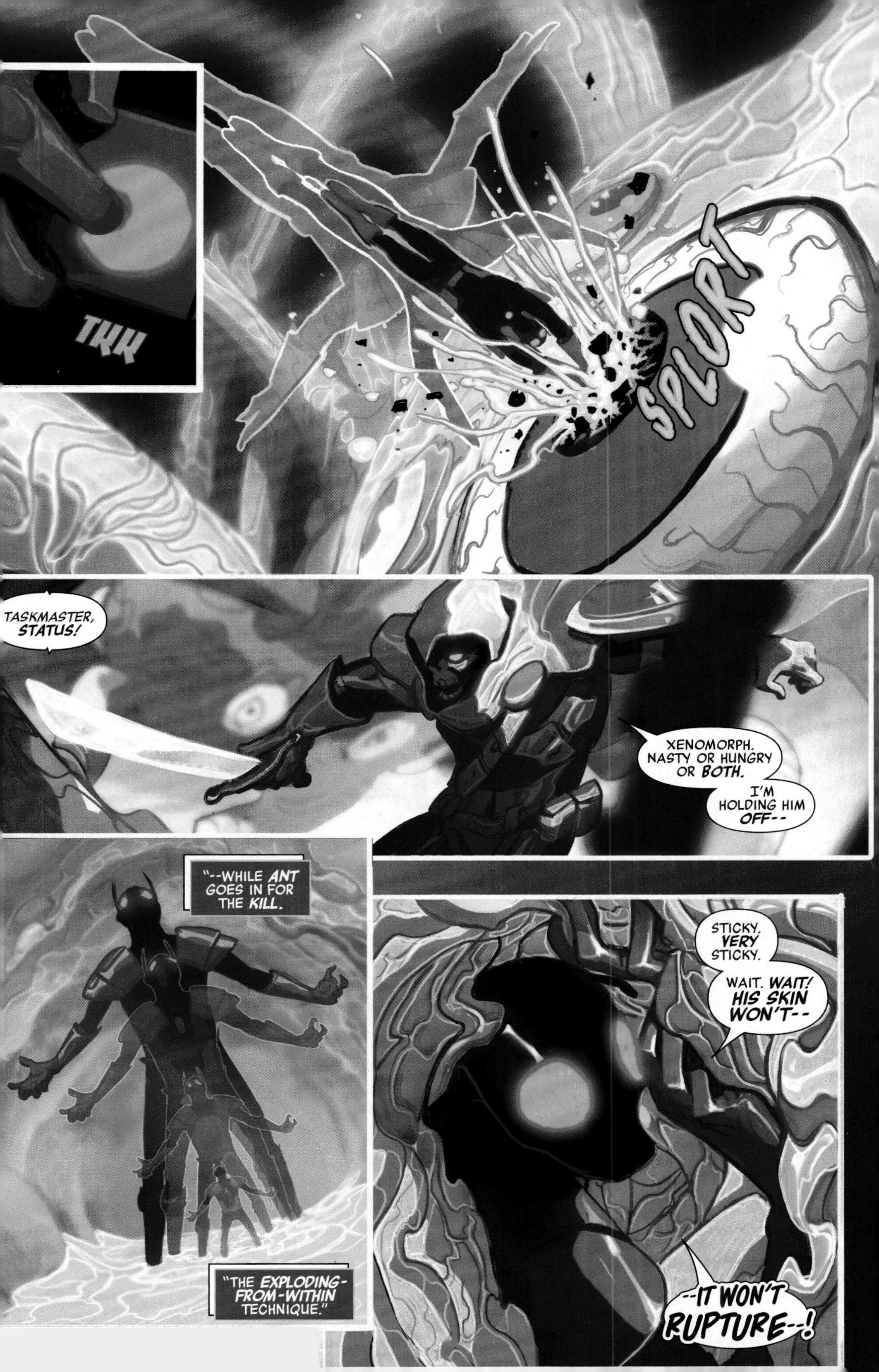
TKK
SPLORT
TASKMASTER, STATUS!
XENOMORPH. NASTY OR HUNGRY OR BOTH.
I'M HOLDING HIM OFF--
"--WHILE ANT GOES IN FOR THE KILL.
"THE EXPLODING-FROM-WITHIN TECHNIQUE."
STICKY. VERY STICKY.
WAIT. WAIT! HIS SKIN WON'T--
--IT WON'T RUPTURE--!

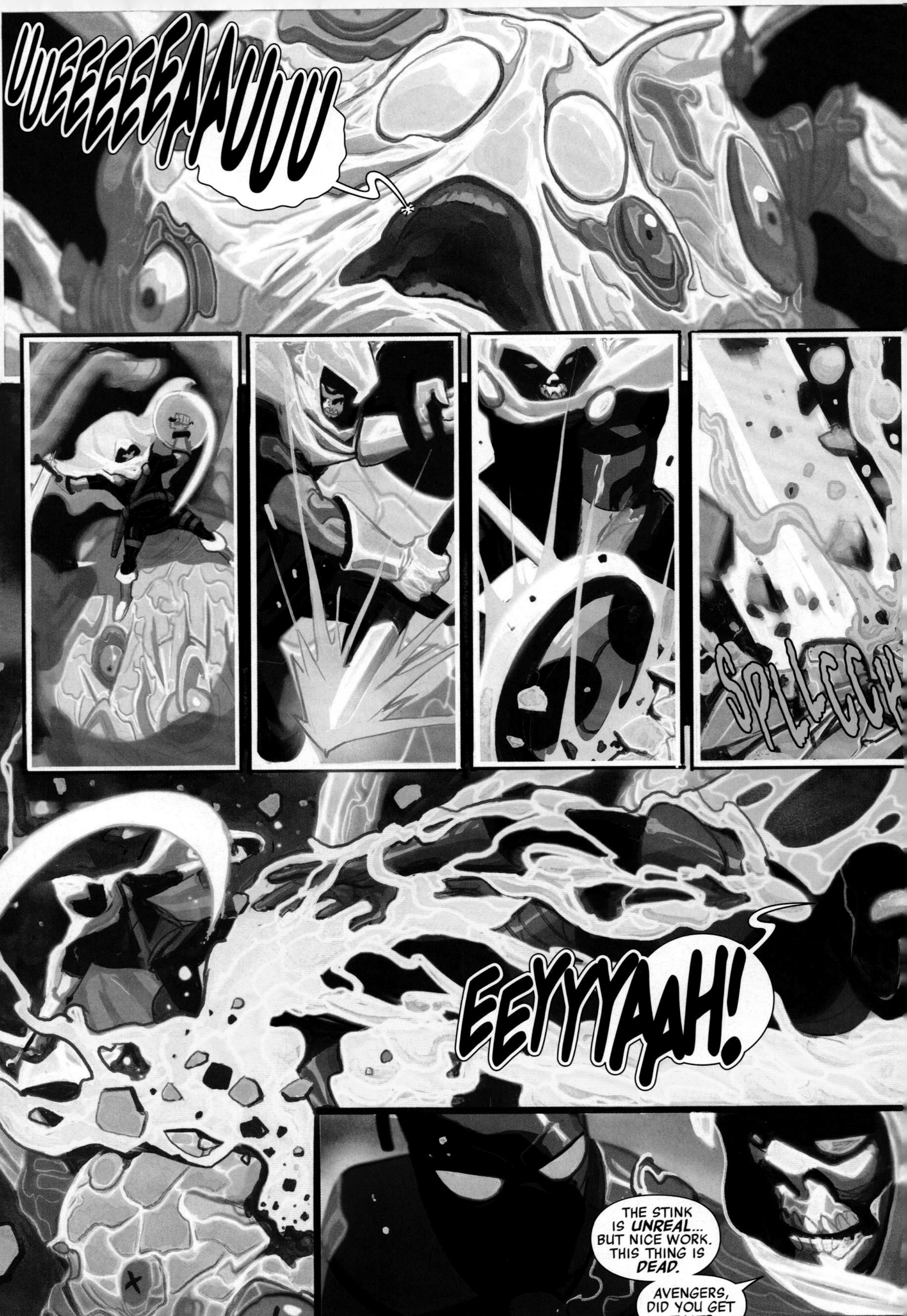
UUEEEEEEAAUUUU
SPLLCCH
EEYYYAAH!
THE STINK IS UNREAL... BUT NICE WORK. THIS THING IS DEAD.
AVENGERS, DID YOU GET THAT?

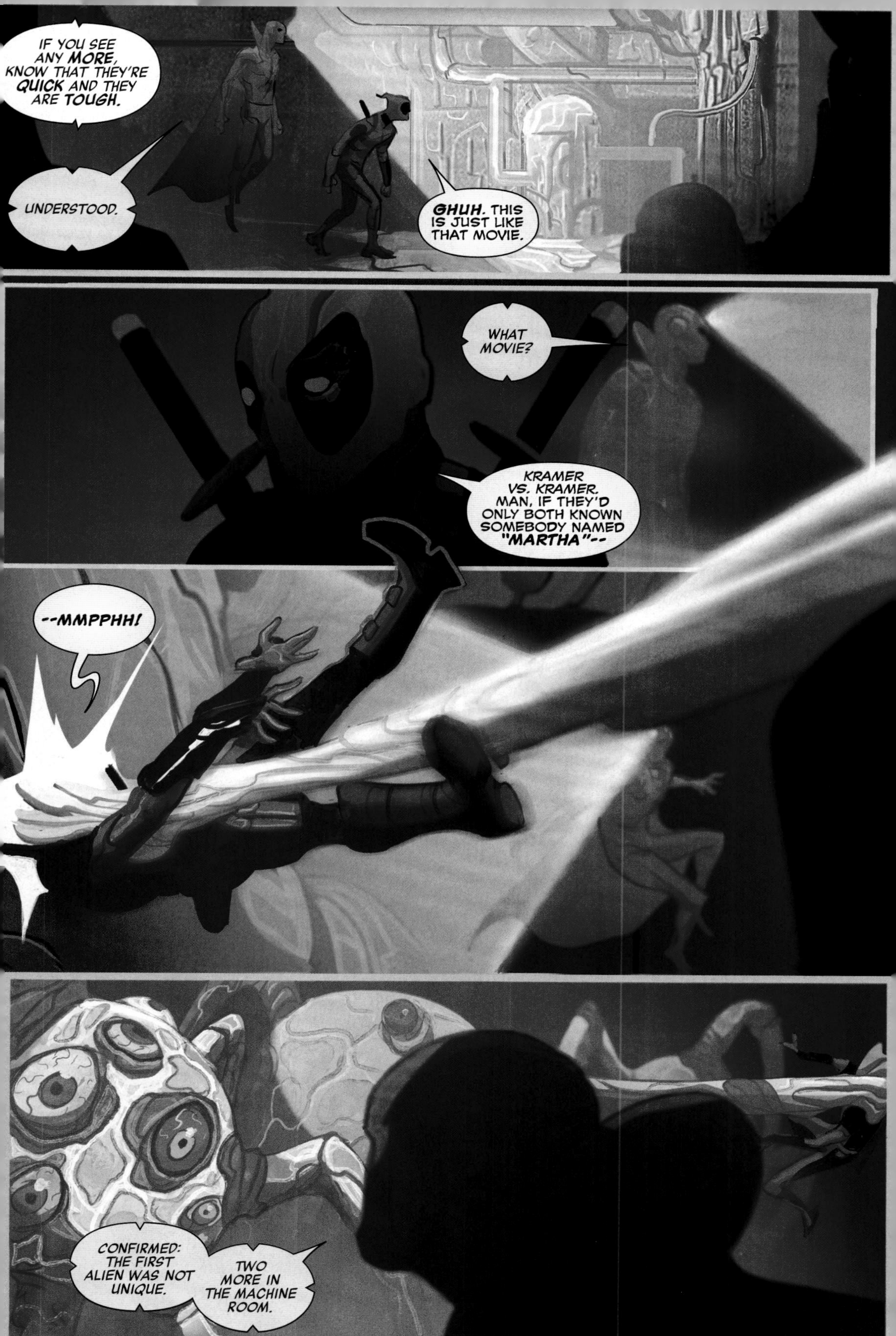
IF YOU SEE ANY MORE, KNOW THAT THEY'RE QUICK AND THEY ARE TOUGH.
UNDERSTOOD.
GHUH. THIS IS JUST LIKE THAT MOVIE.
WHAT MOVIE?
KRAMER VS. KRAMER. MAN, IF THEY'D ONLY BOTH KNOWN SOMEBODY NAMED "MARTHA"--
--MMPPHH!
CONFIRMED: THE FIRST ALIEN WAS NOT UNIQUE.
TWO MORE IN THE MACHINE ROOM.

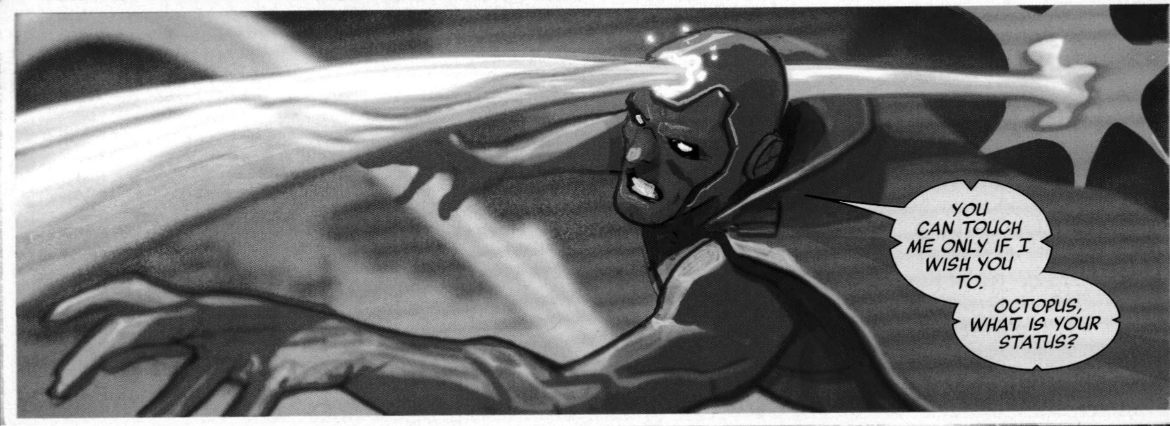
YOU CAN TOUCH ME ONLY IF I WISH YOU TO.
OCTOPUS, WHAT IS YOUR STATUS?

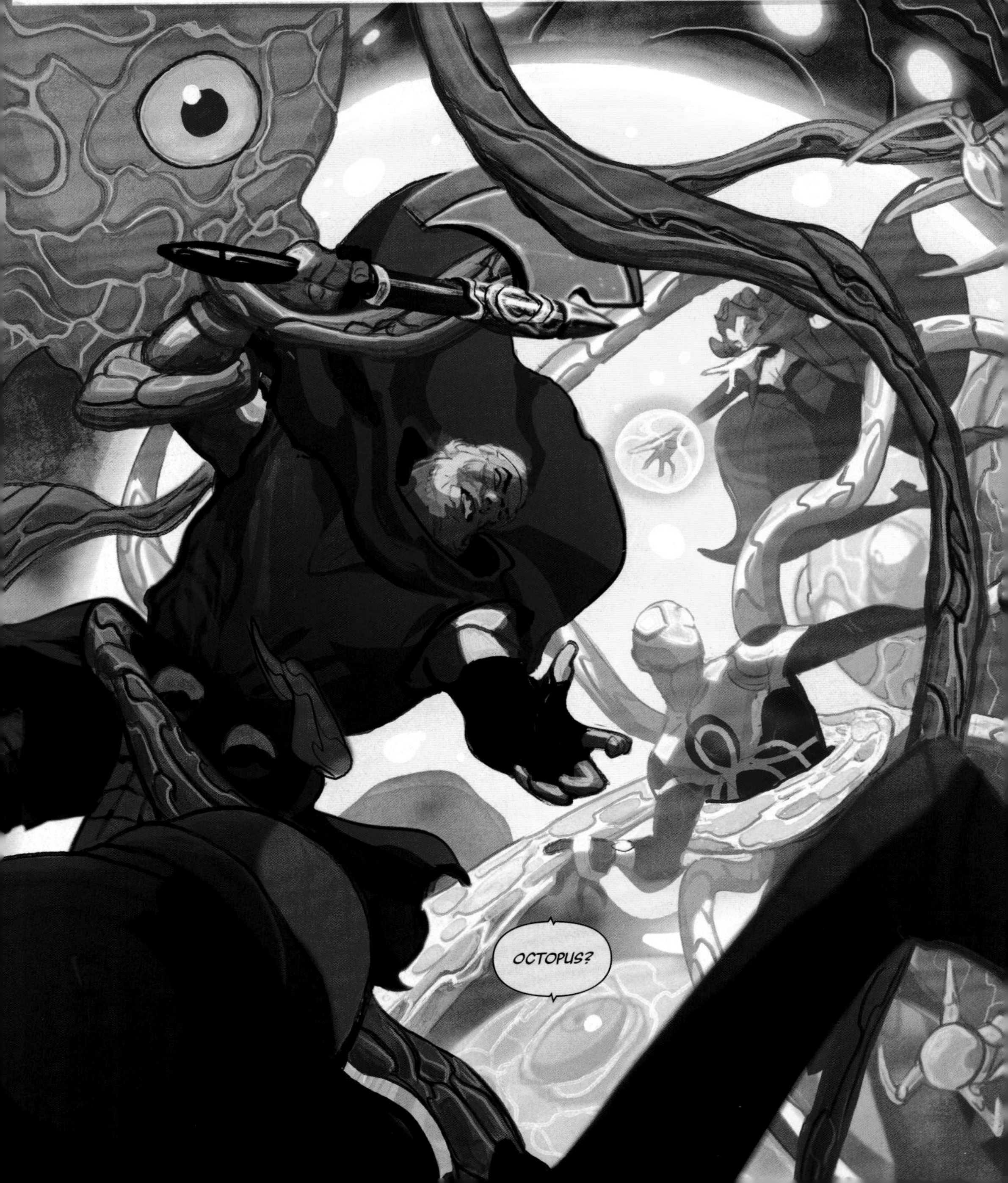
OCTOPUS?

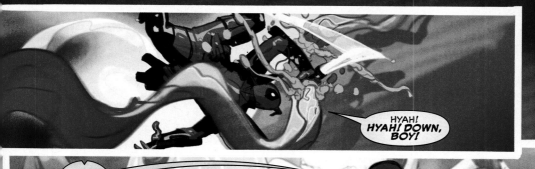

HYAH! HYAH! DOWN, BOY!

ARE YOU ALL RIGHT?

EXCEPT FOR THE VOICES IN MY HEAD. THEN AGAIN, THAT'S A STANDING PROBLEM.

WE COULD PLAY *STABBY-STAB* AND *NO-TAG* ALL DAY, BUT I DON'T FIGURE THAT'LL GET US FAR. VÁMONOS.

OCTOPUS, ARE YOU THERE?

YES--WE COULD USE YOUR *ASSISTANCE.*

HE'S UNDERSELLING THE *DANGER!* **AVENGERS ASSEMBLE!**

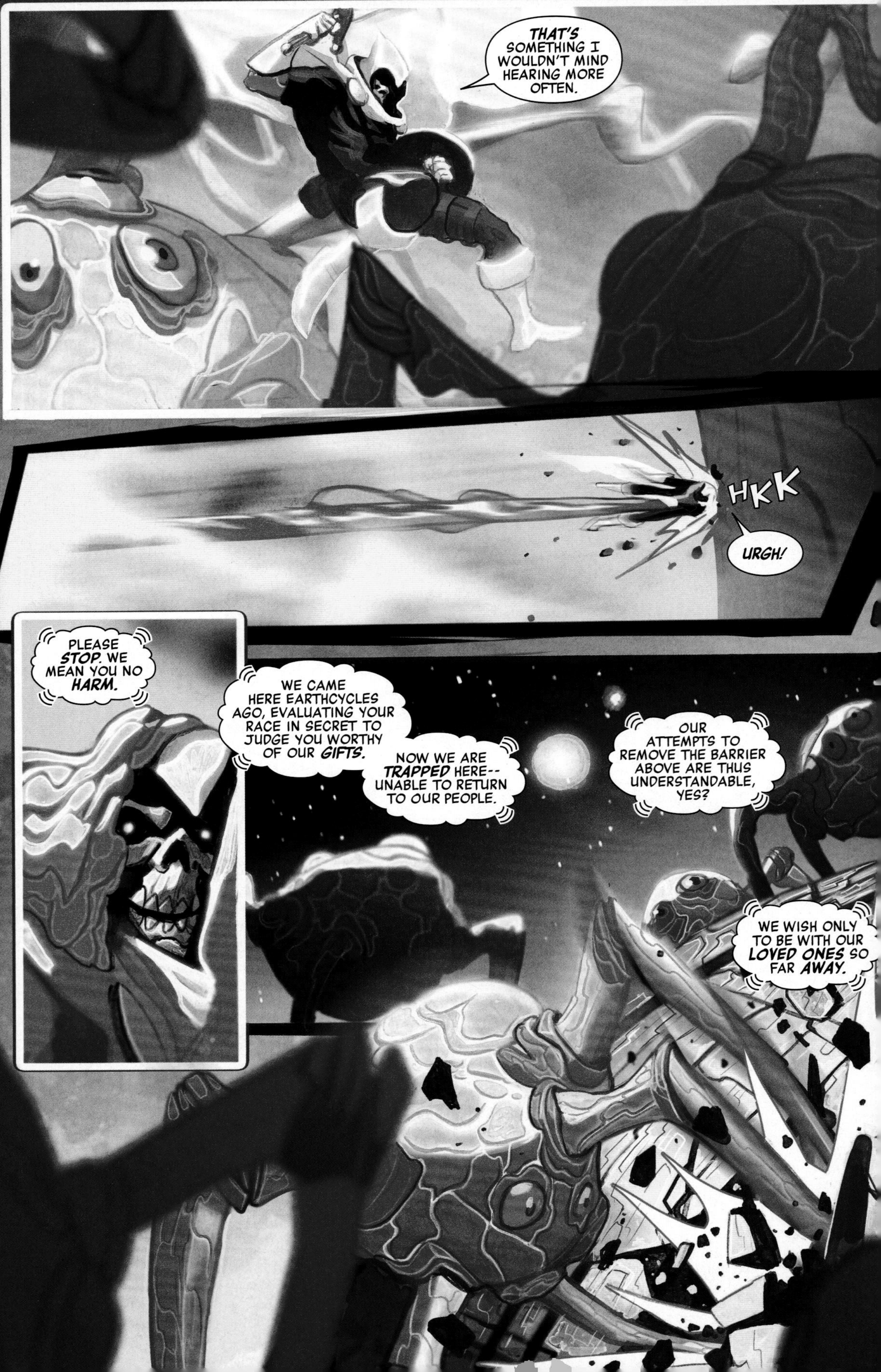
THAT'S SOMETHING I WOULDN'T MIND HEARING MORE OFTEN.
HKK
URGH!
PLEASE STOP. WE MEAN YOU NO HARM.
WE CAME HERE EARTHCYCLES AGO, EVALUATING YOUR RACE IN SECRET TO JUDGE YOU WORTHY OF OUR GIFTS.
NOW WE ARE TRAPPED HERE--UNABLE TO RETURN TO OUR PEOPLE.
OUR ATTEMPTS TO REMOVE THE BARRIER ABOVE ARE THUS UNDERSTANDABLE, YES?
WE WISH ONLY TO BE WITH OUR LOVED ONES SO FAR AWAY.

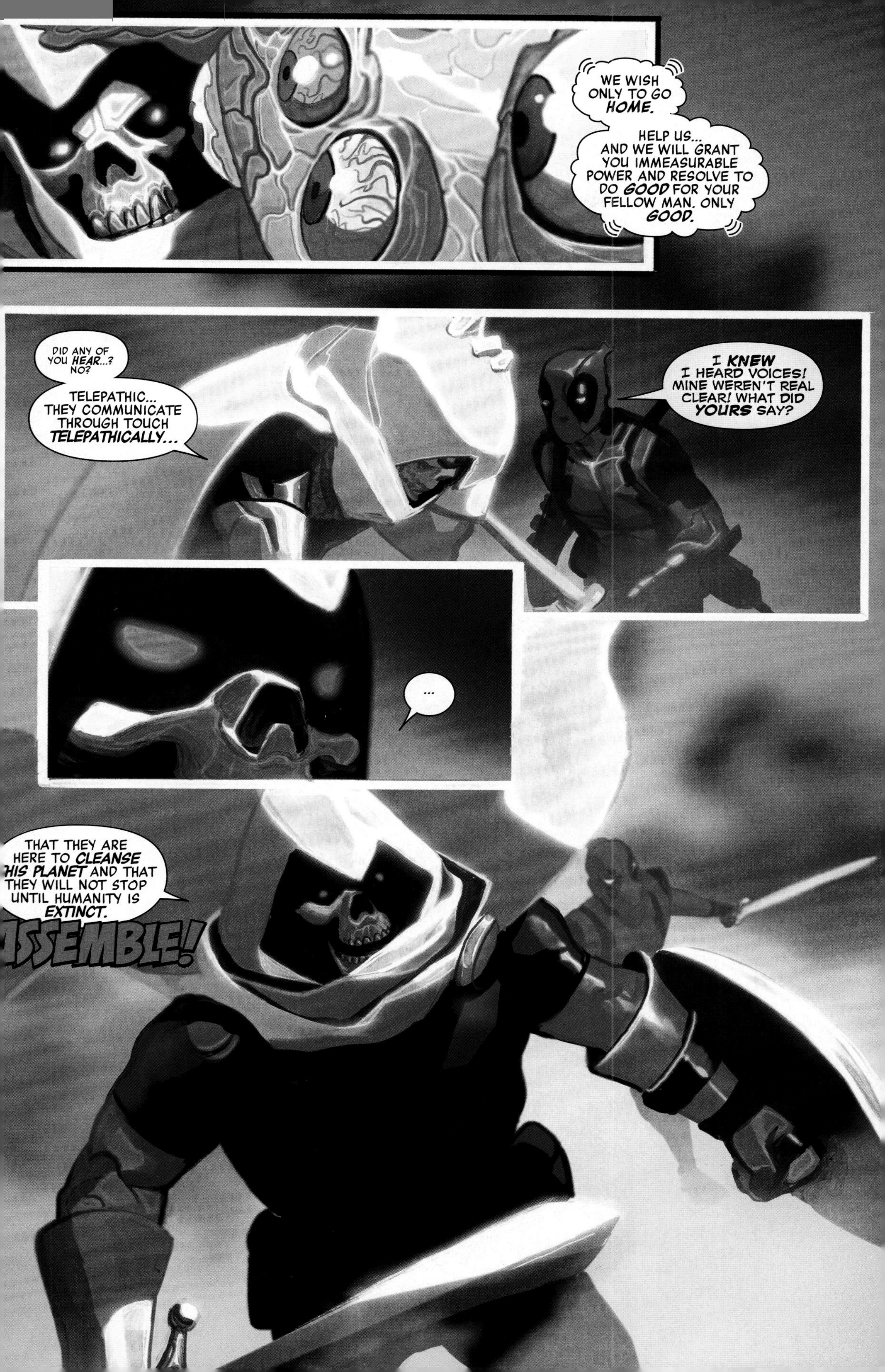
WE WISH ONLY TO GO HOME.
HELP US... AND WE WILL GRANT YOU IMMEASURABLE POWER AND RESOLVE TO DO GOOD FOR YOUR FELLOW MAN. ONLY GOOD.
DID ANY OF YOU HEAR...? NO?
TELEPATHIC... THEY COMMUNICATE THROUGH TOUCH TELEPATHICALLY...
I KNEW I HEARD VOICES! MINE WEREN'T REAL CLEAR! WHAT DID YOURS SAY?
...
THAT THEY ARE HERE TO CLEANSE HIS PLANET AND THAT THEY WILL NOT STOP UNTIL HUMANITY IS EXTINCT.
SSEMBLE!

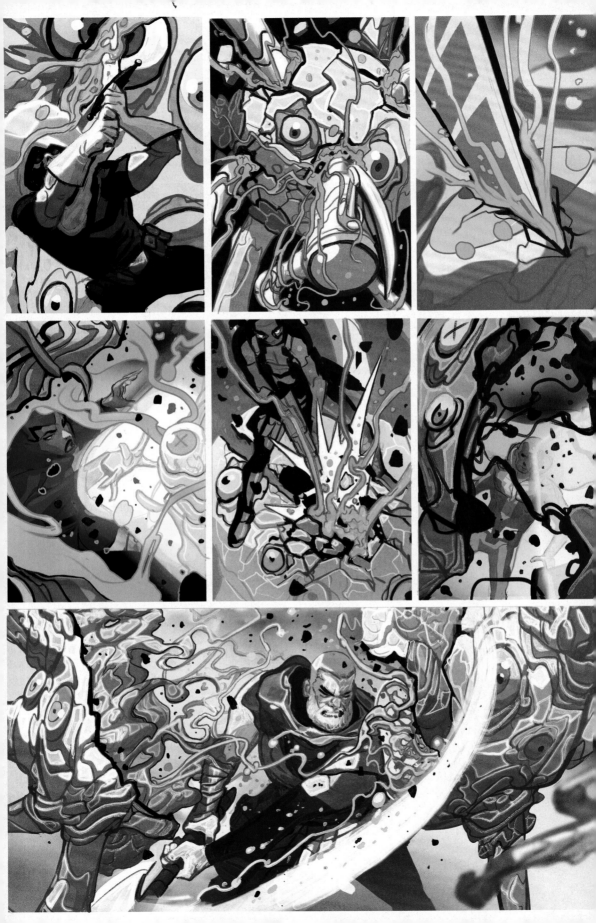

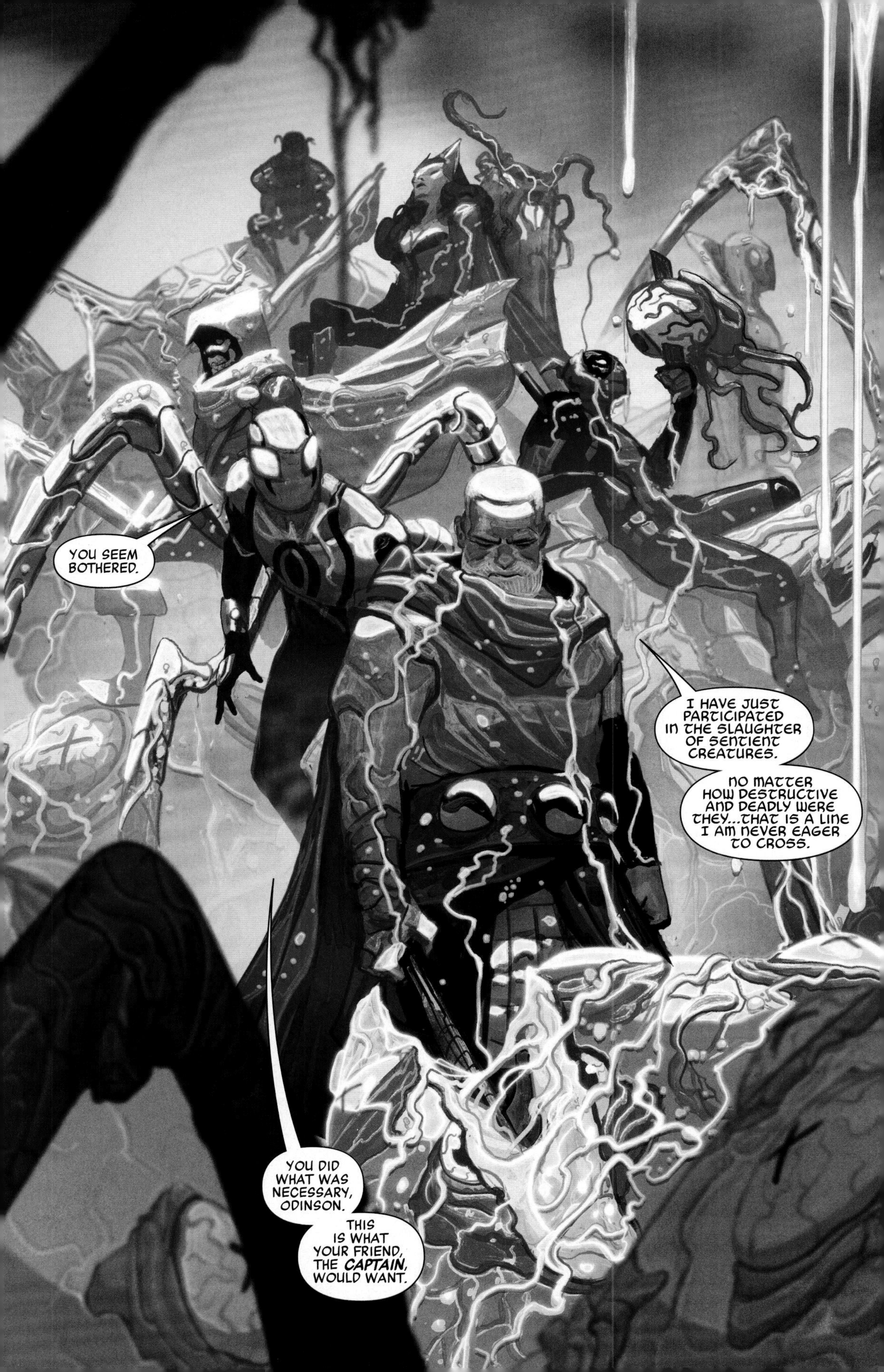
YOU SEEM BOTHERED.
I HAVE JUST PARTICIPATED IN THE SLAUGHTER OF SENTIENT CREATURES.
NO MATTER HOW DESTRUCTIVE AND DEADLY WERE THEY...THAT IS A LINE I AM NEVER EAGER TO CROSS.
YOU DID WHAT WAS NECESSARY, ODINSON.
THIS IS WHAT YOUR FRIEND, THE CAPTAIN, WOULD WANT.

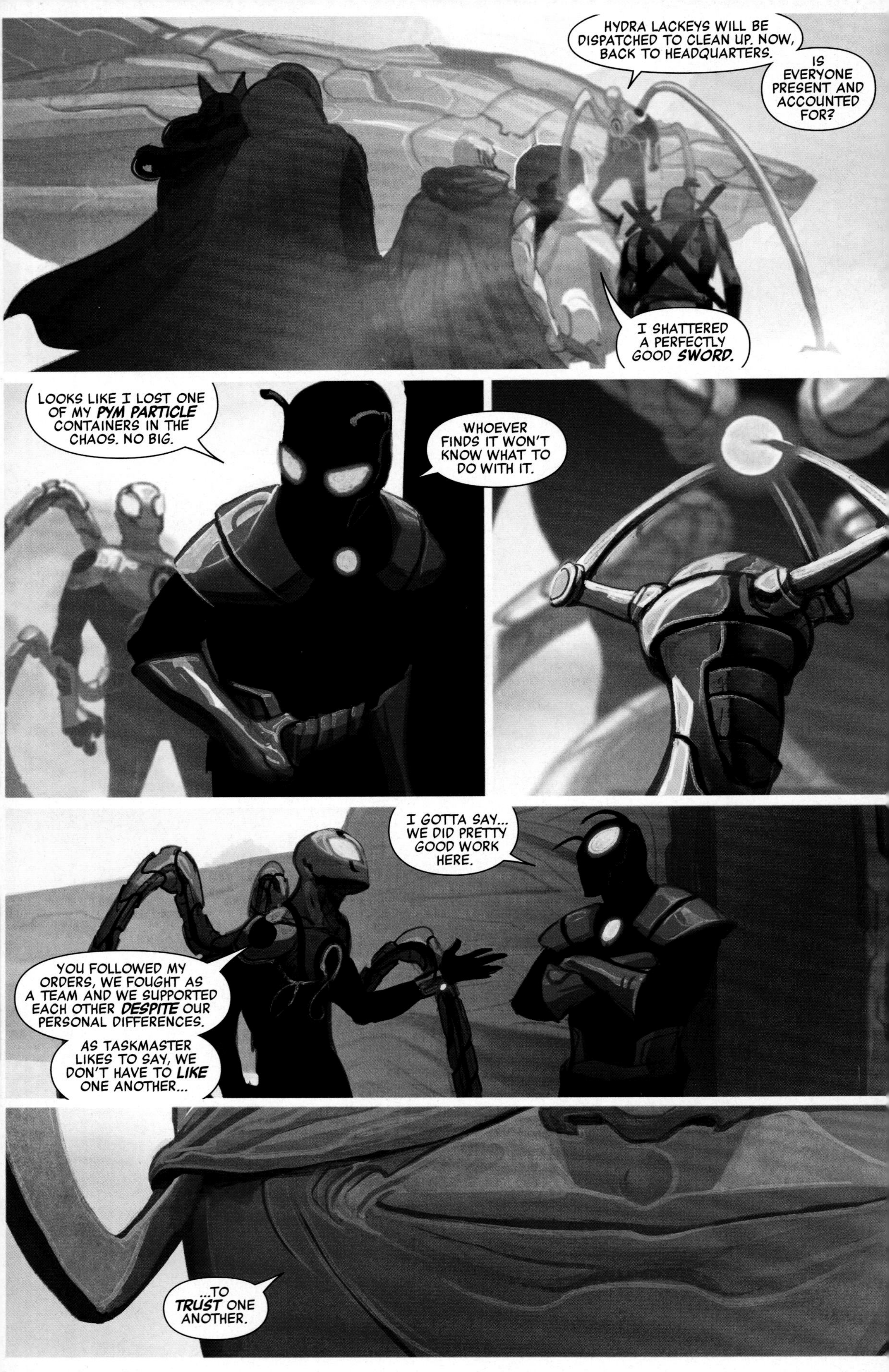
HYDRA LACKEYS WILL BE DISPATCHED TO CLEAN UP. NOW, BACK TO HEADQUARTERS.
IS EVERYONE PRESENT AND ACCOUNTED FOR?
I SHATTERED A PERFECTLY GOOD SWORD.
LOOKS LIKE I LOST ONE OF MY PYM PARTICLE CONTAINERS IN THE CHAOS. NO BIG.
WHOEVER FINDS IT WON'T KNOW WHAT TO DO WITH IT.
I GOTTA SAY... WE DID PRETTY GOOD WORK HERE.
YOU FOLLOWED MY ORDERS, WE FOUGHT AS A TEAM AND WE SUPPORTED EACH OTHER DESPITE OUR PERSONAL DIFFERENCES.
AS TASKMASTER LIKES TO SAY, WE DON'T HAVE TO LIKE ONE ANOTHER...
...TO TRUST ONE ANOTHER.

[11]

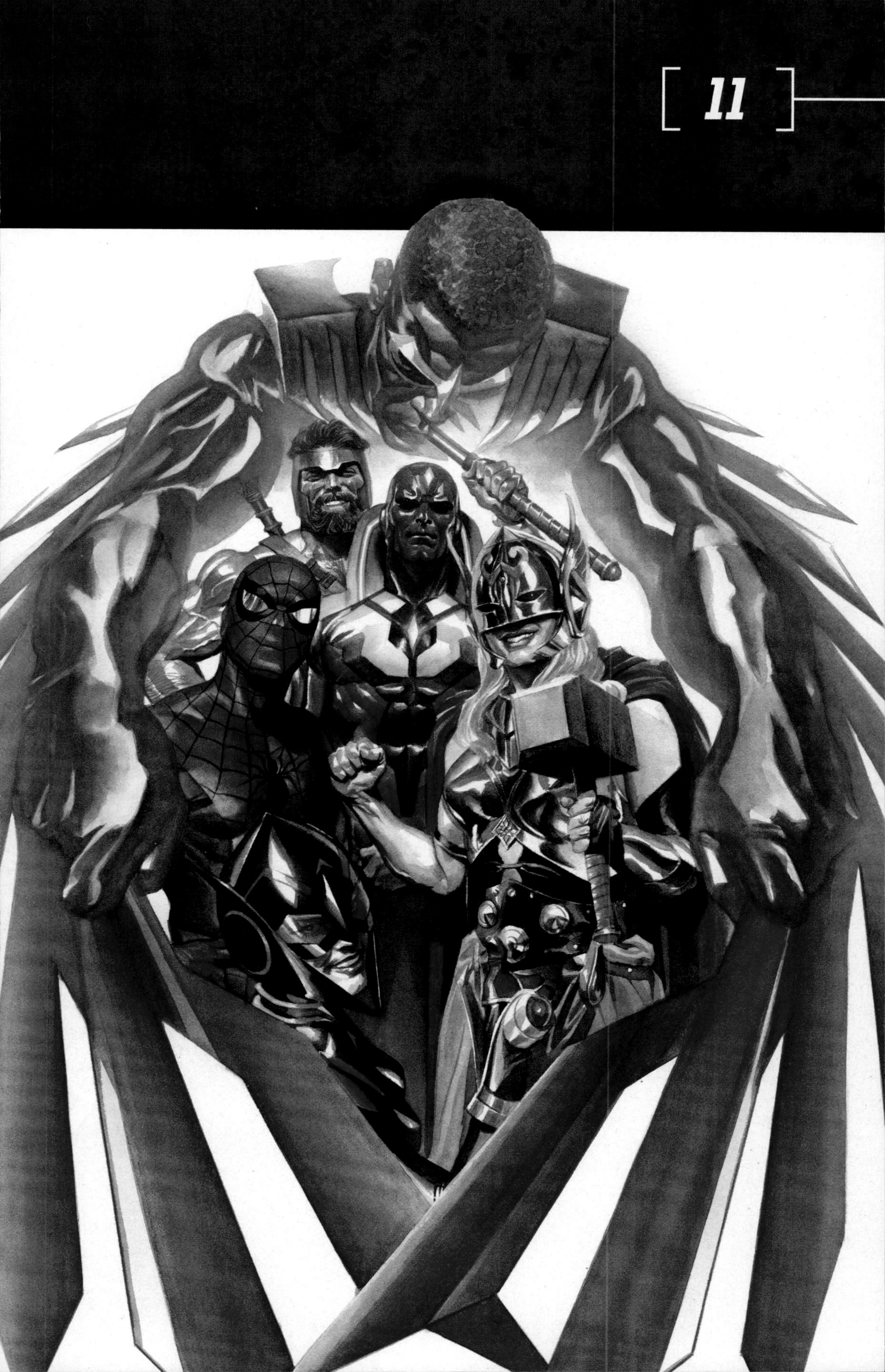

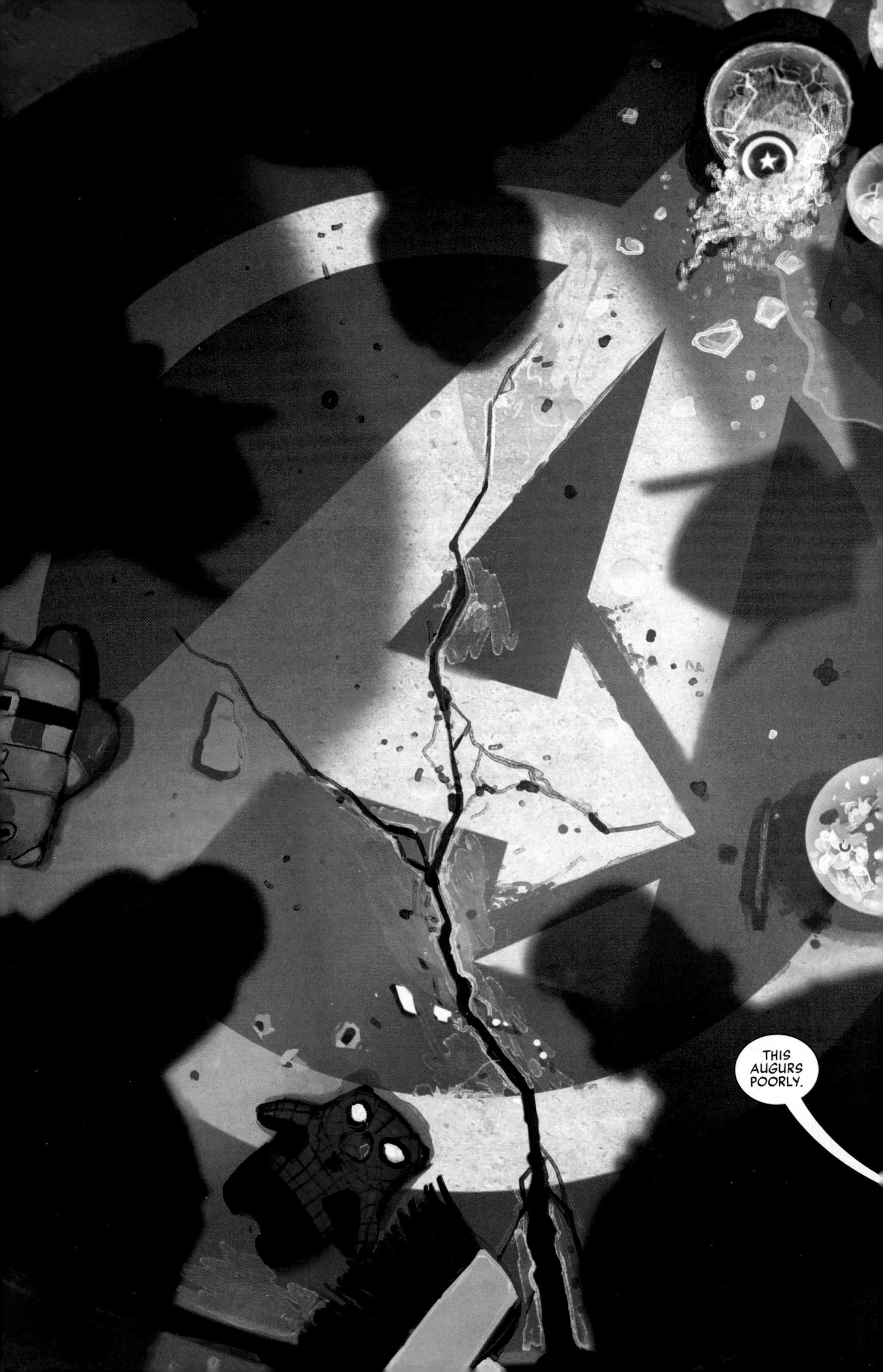
THIS AUGURS POORLY.

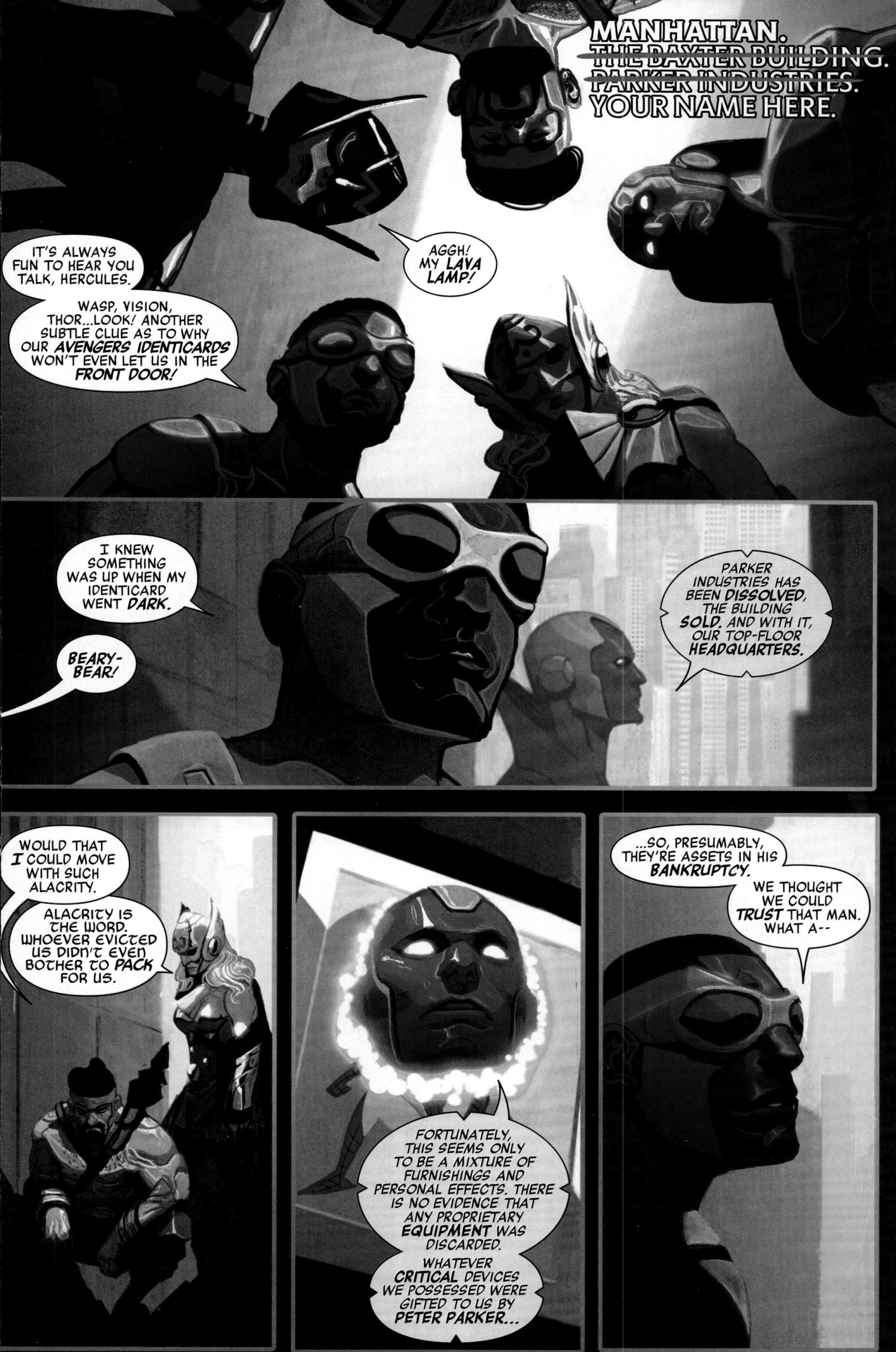
MANHATTAN.
THE BAXTER BUILDING.
PARKER INDUSTRIES.
YOUR NAME HERE.
IT'S ALWAYS FUN TO HEAR YOU TALK, HERCULES.
AGGH! MY LAVA LAMP!
WASP, VISION, THOR...LOOK! ANOTHER SUBTLE CLUE AS TO WHY OUR AVENGERS IDENTICARDS WON'T EVEN LET US IN THE FRONT DOOR!
I KNEW SOMETHING WAS UP WHEN MY IDENTICARD WENT DARK.
BEARY-BEAR!
PARKER INDUSTRIES HAS BEEN DISSOLVED, THE BUILDING SOLD. AND WITH IT, OUR TOP-FLOOR HEADQUARTERS.
WOULD THAT I COULD MOVE WITH SUCH ALACRITY.
ALACRITY IS THE WORD. WHOEVER EVICTED US DIDN'T EVEN BOTHER TO PACK FOR US.
FORTUNATELY, THIS SEEMS ONLY TO BE A MIXTURE OF FURNISHINGS AND PERSONAL EFFECTS. THERE IS NO EVIDENCE THAT ANY PROPRIETARY EQUIPMENT WAS DISCARDED.
WHATEVER CRITICAL DEVICES WE POSSESSED WERE GIFTED TO US BY PETER PARKER...
...SO, PRESUMABLY, THEY'RE ASSETS IN HIS BANKRUPTCY.
WE THOUGHT WE COULD TRUST THAT MAN. WHAT A--

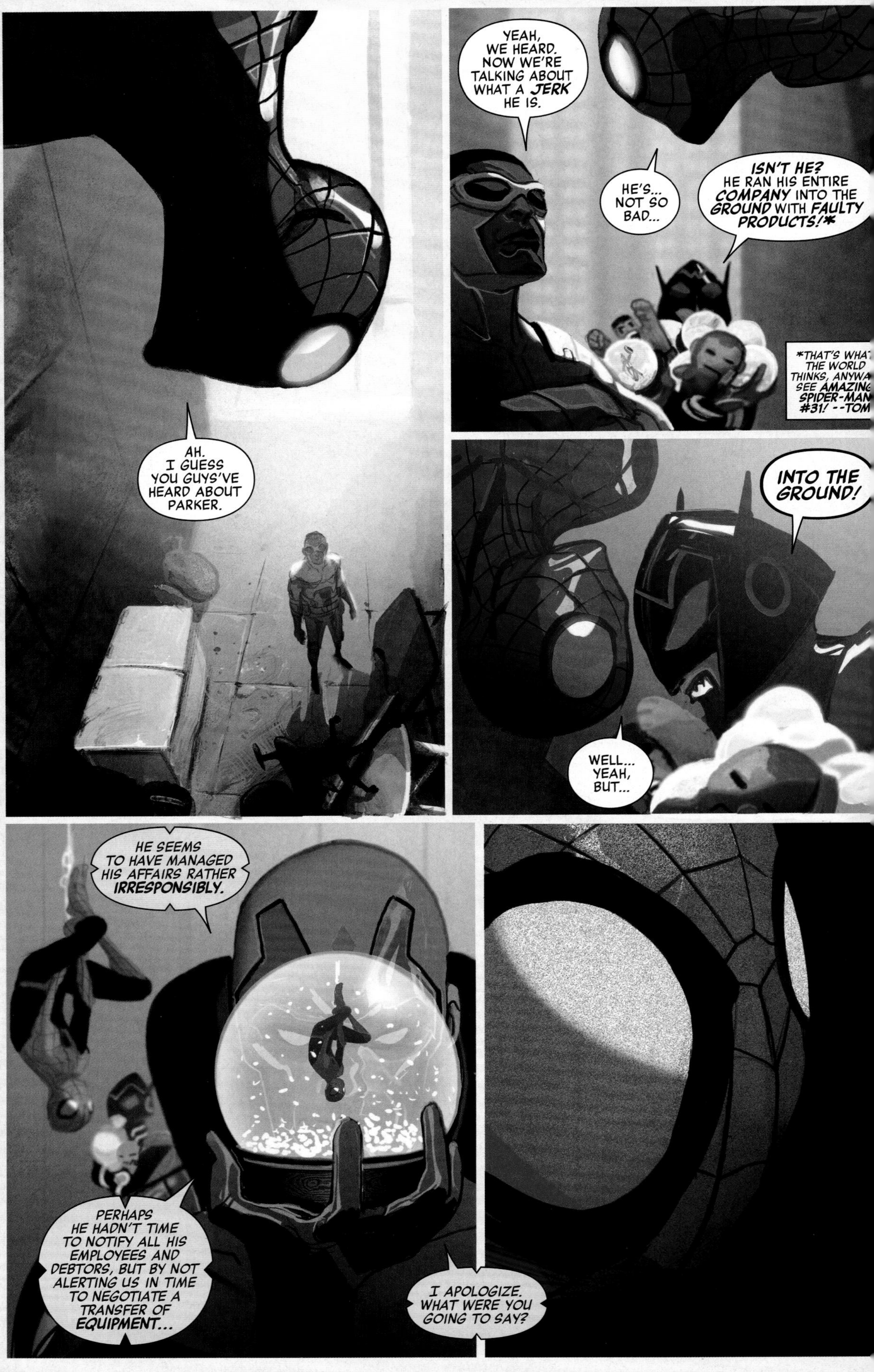
AH. I GUESS YOU GUYS'VE HEARD ABOUT PARKER.
YEAH, WE HEARD. NOW WE'RE TALKING ABOUT WHAT A JERK HE IS.
HE'S... NOT SO BAD...
ISN'T HE? HE RAN HIS ENTIRE COMPANY INTO THE GROUND WITH FAULTY PRODUCTS!*
*THAT'S WHAT THE WORLD THINKS, ANYWA SEE AMAZING SPIDER-MAN #31! --TOM
INTO THE GROUND!
WELL... YEAH, BUT...
HE SEEMS TO HAVE MANAGED HIS AFFAIRS RATHER IRRESPONSIBLY.
PERHAPS HE HADN'T TIME TO NOTIFY ALL HIS EMPLOYEES AND DEBTORS, BUT BY NOT ALERTING US IN TIME TO NEGOTIATE A TRANSFER OF EQUIPMENT...
I APOLOGIZE. WHAT WERE YOU GOING TO SAY?

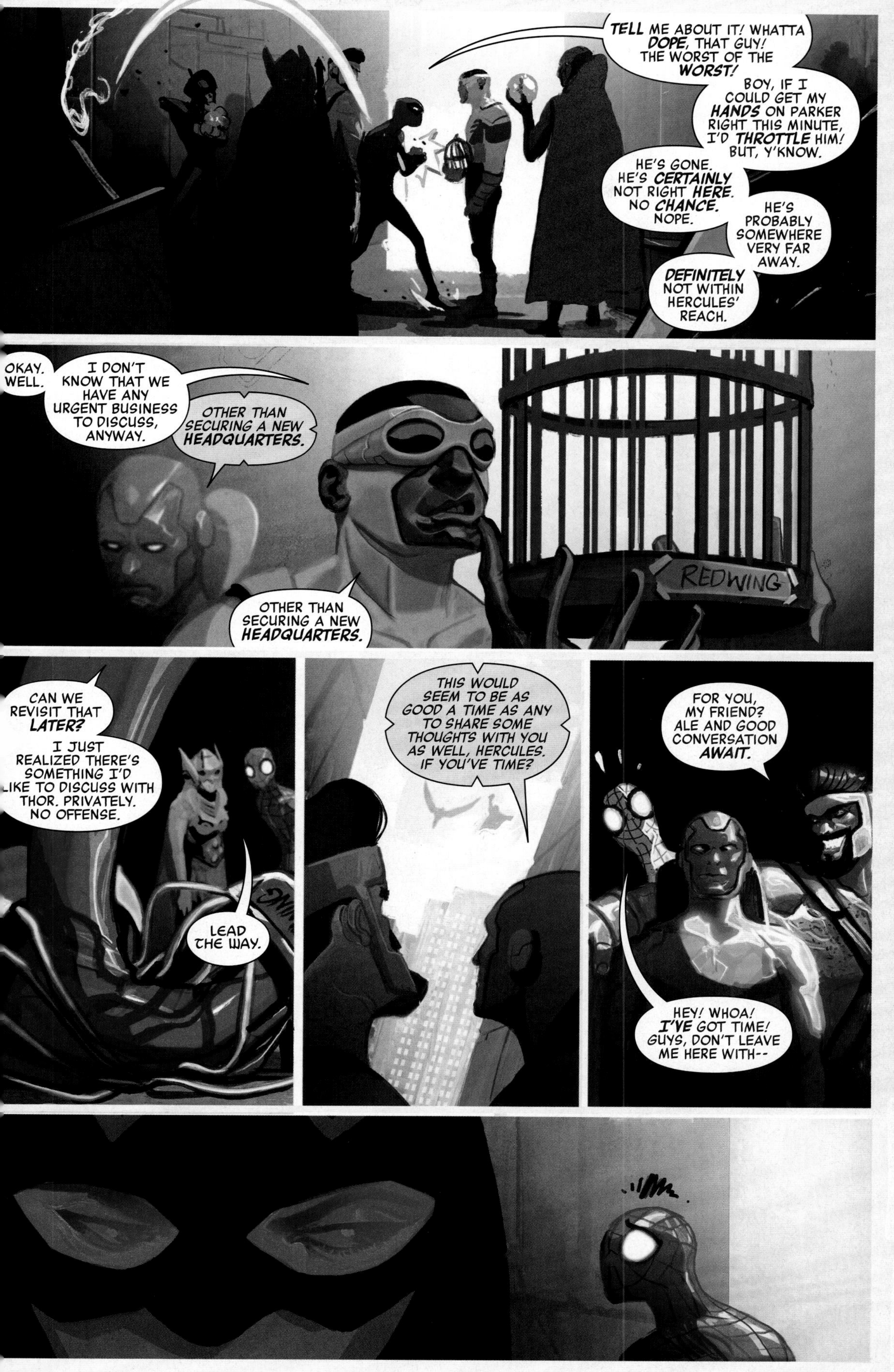

TELL ME ABOUT IT! WHATTA DOPE, THAT GUY! THE WORST OF THE WORST!
BOY, IF I COULD GET MY HANDS ON PARKER RIGHT THIS MINUTE, I'D THROTTLE HIM! BUT, Y'KNOW.
HE'S GONE. HE'S CERTAINLY NOT RIGHT HERE. NO CHANCE. NOPE.
HE'S PROBABLY SOMEWHERE VERY FAR AWAY.
DEFINITELY NOT WITHIN HERCULES' REACH.
OKAY. WELL.
I DON'T KNOW THAT WE HAVE ANY URGENT BUSINESS TO DISCUSS, ANYWAY.
OTHER THAN SECURING A NEW HEADQUARTERS.
OTHER THAN SECURING A NEW HEADQUARTERS.
REDWING
CAN WE REVISIT THAT LATER?
I JUST REALIZED THERE'S SOMETHING I'D LIKE TO DISCUSS WITH THOR. PRIVATELY. NO OFFENSE.
LEAD THE WAY.
THIS WOULD SEEM TO BE AS GOOD A TIME AS ANY TO SHARE SOME THOUGHTS WITH YOU AS WELL, HERCULES. IF YOU'VE TIME?
FOR YOU, MY FRIEND? ALE AND GOOD CONVERSATION AWAIT.
HEY! WHOA! I'VE GOT TIME! GUYS, DON'T LEAVE ME HERE WITH--

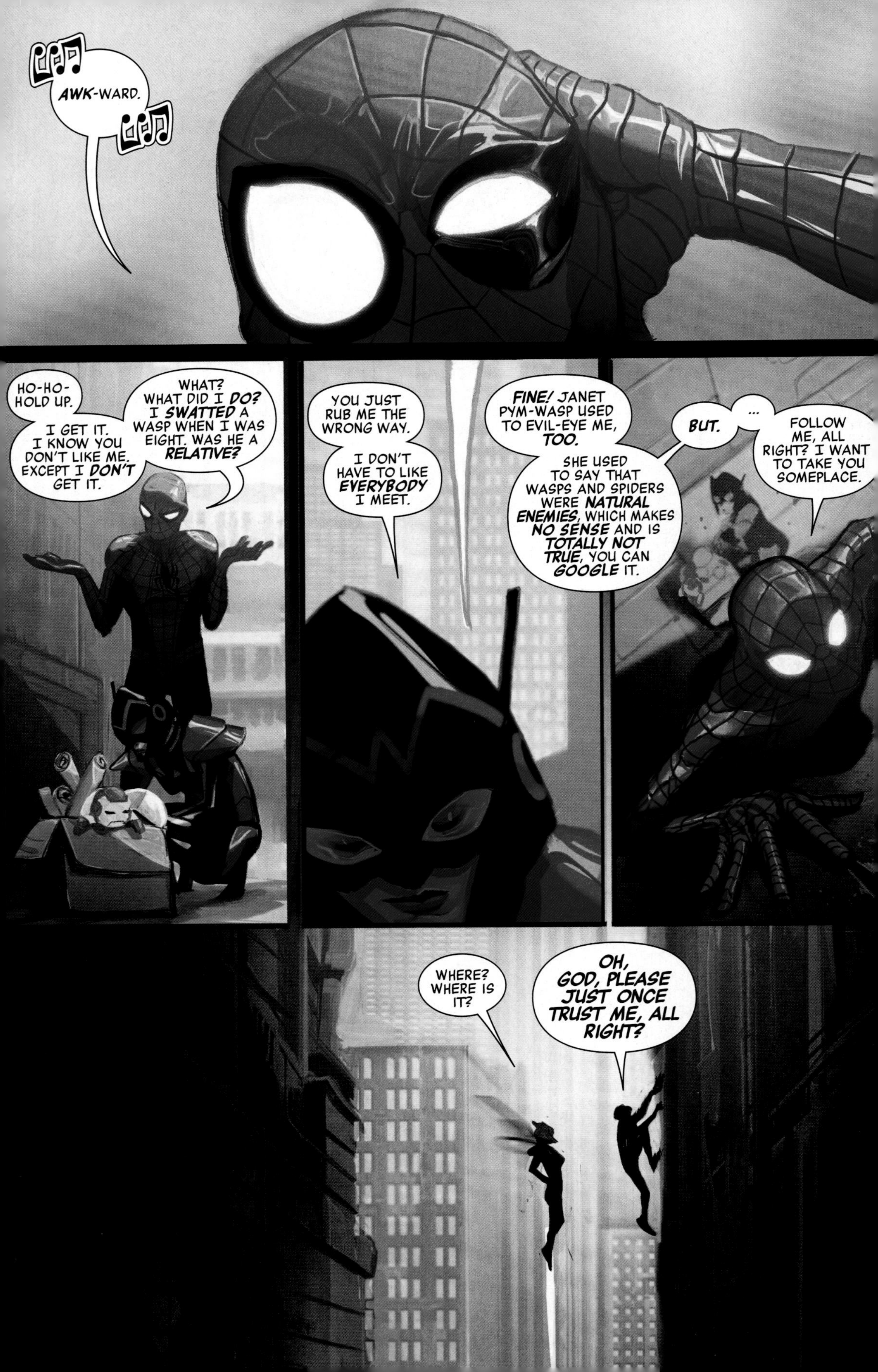
AWK-WARD.
HO-HO-HOLD UP.
I GET IT. I KNOW YOU DON'T LIKE ME. EXCEPT I DON'T GET IT.
WHAT? WHAT DID I DO? I SWATTED A WASP WHEN I WAS EIGHT. WAS HE A RELATIVE?
YOU JUST RUB ME THE WRONG WAY.
I DON'T HAVE TO LIKE EVERYBODY I MEET.
FINE! JANET PYM-WASP USED TO EVIL-EYE ME, TOO.
SHE USED TO SAY THAT WASPS AND SPIDERS WERE NATURAL ENEMIES, WHICH MAKES NO SENSE AND IS TOTALLY NOT TRUE, YOU CAN GOOGLE IT.
BUT.
...
FOLLOW ME, ALL RIGHT? I WANT TO TAKE YOU SOMEPLACE.
WHERE? WHERE IS IT?
OH, GOD, PLEASE JUST ONCE TRUST ME, ALL RIGHT?

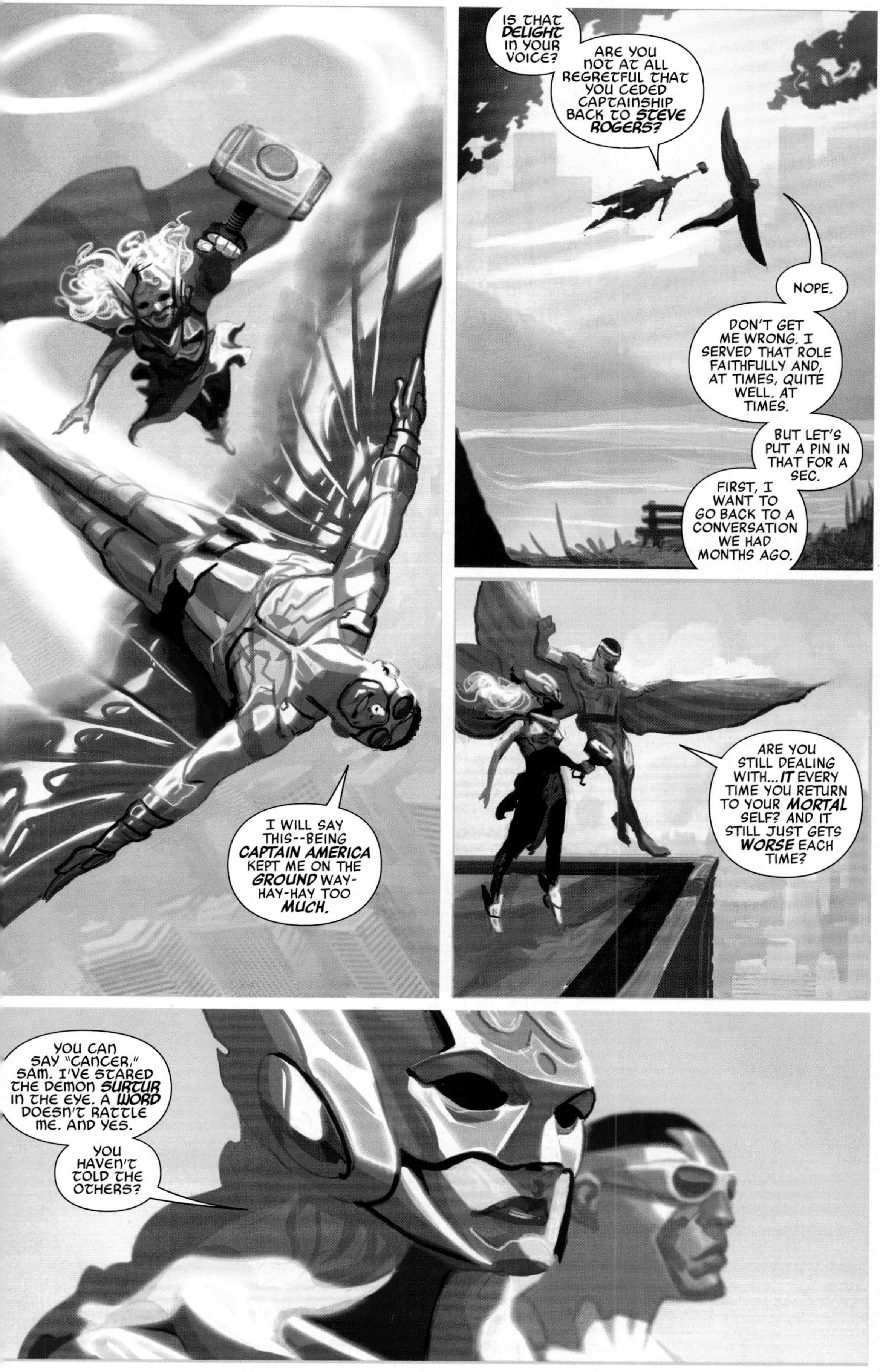
I WILL SAY THIS--BEING CAPTAIN AMERICA KEPT ME ON THE GROUND WAY-HAY-HAY TOO MUCH.
IS THAT DELIGHT IN YOUR VOICE?
ARE YOU NOT AT ALL REGRETFUL THAT YOU CEDED CAPTAINSHIP BACK TO STEVE ROGERS?
NOPE.
DON'T GET ME WRONG. I SERVED THAT ROLE FAITHFULLY AND, AT TIMES, QUITE WELL. AT TIMES.
BUT LET'S PUT A PIN IN THAT FOR A SEC.
FIRST, I WANT TO GO BACK TO A CONVERSATION WE HAD MONTHS AGO.
ARE YOU STILL DEALING WITH...IT EVERY TIME YOU RETURN TO YOUR MORTAL SELF? AND IT STILL JUST GETS WORSE EACH TIME?
YOU CAN SAY "CANCER," SAM. I'VE STARED THE DEMON SURTUR IN THE EYE. A WORD DOESN'T RATTLE ME. AND YES.
YOU HAVEN'T TOLD THE OTHERS?

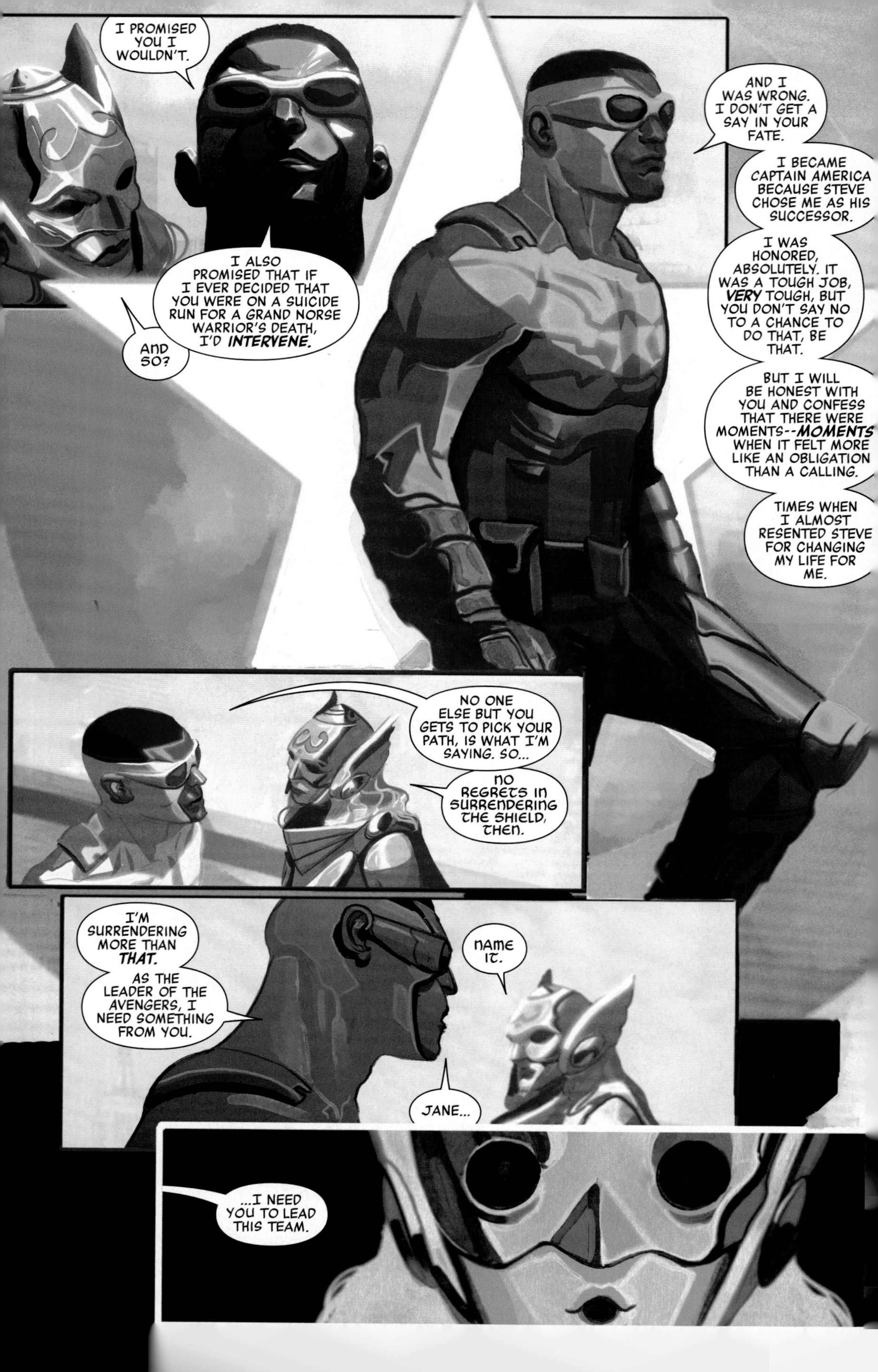
I PROMISED YOU I WOULDN'T.
I ALSO PROMISED THAT IF I EVER DECIDED THAT YOU WERE ON A SUICIDE RUN FOR A GRAND NORSE WARRIOR'S DEATH, I'D INTERVENE.
AND SO?
AND I WAS WRONG. I DON'T GET A SAY IN YOUR FATE.
I BECAME CAPTAIN AMERICA BECAUSE STEVE CHOSE ME AS HIS SUCCESSOR.
I WAS HONORED, ABSOLUTELY. IT WAS A TOUGH JOB, VERY TOUGH, BUT YOU DON'T SAY NO TO A CHANCE TO DO THAT, BE THAT.
BUT I WILL BE HONEST WITH YOU AND CONFESS THAT THERE WERE MOMENTS--MOMENTS WHEN IT FELT MORE LIKE AN OBLIGATION THAN A CALLING.
TIMES WHEN I ALMOST RESENTED STEVE FOR CHANGING MY LIFE FOR ME.
NO ONE ELSE BUT YOU GETS TO PICK YOUR PATH, IS WHAT I'M SAYING. SO...
NO REGRETS IN SURRENDERING THE SHIELD, THEN.
I'M SURRENDERING MORE THAN THAT.
AS THE LEADER OF THE AVENGERS, I NEED SOMETHING FROM YOU.
NAME IT.
JANE...
...I NEED YOU TO LEAD THIS TEAM.

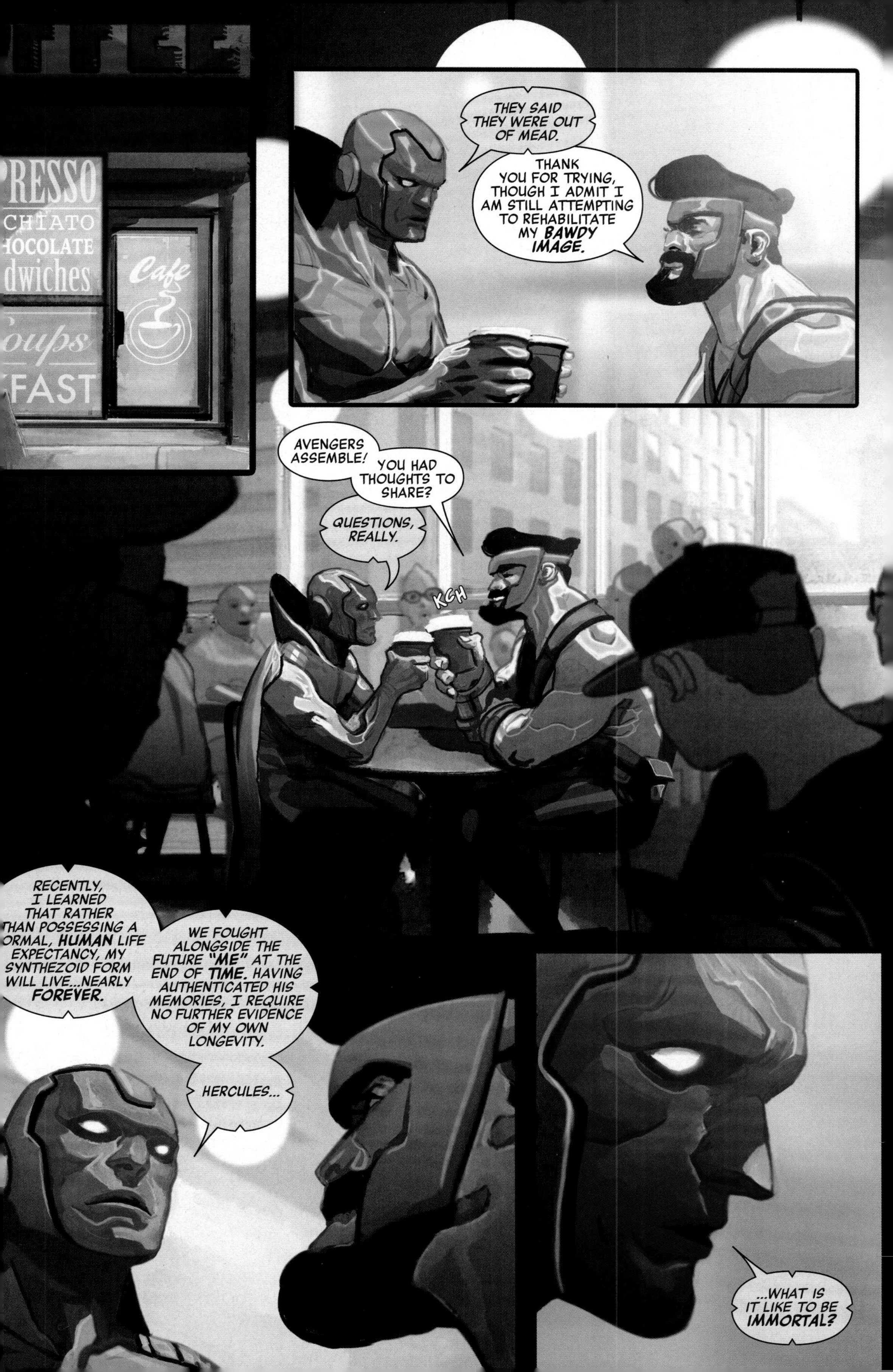

THEY SAID THEY WERE OUT OF MEAD.
THANK YOU FOR TRYING, THOUGH I ADMIT I AM STILL ATTEMPTING TO REHABILITATE MY BAWDY IMAGE.
AVENGERS ASSEMBLE!
YOU HAD THOUGHTS TO SHARE?
QUESTIONS, REALLY.
KCH
RECENTLY, I LEARNED THAT RATHER THAN POSSESSING A NORMAL, HUMAN LIFE EXPECTANCY, MY SYNTHEZOID FORM WILL LIVE...NEARLY FOREVER.
WE FOUGHT ALONGSIDE THE FUTURE "ME" AT THE END OF TIME. HAVING AUTHENTICATED HIS MEMORIES, I REQUIRE NO FURTHER EVIDENCE OF MY OWN LONGEVITY.
HERCULES...
...WHAT IS IT LIKE TO BE IMMORTAL?

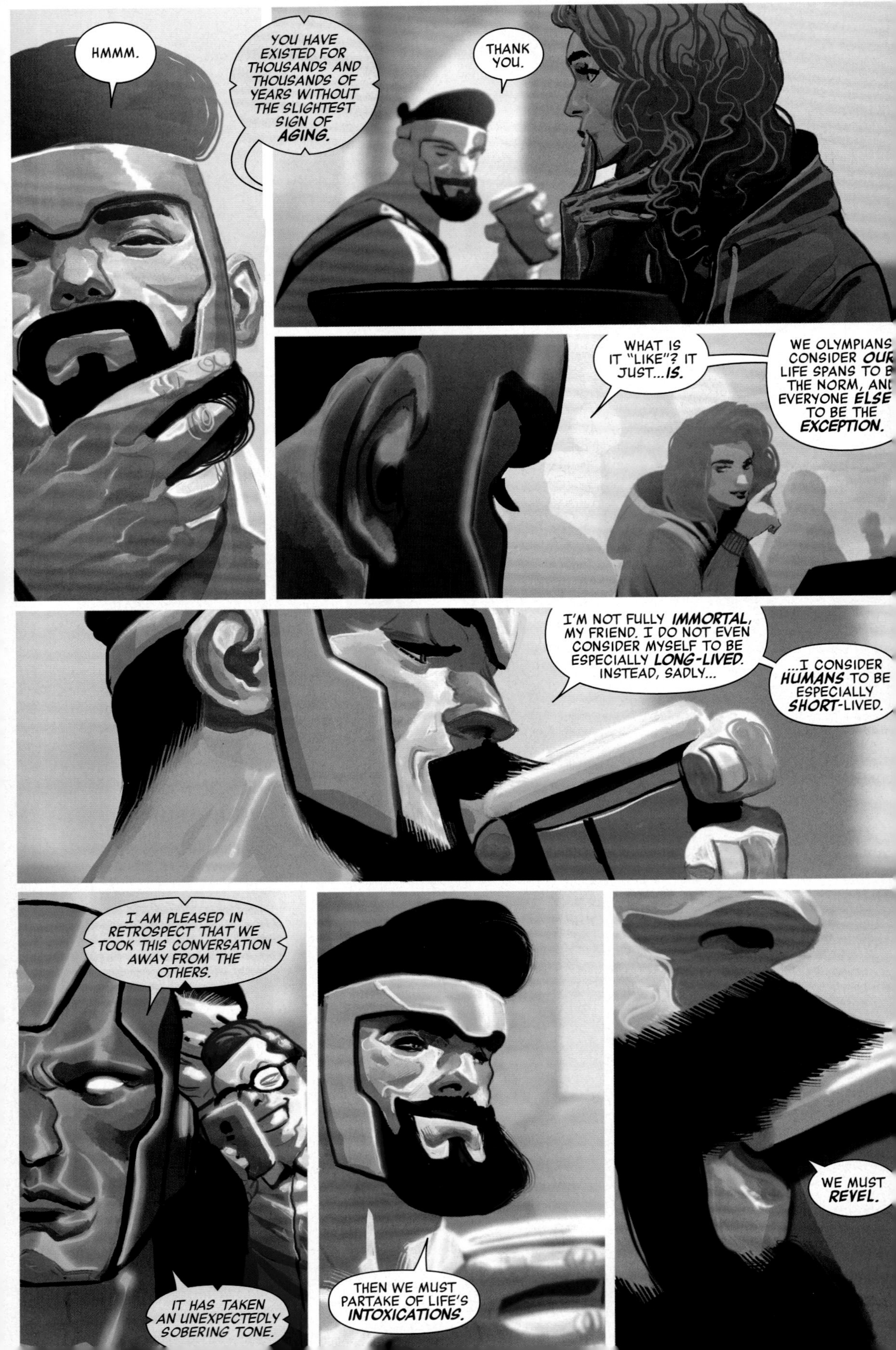
HMMM.
YOU HAVE EXISTED FOR THOUSANDS AND THOUSANDS OF YEARS WITHOUT THE SLIGHTEST SIGN OF AGING.
THANK YOU.
WHAT IS IT "LIKE"? IT JUST...IS.
WE OLYMPIANS CONSIDER OUR LIFE SPANS TO BE THE NORM, AND EVERYONE ELSE TO BE THE EXCEPTION.
I'M NOT FULLY IMMORTAL, MY FRIEND. I DO NOT EVEN CONSIDER MYSELF TO BE ESPECIALLY LONG-LIVED. INSTEAD, SADLY...
...I CONSIDER HUMANS TO BE ESPECIALLY SHORT-LIVED.
I AM PLEASED IN RETROSPECT THAT WE TOOK THIS CONVERSATION AWAY FROM THE OTHERS.
IT HAS TAKEN AN UNEXPECTEDLY SOBERING TONE.
THEN WE MUST PARTAKE OF LIFE'S INTOXICATIONS.
WE MUST REVEL.

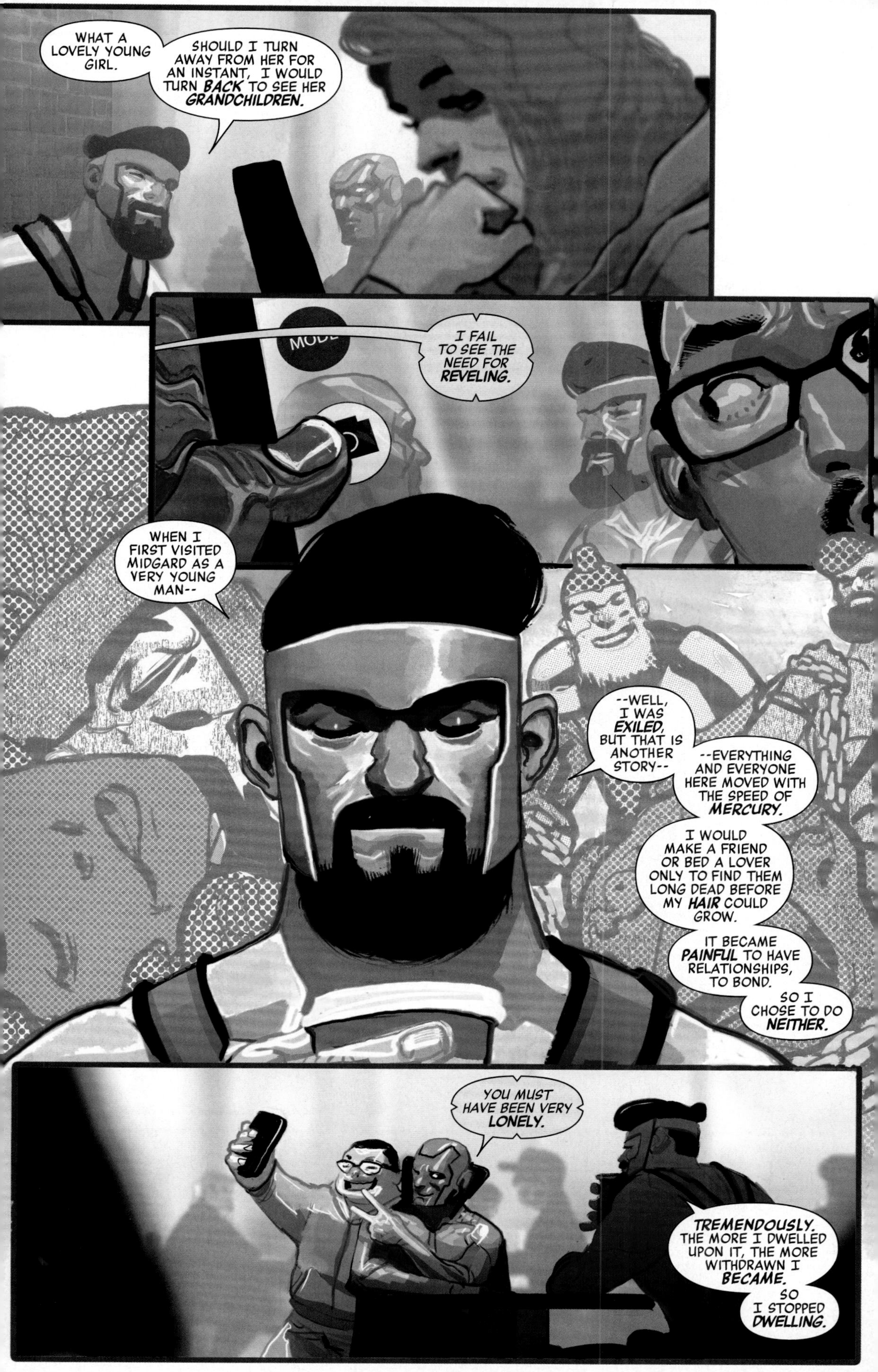
WHAT A LOVELY YOUNG GIRL.
SHOULD I TURN AWAY FROM HER FOR AN INSTANT, I WOULD TURN BACK TO SEE HER GRANDCHILDREN.
MODE
I FAIL TO SEE THE NEED FOR REVELING.
WHEN I FIRST VISITED MIDGARD AS A VERY YOUNG MAN--
--WELL, I WAS EXILED, BUT THAT IS ANOTHER STORY--
--EVERYTHING AND EVERYONE HERE MOVED WITH THE SPEED OF MERCURY.
I WOULD MAKE A FRIEND OR BED A LOVER ONLY TO FIND THEM LONG DEAD BEFORE MY HAIR COULD GROW.
IT BECAME PAINFUL TO HAVE RELATIONSHIPS, TO BOND.
SO I CHOSE TO DO NEITHER.
YOU MUST HAVE BEEN VERY LONELY.
TREMENDOUSLY. THE MORE I DWELLED UPON IT, THE MORE WITHDRAWN I BECAME.
SO I STOPPED DWELLING.

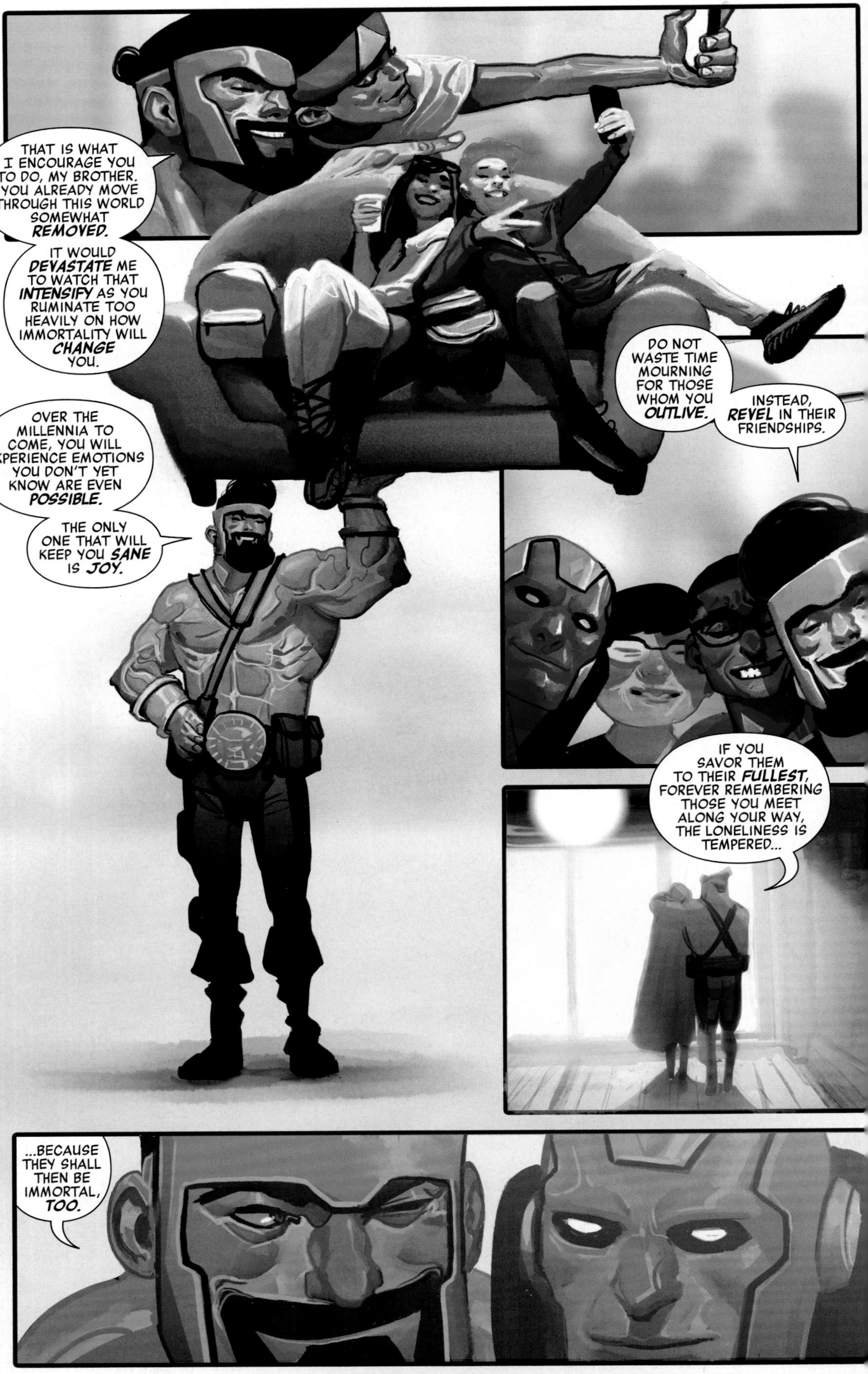
THAT IS WHAT I ENCOURAGE YOU TO DO, MY BROTHER. YOU ALREADY MOVE THROUGH THIS WORLD SOMEWHAT REMOVED.
IT WOULD DEVASTATE ME TO WATCH THAT INTENSIFY AS YOU RUMINATE TOO HEAVILY ON HOW IMMORTALITY WILL CHANGE YOU.
OVER THE MILLENNIA TO COME, YOU WILL EXPERIENCE EMOTIONS YOU DON'T YET KNOW ARE EVEN POSSIBLE.
THE ONLY ONE THAT WILL KEEP YOU SANE IS JOY.
DO NOT WASTE TIME MOURNING FOR THOSE WHOM YOU OUTLIVE.
INSTEAD, REVEL IN THEIR FRIENDSHIPS.
IF YOU SAVOR THEM TO THEIR FULLEST, FOREVER REMEMBERING THOSE YOU MEET ALONG YOUR WAY, THE LONELINESS IS TEMPERED...
...BECAUSE THEY SHALL THEN BE IMMORTAL, TOO.

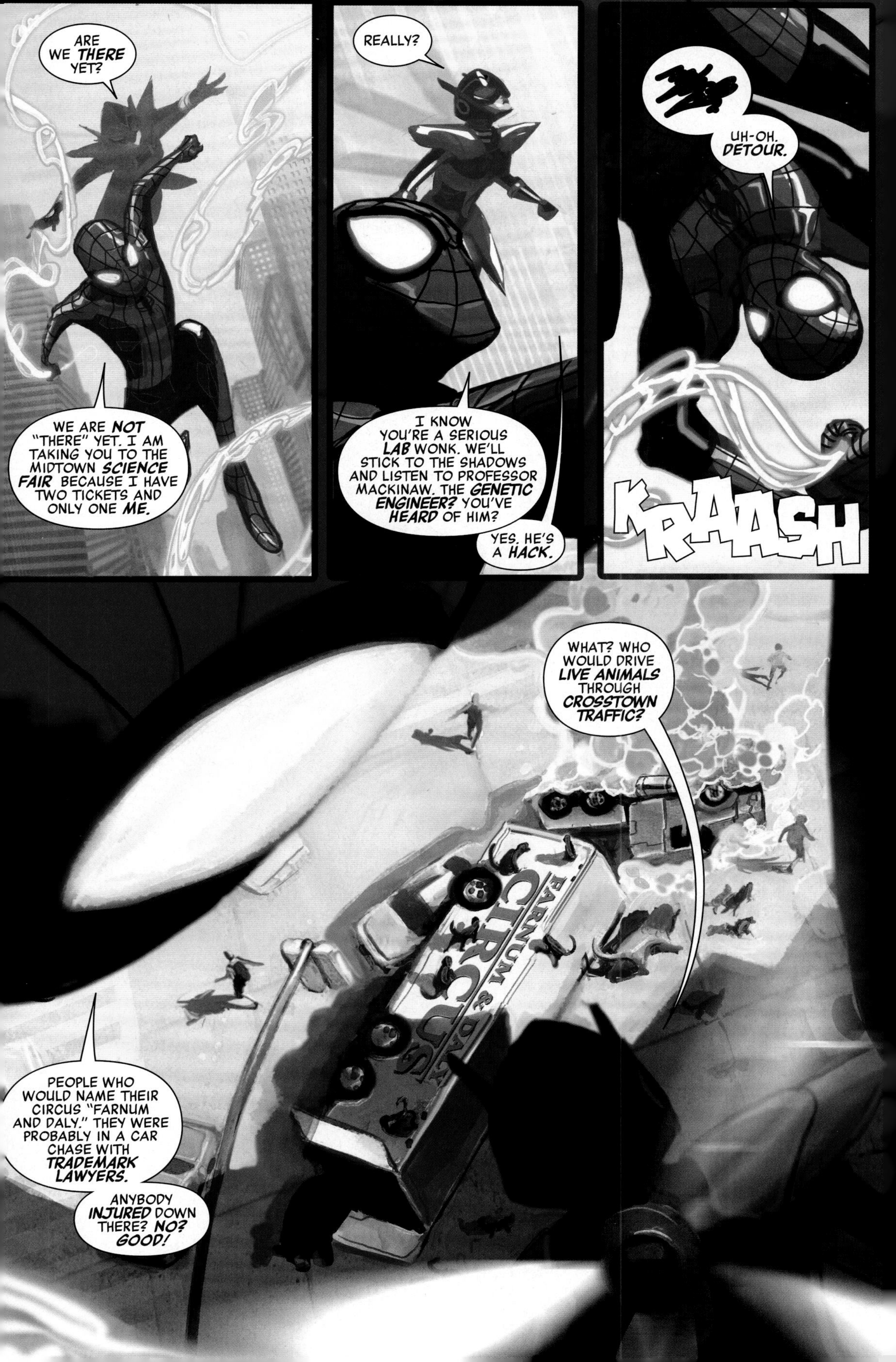
ARE WE THERE YET?
WE ARE NOT "THERE" YET. I AM TAKING YOU TO THE MIDTOWN SCIENCE FAIR BECAUSE I HAVE TWO TICKETS AND ONLY ONE ME.
REALLY?
I KNOW YOU'RE A SERIOUS LAB WONK. WE'LL STICK TO THE SHADOWS AND LISTEN TO PROFESSOR MACKINAW. THE GENETIC ENGINEER? YOU'VE HEARD OF HIM?
YES. HE'S A HACK.
UH-OH. DETOUR.
KRAAASH
WHAT? WHO WOULD DRIVE LIVE ANIMALS THROUGH CROSSTOWN TRAFFIC?
PEOPLE WHO WOULD NAME THEIR CIRCUS "FARNUM AND DALY." THEY WERE PROBABLY IN A CAR CHASE WITH TRADEMARK LAWYERS.
ANYBODY INJURED DOWN THERE? NO? GOOD!
FARNUM & DALY CIRCUS

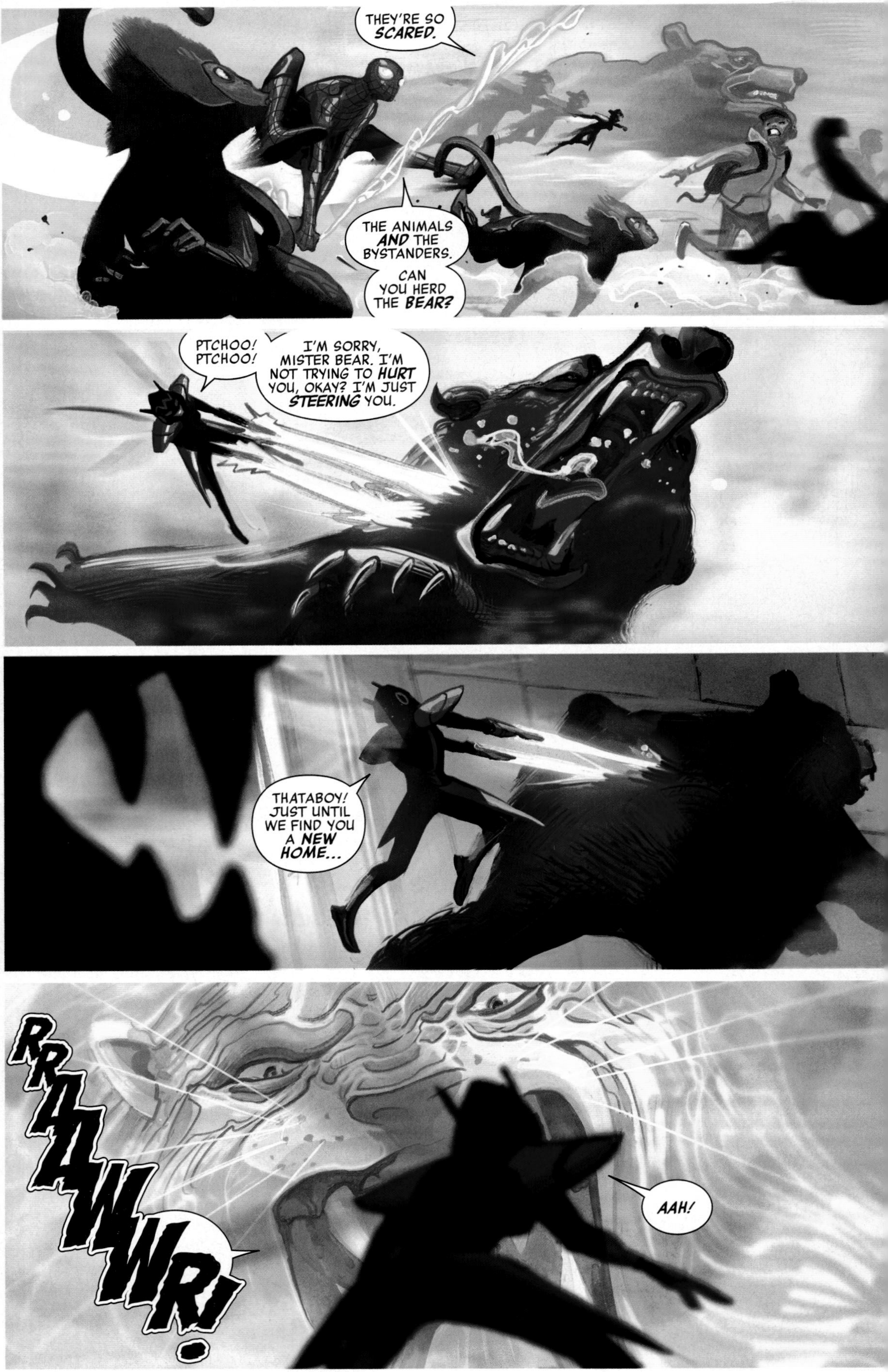
THEY'RE SO SCARED.
THE ANIMALS AND THE BYSTANDERS.
CAN YOU HERD THE BEAR?
PTCHOO! PTCHOO!
I'M SORRY, MISTER BEAR. I'M NOT TRYING TO HURT YOU, OKAY? I'M JUST STEERING YOU.
THATABOY! JUST UNTIL WE FIND YOU A NEW HOME...
RRAAWWR!
AAH!

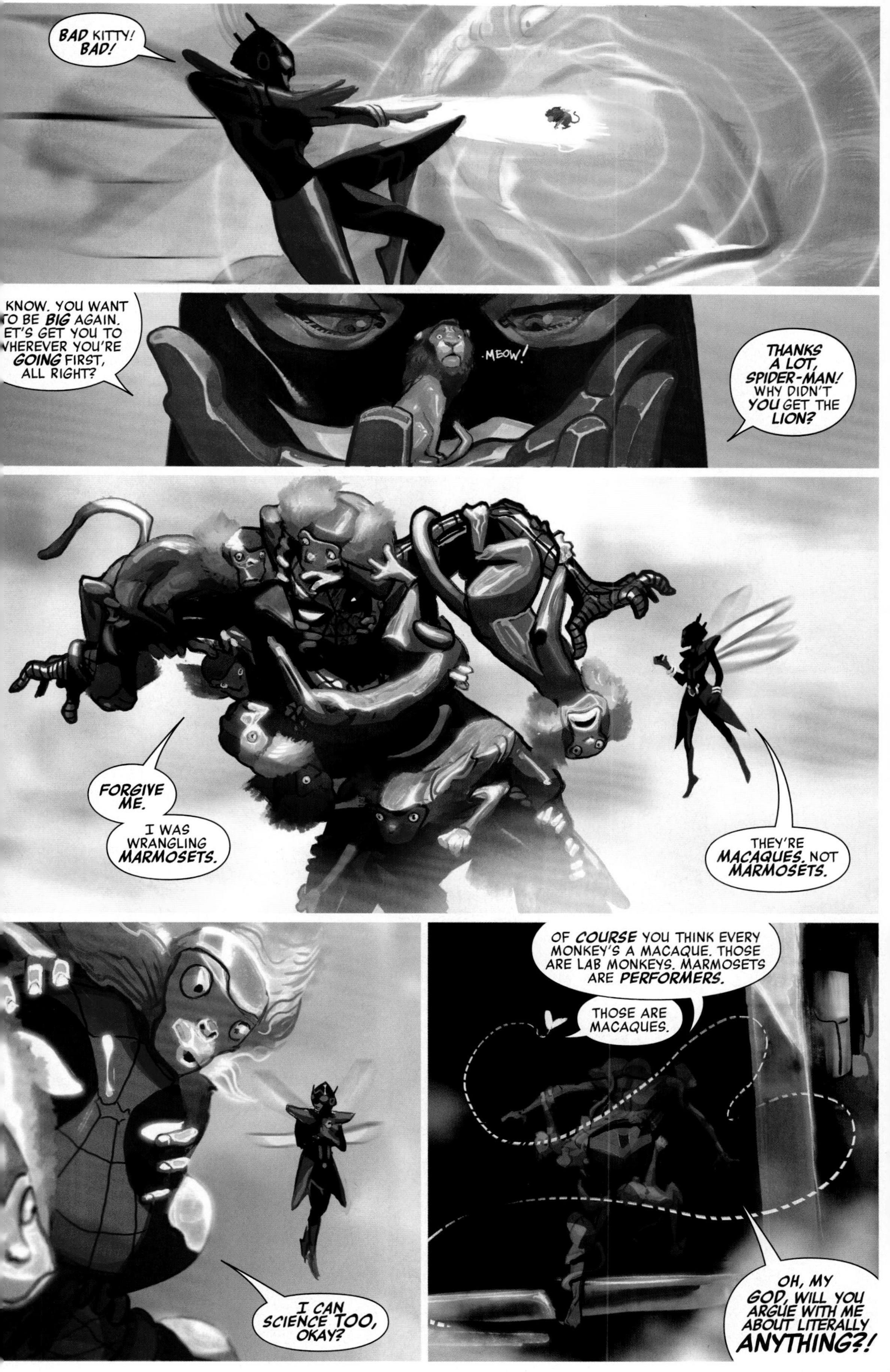

BAD KITTY! BAD!
KNOW. YOU WANT TO BE BIG AGAIN. ET'S GET YOU TO VHEREVER YOU'RE GOING FIRST, ALL RIGHT?
MEOW!
THANKS A LOT, SPIDER-MAN! WHY DIDN'T YOU GET THE LION?
FORGIVE ME.
I WAS WRANGLING MARMOSETS.
THEY'RE MACAQUES, NOT MARMOSETS.
I CAN SCIENCE TOO, OKAY?
OF COURSE YOU THINK EVERY MONKEY'S A MACAQUE. THOSE ARE LAB MONKEYS. MARMOSETS ARE PERFORMERS.
THOSE ARE MACAQUES.
OH, MY GOD, WILL YOU ARGUE WITH ME ABOUT LITERALLY ANYTHING?!

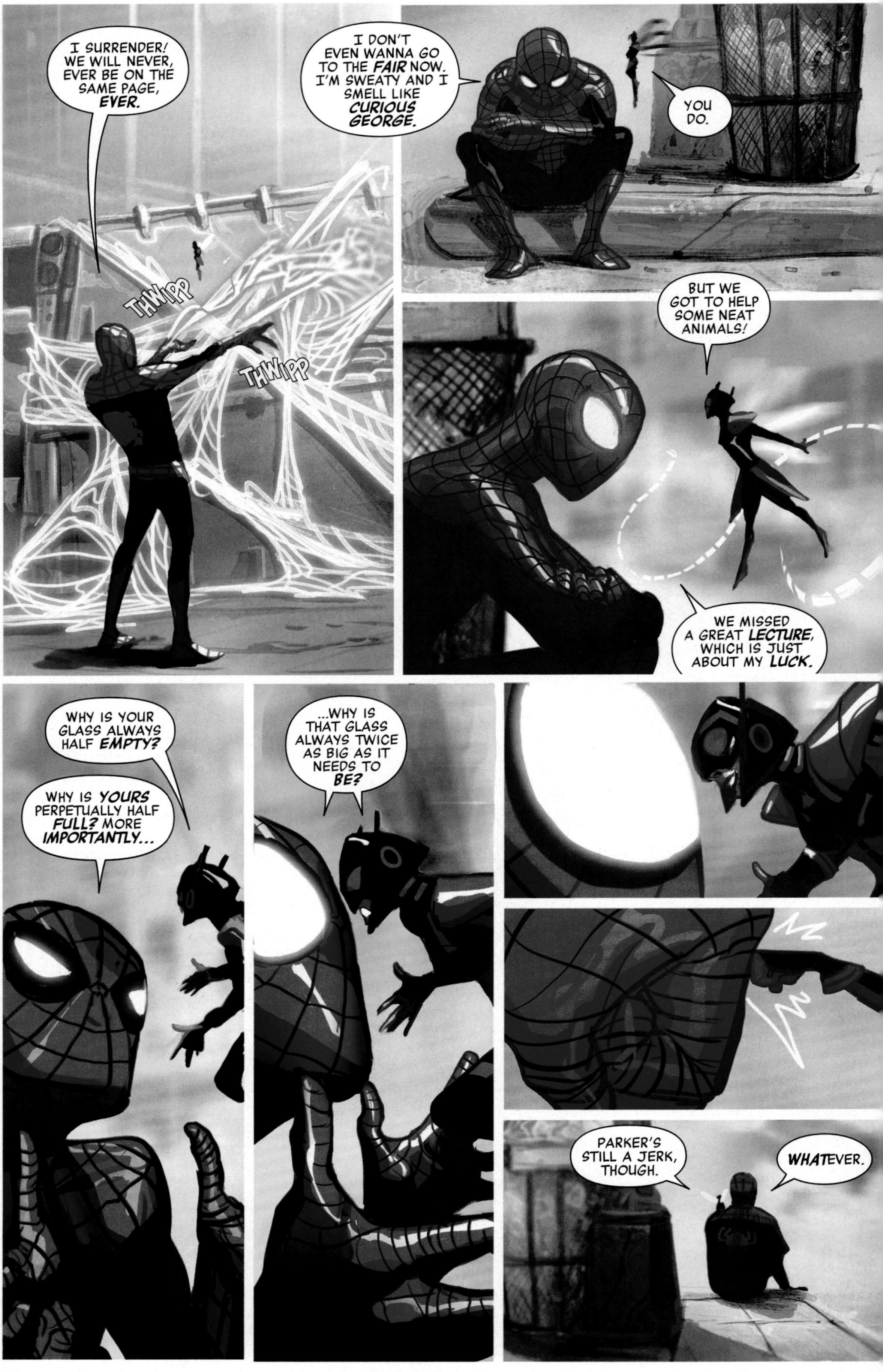
I SURRENDER! WE WILL NEVER, EVER BE ON THE SAME PAGE, **EVER.**
THWIPP
THWIPP
I DON'T EVEN WANNA GO TO THE **FAIR** NOW. I'M SWEATY AND I SMELL LIKE **CURIOUS GEORGE.**
YOU DO.
BUT WE GOT TO HELP SOME NEAT ANIMALS!
WE MISSED A GREAT **LECTURE,** WHICH IS JUST ABOUT MY **LUCK.**
WHY IS YOUR GLASS ALWAYS HALF **EMPTY?**
WHY IS **YOURS** PERPETUALLY HALF **FULL?** MORE **IMPORTANTLY...**
...WHY IS THAT GLASS ALWAYS TWICE AS BIG AS IT NEEDS TO **BE?**
PARKER'S STILL A JERK, THOUGH.
WHATEVER.

YOU WANT *ME* TO LEAD.

ARE YOU *RETIRING* AS *CAPTAIN AMERICA* AND THE *FALCON?*

NO. WHY WOULD YOU THINK *THAT?*

BECAUSE THE ONLY OTHER EXCUSE IS *ASININE.*

PARDON ME, BUT YOU'RE NOT A *MIND READER.* YOU DON'T *KNOW* WHY I'M ASKING YOU TO--

YOU'VE TOLD YOURSELF THAT IF YOU'RE NOT *CAPTAIN AMERICA,* YOU'RE NOT CAPABLE OF *RUNNING* THE *TEAM.*

WOW. YOU *ARE* A MIND READER. WHAT NUMBER AM I THINKING OF?

FIVE.

THIRTY-TWO.

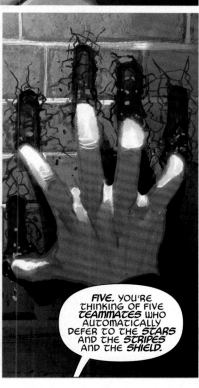

FIVE. YOU'RE THINKING OF FIVE *TEAMMATES* WHO AUTOMATICALLY DEFER TO THE *STARS* AND THE *STRIPES* AND THE *SHIELD.*

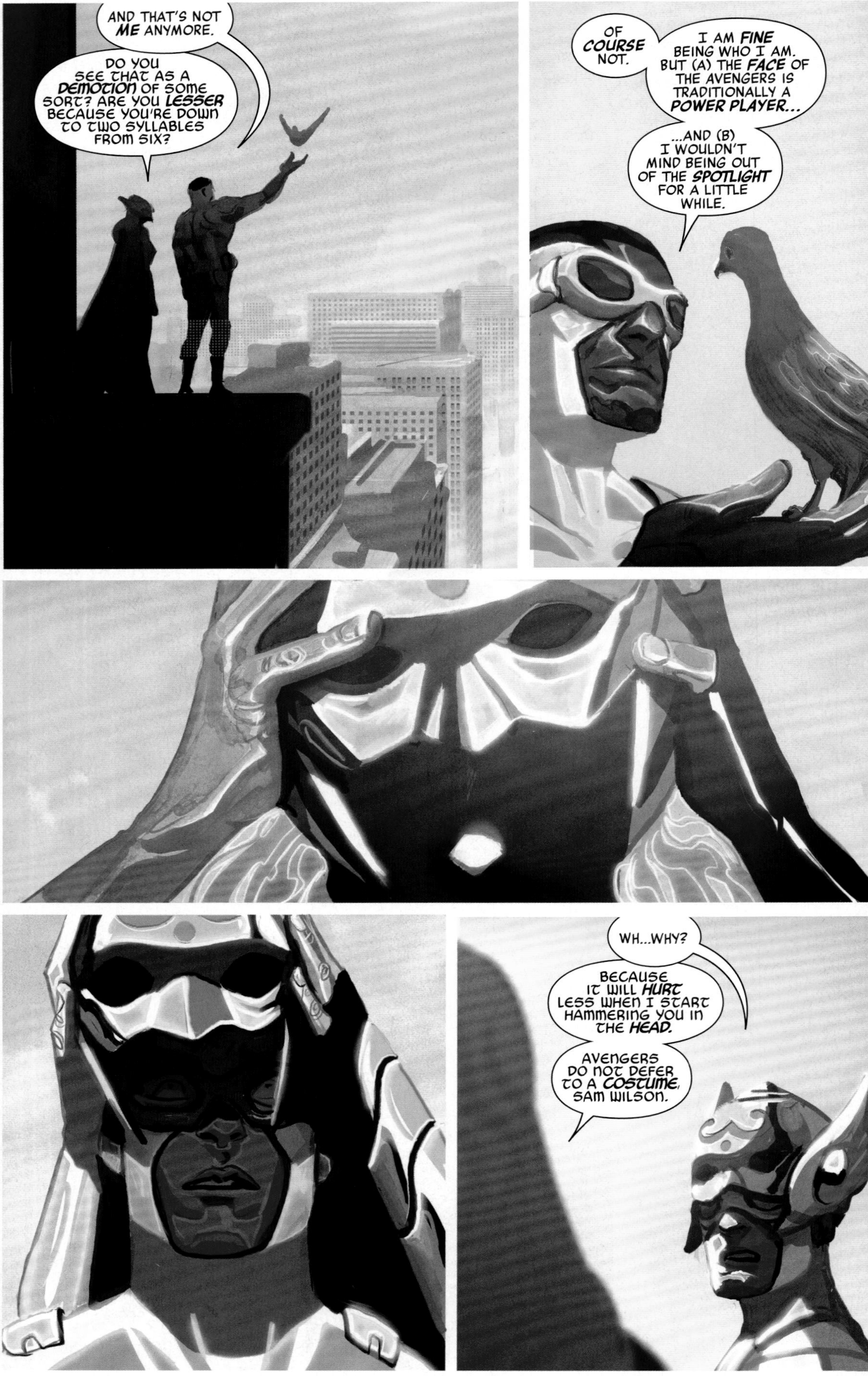
AND THAT'S NOT ME ANYMORE.
DO YOU SEE THAT AS A DEMOTION OF SOME SORT? ARE YOU LESSER BECAUSE YOU'RE DOWN TO TWO SYLLABLES FROM SIX?
OF COURSE NOT.
I AM FINE BEING WHO I AM. BUT (A) THE FACE OF THE AVENGERS IS TRADITIONALLY A POWER PLAYER...
...AND (B) I WOULDN'T MIND BEING OUT OF THE SPOTLIGHT FOR A LITTLE WHILE.
WH...WHY?
BECAUSE IT WILL HURT LESS WHEN I START HAMMERING YOU IN THE HEAD.
AVENGERS DO NOT DEFER TO A COSTUME, SAM WILSON.

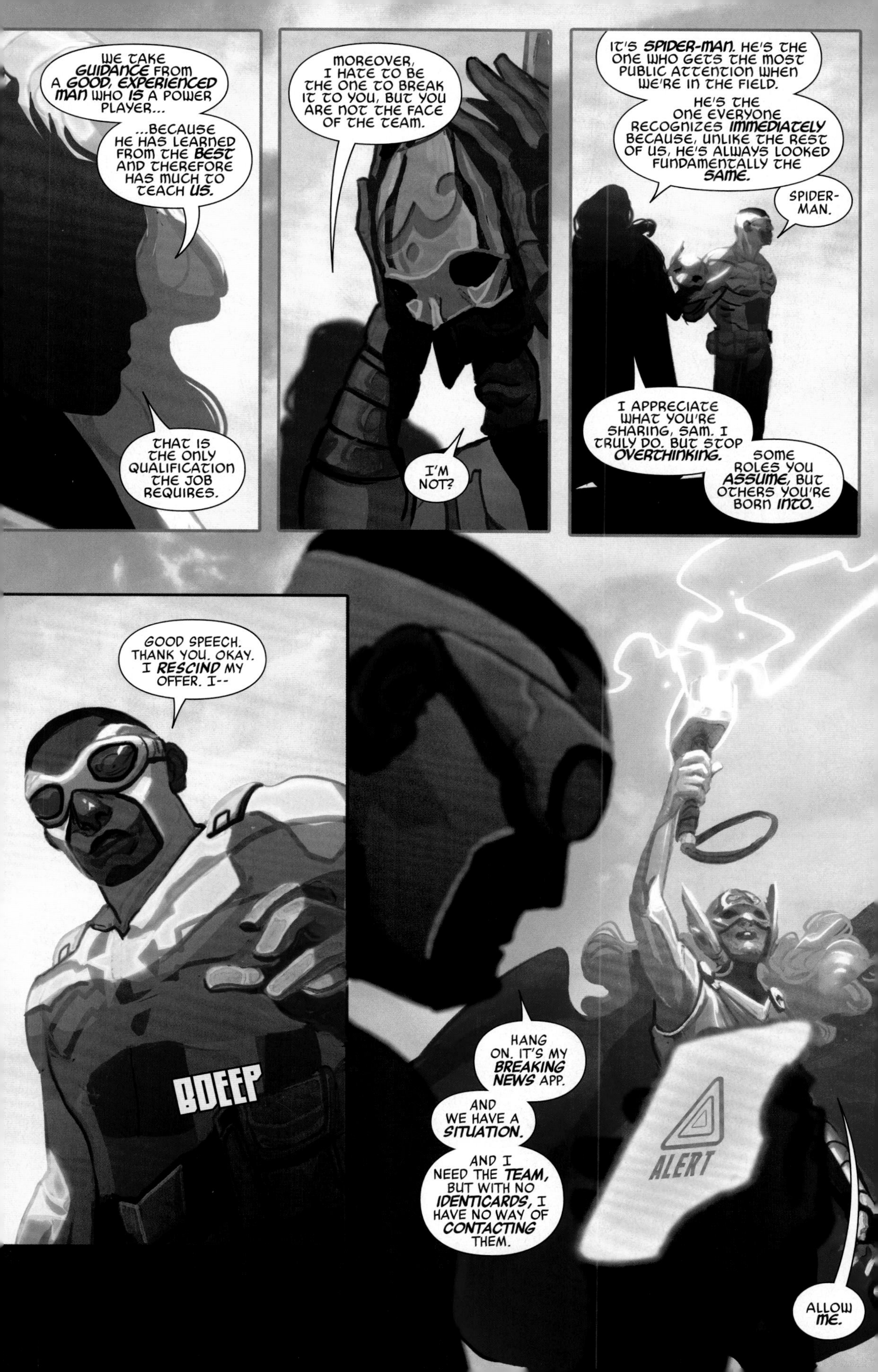
WE TAKE GUIDANCE FROM A GOOD, EXPERIENCED MAN WHO IS A POWER PLAYER...
...BECAUSE HE HAS LEARNED FROM THE BEST AND THEREFORE HAS MUCH TO TEACH US.
THAT IS THE ONLY QUALIFICATION THE JOB REQUIRES.
MOREOVER, I HATE TO BE THE ONE TO BREAK IT TO YOU, BUT YOU ARE NOT THE FACE OF THE TEAM.
I'M NOT?
IT'S SPIDER-MAN. HE'S THE ONE WHO GETS THE MOST PUBLIC ATTENTION WHEN WE'RE IN THE FIELD.
HE'S THE ONE EVERYONE RECOGNIZES IMMEDIATELY BECAUSE, UNLIKE THE REST OF US, HE'S ALWAYS LOOKED FUNDAMENTALLY THE SAME.
SPIDER-MAN.
I APPRECIATE WHAT YOU'RE SHARING, SAM. I TRULY DO. BUT STOP OVERTHINKING.
SOME ROLES YOU ASSUME, BUT OTHERS YOU'RE BORN INTO.
GOOD SPEECH. THANK YOU. OKAY. I RESCIND MY OFFER. I--
BOEEP
HANG ON. IT'S MY BREAKING NEWS APP.
AND WE HAVE A SITUATION.
AND I NEED THE TEAM, BUT WITH NO IDENTICARDS, I HAVE NO WAY OF CONTACTING THEM.
ALERT
ALLOW ME.

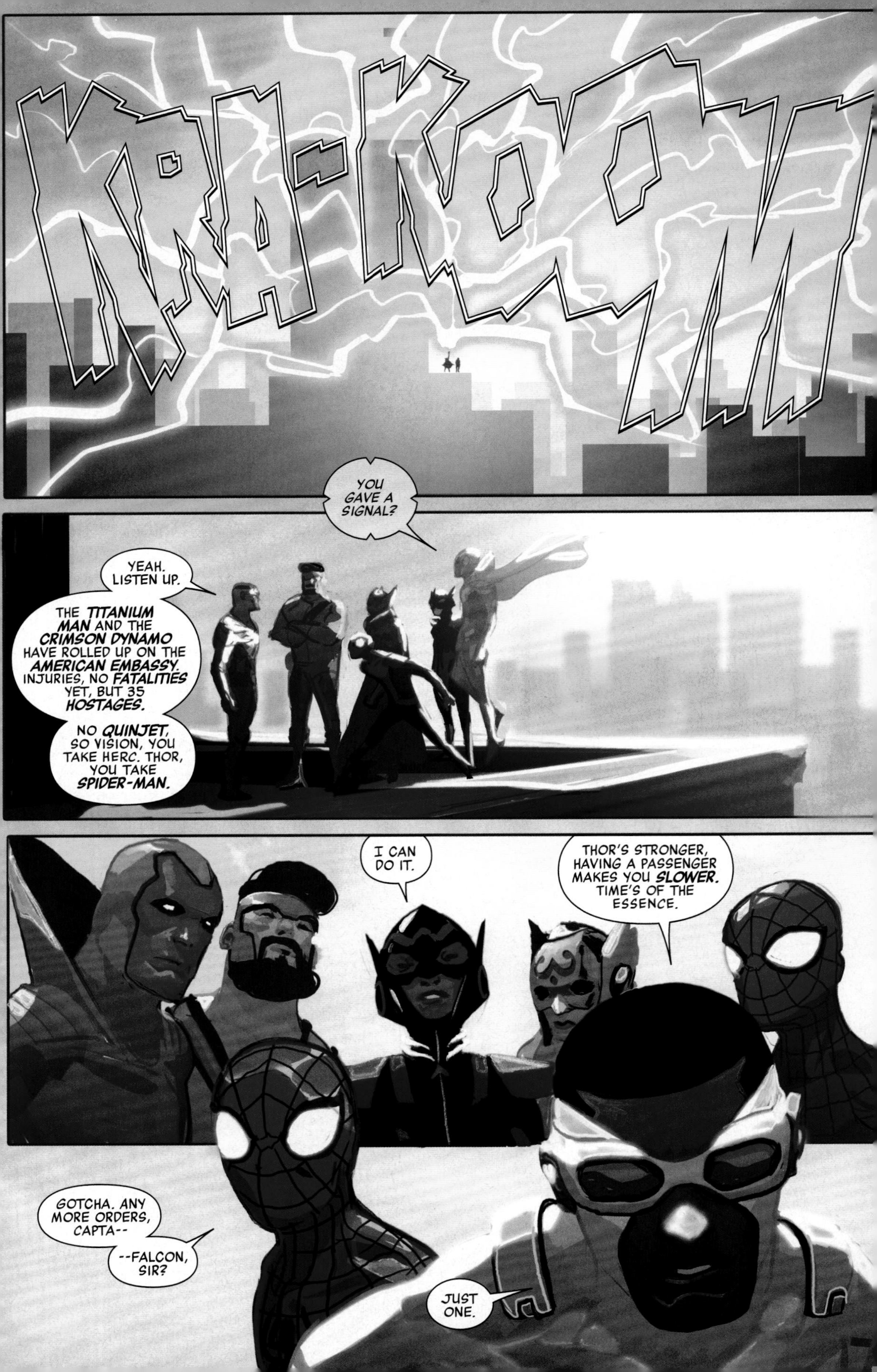
KRA-KOOOM
YOU GAVE A SIGNAL?
YEAH. LISTEN UP.
THE TITANIUM MAN AND THE CRIMSON DYNAMO HAVE ROLLED UP ON THE AMERICAN EMBASSY. INJURIES, NO FATALITIES YET, BUT 35 HOSTAGES.
NO QUINJET, SO VISION, YOU TAKE HERC. THOR, YOU TAKE SPIDER-MAN.
I CAN DO IT.
THOR'S STRONGER, HAVING A PASSENGER MAKES YOU SLOWER. TIME'S OF THE ESSENCE.
GOTCHA. ANY MORE ORDERS, CAPTA--
--FALCON, SIR?
JUST ONE.

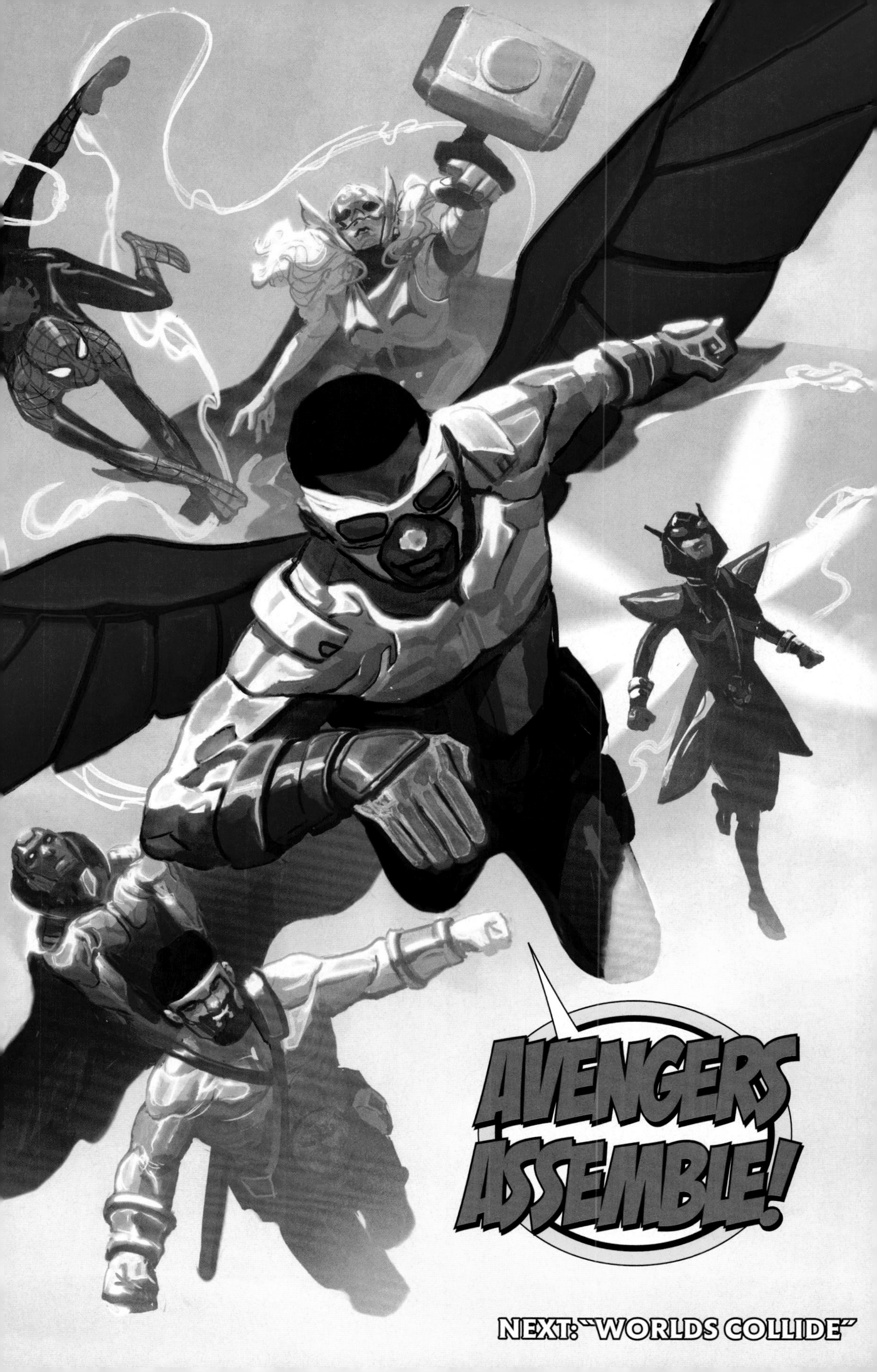
AVENGERS ASSEMBLE!
NEXT: "WORLDS COLLIDE"

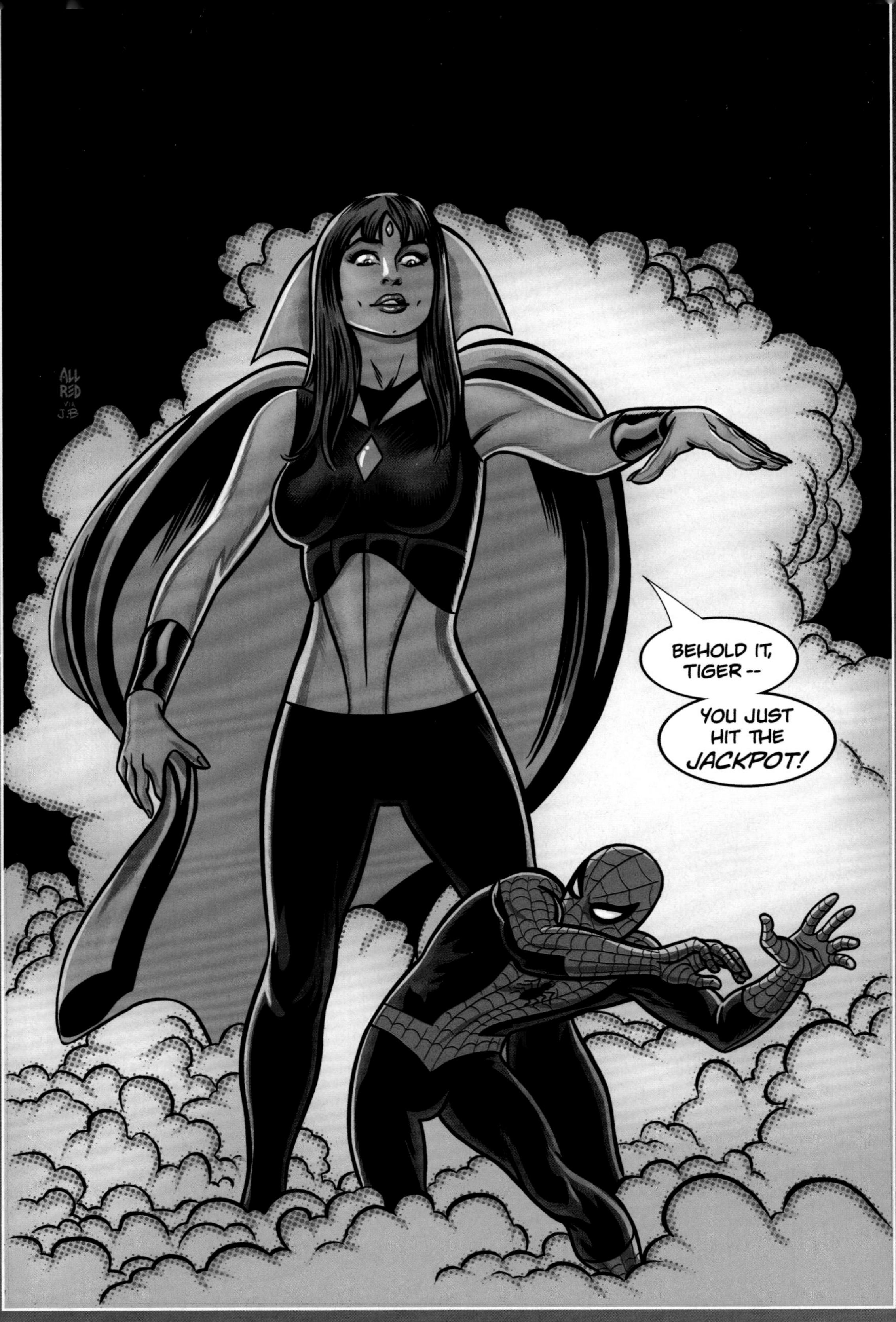
ALL RED VIA J.B
BEHOLD IT, TIGER --
YOU JUST HIT THE JACKPOT!

#8 MARY JANE VARIANT BY
MICHAEL ALLRED & LAURA ALLRED

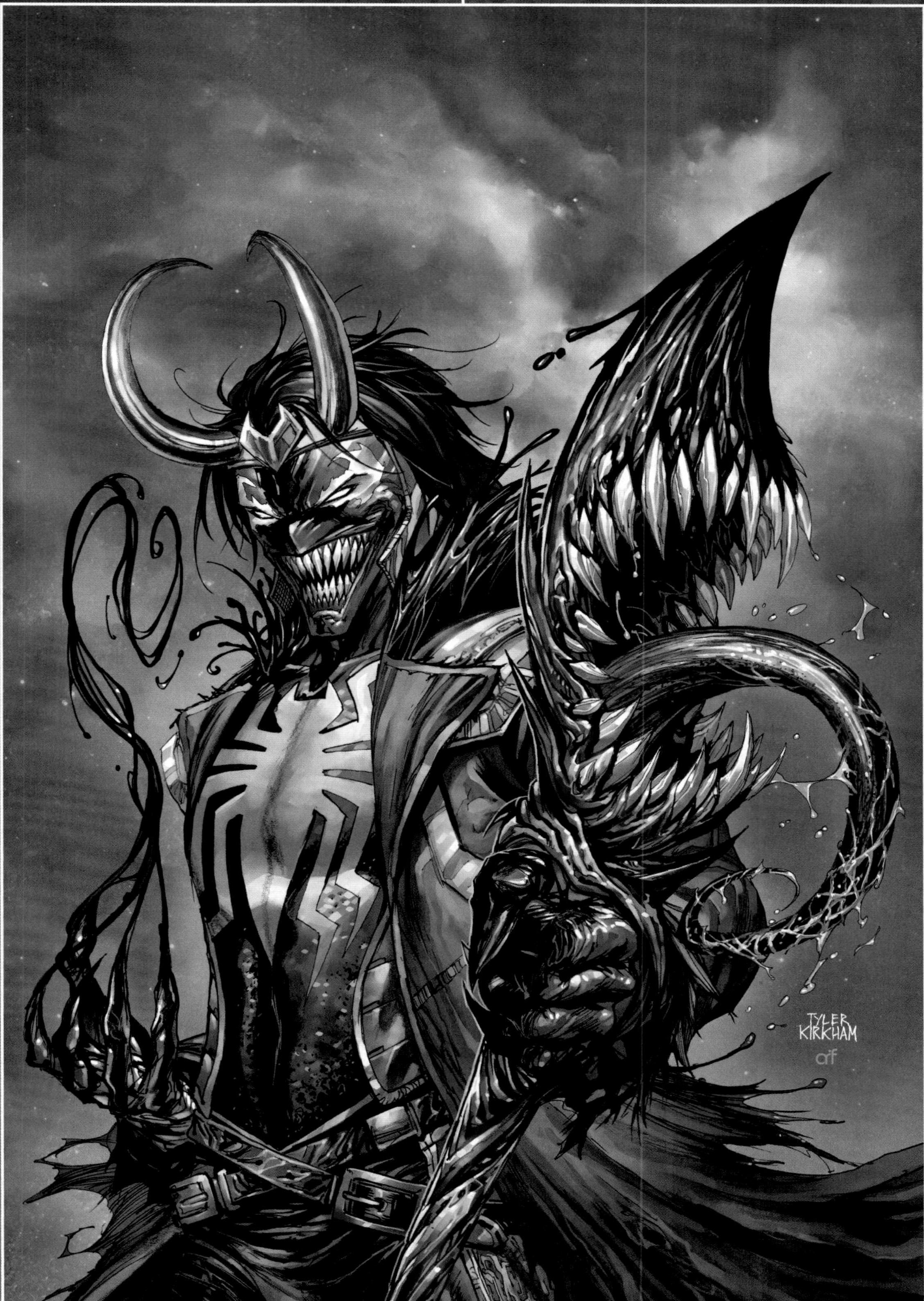
TYLER KIRKHAM
af

#11 VENOMIZED VILLAINS VARIANT BY
TYLER KIRKMAN & ARIF PRIANTO

#9 LAYOUTS BY MIKE DEL MUNDO

1

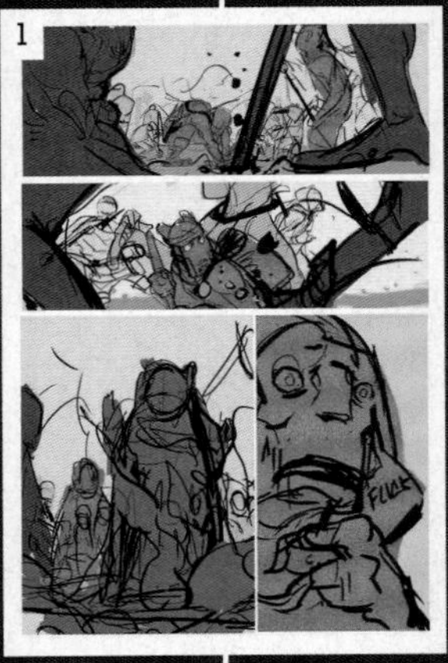

2

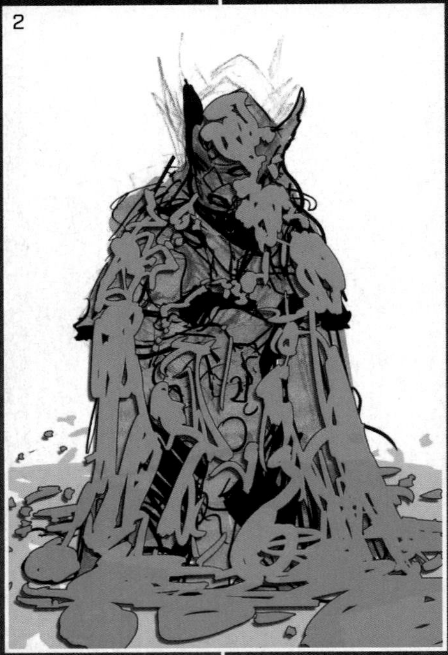

3

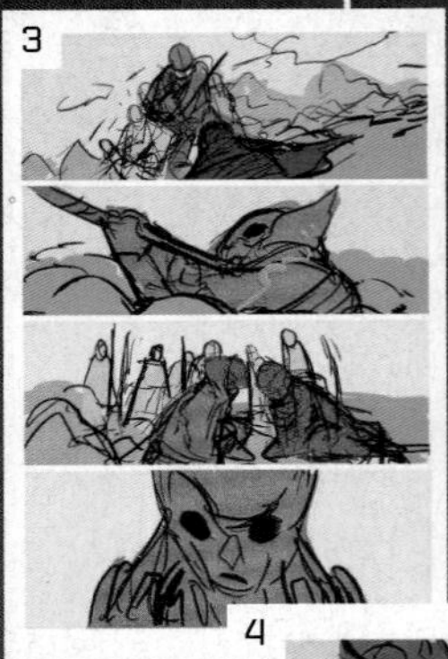

4

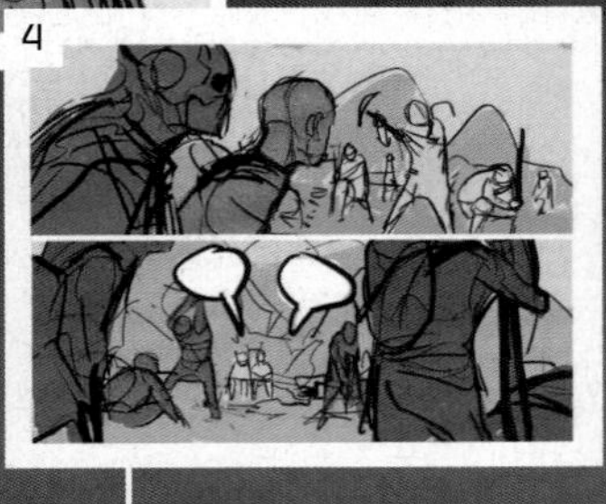

5

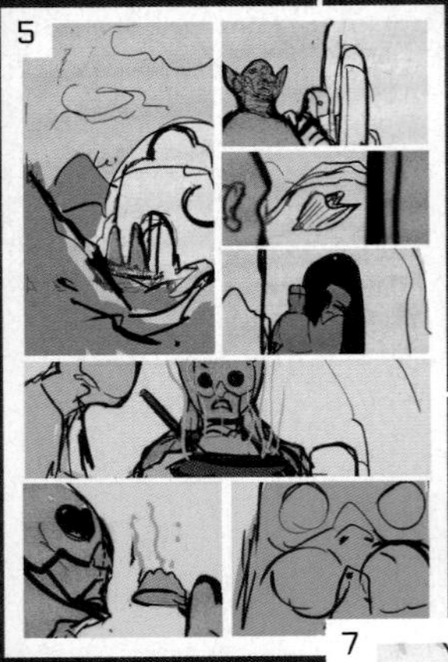

6

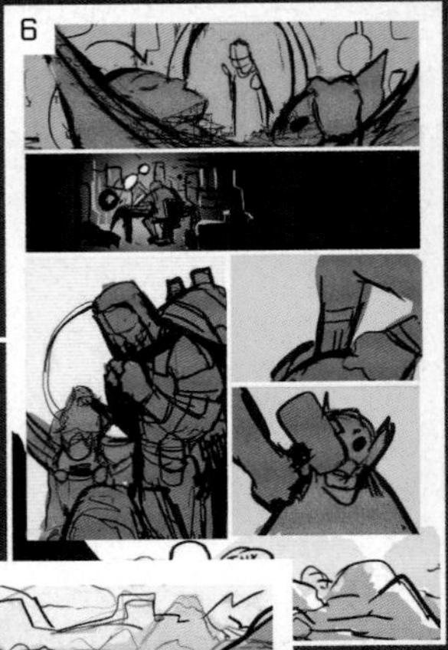

7

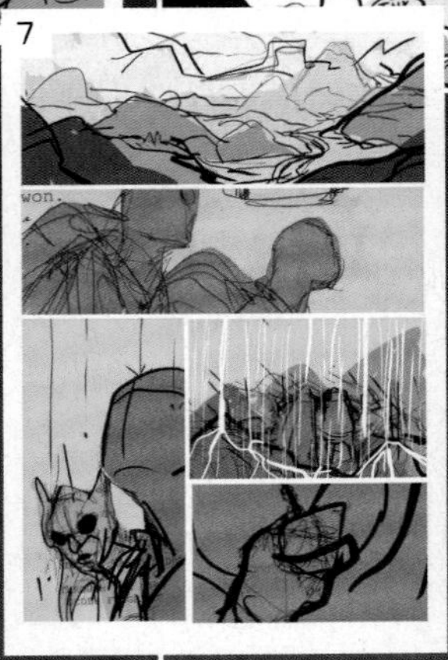
won.

8

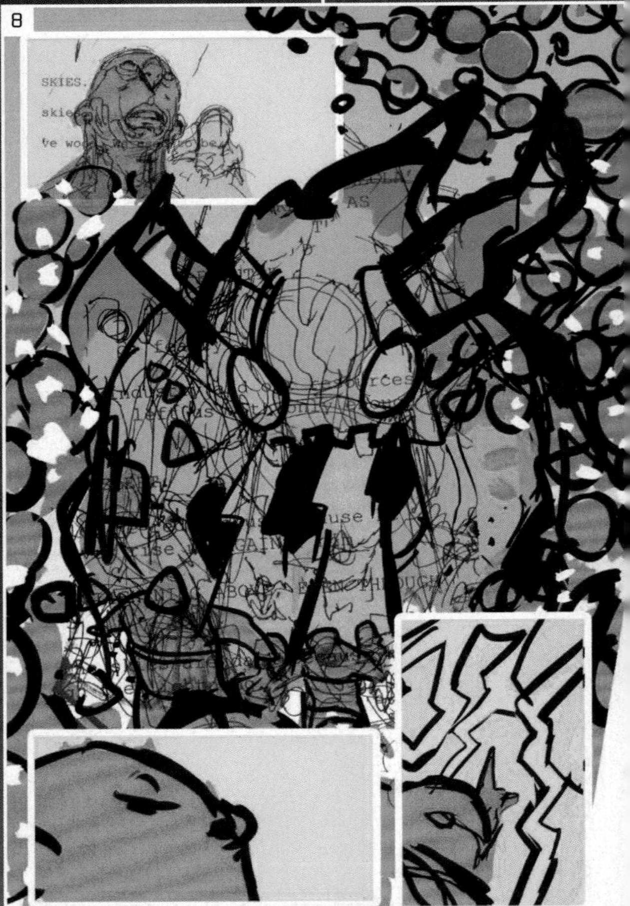
SKIES.

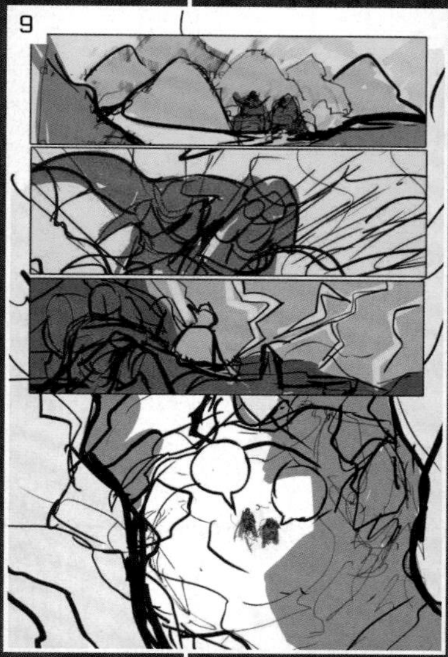
9

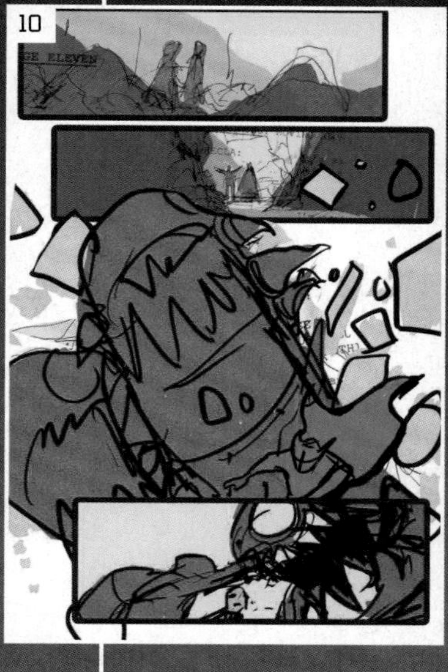
10

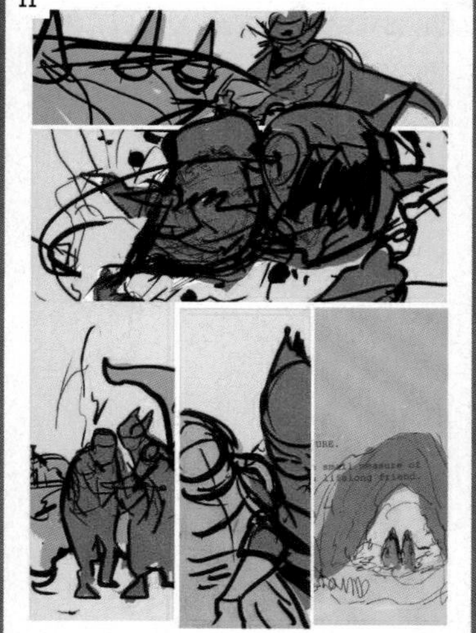
11

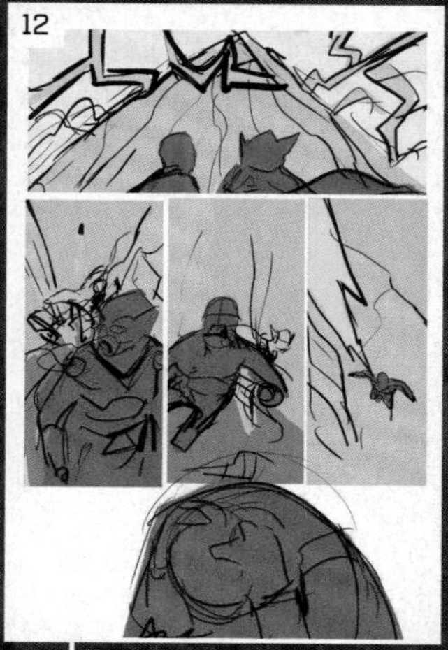
12

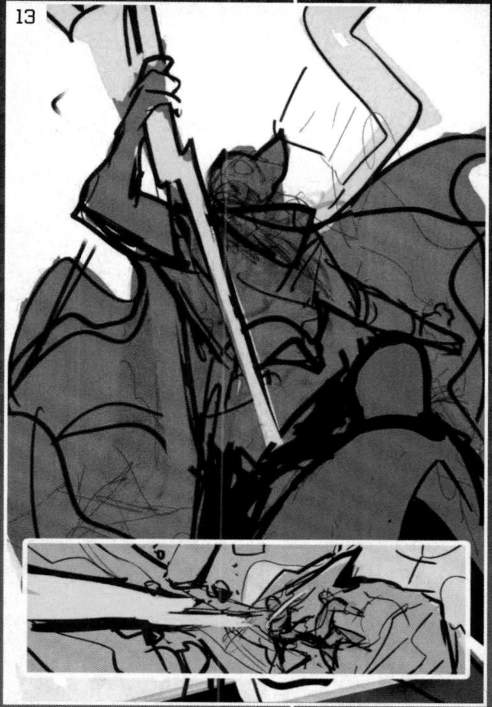
13

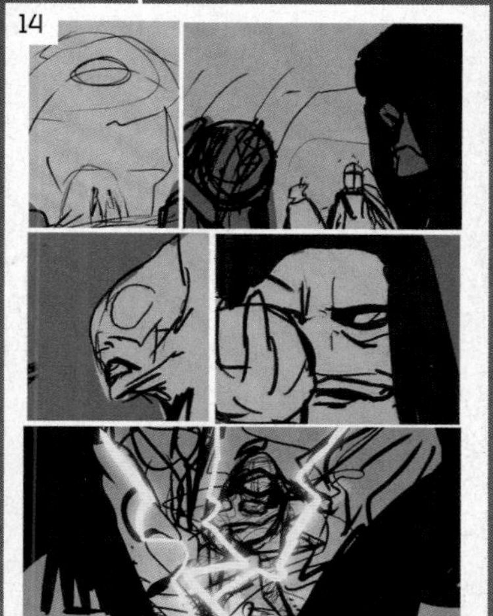
14

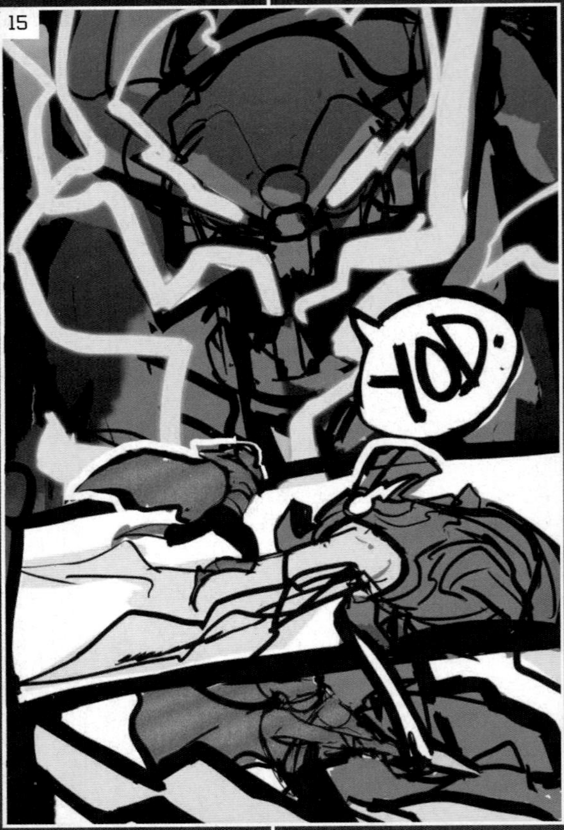
15

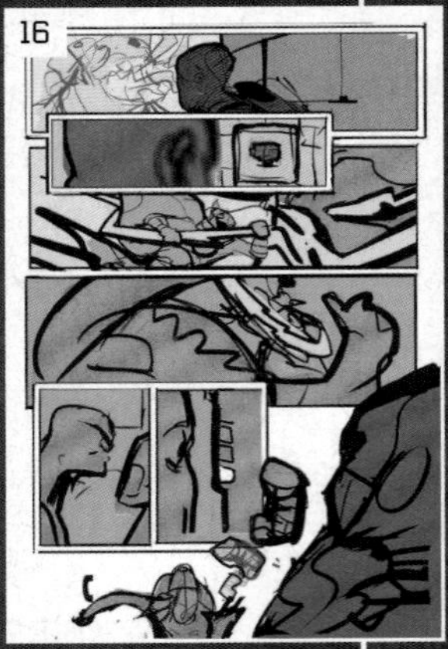
16

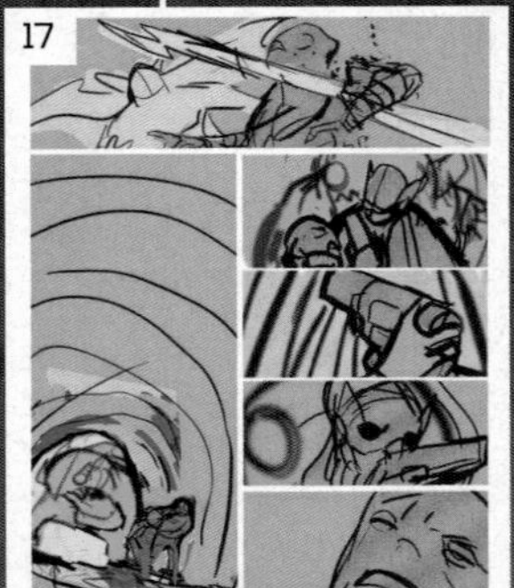
17

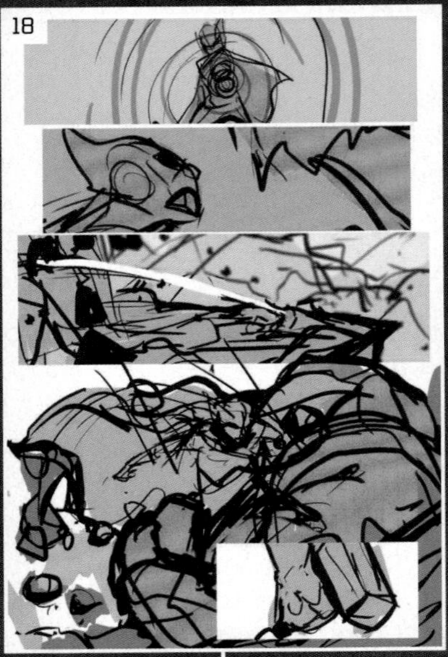
18

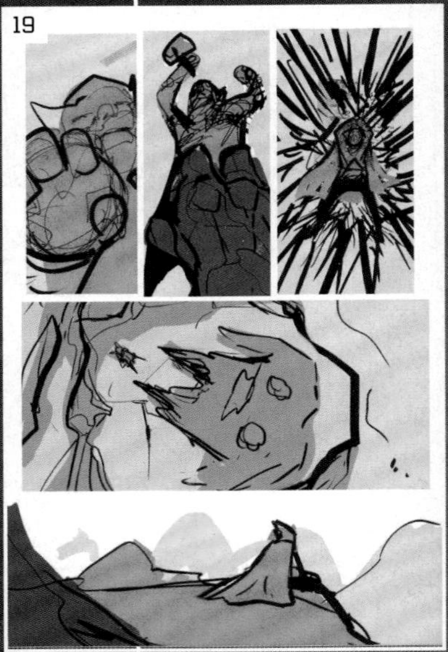
19

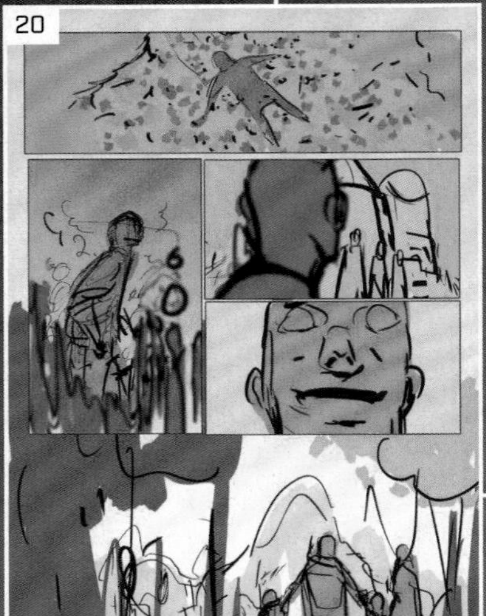
20

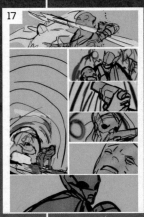